Multicultural Artworlds: Enduring, Evolving, and Overlapping Traditions

Edited by Mary Erickson and Bernard Young

2002

National Art Education Association

About the National Art Education Associaton

The National Art Education Association is the world's largest professional art education association and a leader in educational research, policy, and practice for art education. NAEA's mission is to advance art education through professional development, service, advancement of knowledge, and leadership.

Membership (approximately 40,000) includes elementary and secondary art teachers (and middle and senior high students in the National Art Honor Society programs), artists, administrators, museum educators, arts council staff, and university professors from throughout the United States and several foreign countries. It also includes publishers, manufacturers and suppliers of art materials, parents, students, retired art educators, and others concerned about quality art education in our schools.

The Association publishes several journals, papers, and flyers on art education; holds an annual convention; conducts research; sponsors a teacher awards program; develops standards on student learning, school programs and teacher preparation; and cosponsors workshops, seminars and institutes on art education. For further information, contact our web site at www.naea-reston.org.

© 2002 National Art Educaton Association
1916 Association Drive
Reston, VA 20191

Order No. 275
ISBN 1-890160-20-2

Table of Contents

Contributors

- **Lucy Andrus**, Professor, Art Education, Buffalo State College, Buffalo, New York.

- **Patricia Belleville,** Assistant Professor, Art Education, Eastern Illinois University, Charleston, Illinois.

- **Minuette Byers-Floyd**, Assistant Professor of Art, McMaster College, University of South Carolina, Columbia.

- **Faith Clover**, Faculty, Curriculum and Instruction Department, University of Minnesota.

- **Laurie Eldridge**, Art Teacher, Metropolitan School District of Perry Township, Indianapolis, Indiana.

- **Mary Erickson**, Professor of Art, School of Art, Arizona State University

- **Amy Giles**, Kindergarten Co-Teacher, Hackley Lower School, Tarrytown, New York [recently earned her doctorate at the University of Illinois].

- **Karen Kakas,** Associate Professor and Chair, Division of Art Education/Therapy, School of Art, Bowling Green State University, Ohio.

- **Alice Keppley**, Art Teacher, Penn View Christian School, Souderton, Pennsylvania.

- **Christine Ballangee Morris**, Associate Professor of Art Education, Director of the Multicultural Center, The Ohio State University, Columbus.

- **Mariama Ross**, Assistant Professor of Art Education and African Diaspora Studies, University of Wisconsin-Madison.

- **Mary Stokrocki**, Professor of Art, School of Art, Arizona State University.

- **Rosemary Scheuering**, Art Instructor, Pikes Peak Community College and other schools, Colorado Springs, Colorado.

- **Ilona Szekely**, Elementary Art Teacher, Goodridge Elementary, Hebron, Kentucky.

- **Pamela G. Taylor**, Assistant Professor of Art, Lamar Dodd School of Art, The University of Georgia, Athens.

- **Harriet Walker**, Assistant Professor, Graduate College of Education, University of Massachusetts, Boston.

- **Bernard Young**, Professor of Art, School of Art, Arizona State University.

- **Midge Zimmerman**, Art Specialist, 4-8th grade, Dakota Valley School District, North Sioux City, South Dakota.

Part One: Foundations

Today's teachers of art are charged to offer students opportunities to experience and make art that is meaningful to them and at the same time to focus on standards both in the quality of art students view and also in the quality of art they produce. In addition, teachers of art, like other educators, are increasingly concerned about improving cross-cultural understanding. This book has three foci that we believe can guide art educators in addressing these important concerns: 1) multicultural art education, 2) alternative artworlds, and 3) the maintenance and evolution of art traditions. We believe that attention to these foci can help guide teachers of art in developing art curricula that are inclusive, that promote high standards of art achievement, and that are culturally sensitive.

The purpose of this book is to propose a rationale, introduce a model curriculum unit, present a research base, and offer sample lessons for guiding students in investigating the key people, places, activities, and ideas of some of the historical and contemporary artworlds that make up the complex art traditions of North America.

This book has three parts. The first presents foundations for multicultural art education. The second presents 15 artworld-centered lessons developed by practicing elementary, secondary, and university art educators. The third part presents resources for teaching one multicultural, artworld-centered curriculum unit.

In the first chapter, "Multicultural Challenges in Art Education," Bernard Young defines and argues for multicultural art education and places it within the broader historical contexts of culture, scholarship, art history, and art education. His is a broad definition drawing on African American, Native American, Mexican American and other cultures and art traditions. He concludes with an example of the rich achievements of artists who cross artworld boundaries (African American and Mexican) in pursuit of shared values.

In the second chapter, "What are Multicultural Artworlds and Why are They Important?," Mary Erickson defines artworlds as cultures within larger cultures whose members draw a significant portion of their identity in some way from art. She introduces four questions (focused on artworld people, places, activities, and ideas) as a structure for investigating alternative artworlds and concludes by presenting five key ideas to justify teachers' attention to artworlds as they develop their curricula.

In the third chapter, "How Can an Artworld-Centered Online Curriculum be Used?," Faith Clover outlines an extensive artworld-centered curriculum drawn largely from two online units, which art teachers adapted and taught in their culturally diverse elementary, middle, and high school classes. The eight key African American, Chicana/o, and Mexican prints upon which this unit centers are reproduced in the resources section of this book, along with detailed information about each artwork.

In the fourth chapter, "Teaching about Artworlds: A Collaborative Project," Mary Erickson presents the results of a study of the effectiveness of an artworld-centered unit (outlined in the third chapter) on elementary and secondary students' understanding of their own artworlds. She concludes by proposing student objectives around which artworld instruction might focus and justifications for using artworlds as a key idea in art curriculum development.

The second part of this book is comprised of 15 lesson plans focused on traditional, ethnic artworlds and on everyday and other artworlds not always addressed in art curricula. Teachers responded to an invitation to submit lesson plans that focus, at least in part, on traditionally under-represented artworlds of North America. This book introduces a sampling (certainly not all) of the many often-overlapping artworlds that thrive in North America, especially in the United States. Locations for accessing reproductions of key artworks and information (including artworld information) accompany each lesson. Sample student writing and artwork appear with many of the lessons. The four artworld questions (focused on artworld people, places, activities, and ideas) introduced in the second chapter provide an introductory structure for the 15 diverse lesson plans.

The final part of this book is a set of resources that readers are invited to use to try out the idea of multicultural artworlds in their own classrooms. Resources include: eight reproductions of artworks by African American, Chicana/o and Mexican printmakers intended for classroom display; key information (including artworld information) about each of the eight artworks and Artworld Analysis worksheet to guide students in investigating their own or others' artworlds. These resources are those used to support the artworld-centered unit outlined in chapter three, the effectiveness of which is presented in chapter four.

Chapter 1

Multicultural Challenges in Art Education

by Bernard Young

Introduction

Multicultural education has been adopted in a growing number of educational institutions and school districts' curriculums as a partial solution to transforming the lack of representation of cultural diversity. It serves as an action and theoretical movement to plant the seeds of empowerment and the promoting of complete human dignity in United States schools. This movement has also attempted to deal with the persistent problems of minority underachievement and racial antagonism in schools. The multicultural movement was a result of demands made by African Americans, Latinos, Native Americans, and other marginalized groups for equality of opportunity, and by the efforts of the professional educational community to provide solutions to these problems (McCarthy 1994, p. 81-82). Art education is a highly specialized interdisciplinary field, which counts among its members many who believe the continuing lack of multicultural course content in some art curriculums needs to be changed. This chapter focuses primarily on the multicultural and cultural challenges of art educators and educators in the United States rather than on the specific multicultural challenges of our immediate neighbors on each border in Mexico or Canada, although some overlapping reflections from our neighbors are discussed.

Many multicultural and Afrocentric specialists believe that one of the pressing aims of multicultural education is to restructure schools, colleges, universities so that students from diverse racial, ethnic, and social-class groups will experience an equal opportunity to learn (Banks, 1996, 1994; Banks & Banks, 1993, 1995; Gay, 1992; Grant, 1977; Grant, Sleeter & Anderson, 1986; Benjamin, 1996). Public colleges and universities claim not to discriminate among their applicants based on race or social background or economic status, but in reality the current structure of our institutions of higher learning limits opportunities for a higher education for African Americans and other minorities.

Admission policies are often exclusive and the former affirmative action policies no longer exist in many of our institutions of higher education. Exclusionary policies especially affect those that live in low-income, inner-city communities in the United States. Examples of anti-affirmative action admission policies and the effects of these policies can be found in current books, articles, news stories and on the Internet (Cybercampus, Hacker, 1995; Ezorsky, 1991). This can be especially noticed in the public universities in California and Texas, where some believe these policies are creating unnecessary barriers to minorities.

Insignificant and Significant History

We hope that the selected artworlds introduced in the lessons in this book present diverse brief histories of art that are not prominent in art education. Bolin (1987) states, "what is 'discarded' by one historian as 'insignificant' or 'unhistorical' may be rightly regarded by another as central to his or her historical study" (p.59). A dramatic example of reexamining "insignificant history" is the case of Barbara Chase-Riboud's novel and historical account of Thomas Jefferson, third president of the United States, and his relationship with Sally Hemings (Chase-Riboud, 1979, 1994). Recent DNA testing has provided strong evidence that Bolin and others are correct in assessing there are differences in how historians select and ultimately regard events as being important history. This also holds true in thinking that what is described, as being important in one artworld may not be acceptable or important in another. According to Villeneuve in an editorial written for *Art Education* (2001) the notion that when an art scholar or author of a textbook accepts the challenge to make room in an established text for women and underrepresented cultures, decisions have to be made about what to eliminate to make room for the new. She goes further and points out that time is limited in the classes we teach, and to change an already established curriculum means additional work as well as eliminating something already included.

To some multiculturalists the generally accepted history of Christopher Columbus symbolizes everything that cries out for historical rejection. He stands at the gateway to the Europeanization of the Americas; Columbus has come to represent for some people the most wicked dead white European male of all (Royal, 1992, p. 90). As some multiculturalists would say the study of dead white European males must give way to the study of other cultures and historical figures. To what degree the dispute over Columbus is factual, is not the issue in writing a new multicultural history or curriculum. What is more important is that contemporary students realize that history and curricular materials are highly selected and sometimes the selection process is more political than educational. In addition in some cases textbooks and educational materials have been found with incorrect information. Even art educators should pursue balances and correct imbalances.

The retelling of the Columbus story told by the indigenous people of the Western Hemisphere, who later came to be known as "Indians" and then as Native Americans is certainly as important to read and hear about as the European versions that cover the shelves of our libraries. Views written by Native Americans in general and in specific in an edited book called *Columbus and Beyond: View from Native Americans* (Jorgen 1992), which includes writers such as, Allen, Francis III, Hogan, Ortiz, Revard, and Young Bear, are essential reading for those interested in the view of Native Americans. Anderson, a Native American, gives us a different point of view on Columbus discovering America:

> That was All Indian Elementary school I went to, though… they taught White History. I remember later on they had in there Columbus discovered America an' I said, "Why am I saying Columbus discovered America? Hell," I said, "I'm the one discovered America." (Jorgen, 1992, p. 57)

Native Americans are among the most articulate people protesting and reevaluating our history about Columbus. Some believe they have good reason to dethrone this American folk hero, the myth, his legend, his mission, and his accomplishments. Some scholars believe a reexamination of Columbus and the more than 500 years of European presence in the Americas is long overdue (Jorgen, 1992). A native author, White Deer of Autumn, focuses on the Native Americans' life with the European settlers after Columbus. He and other Native Americans have a unique perspective on their culture and traditions.

The quarterly *Rethinking Schools* published a special issued titled, "Rethinking Columbus." The quarterly is dedicated to children of the Americas and the editorial staff and its writers believe Columbus as taught in the public schools is a basic myth and is not an accurate portrayal of history. They state their goal is not to "idealize native people and demonize Europeans, or present a depressing litany of victimization.

We wanted to encourage a deeper understanding of the European invasions consequences, honor the rich legacy of resistance to the injustices it created, and convey some appreciation for the diverse cultures of the original inhabitants of the hemisphere" (Bigelow, Miner, and Peterson, 1991). They further state their goal is to tell the story or "history" that has not been told.

This lack of telling the complete story is also true for other groups that can be categorized as multicultural. Multicultural education is a reform movement that maintains that all students should have equal opportunities to learn regardless of racial, ethnic, social-class, or gender group to which they belong. In seeking justice, equality and freedom the stories of many neglected groups should be told. A survey of demographic structure of the United States reveals the existence of 276 different ethnic groups: 170 of these are Native American groups (Gollnick & Chinn, 1986).

Early Movements in Ethnic and Art Studies
Banks (1993) found that the Black studies movement that emerged in the 1960s and 1970's has historical roots in the early development of education in the United States. The current multicultural education movement is directly related to early African American scholarship. African American scholars such as George Washington Williams (1882-1883), Carter G. Woodson (1922, 1933, 1977), Charles H. Wesley (1922), and W.E.B. DuBois (1935, 1973) were directly connected to this movement as they developed ethnic studies research and teaching materials that were appropriate to the study of their race. African American leaders (such as Sojourner Truth, Harriet Tubman, Frederick Douglas, before and after emancipation and Ida B. Wells-Barnett, Mary McCloud Bethune, Booker T. Washington, W. E. B. DuBois, Malcolm X, Martin Luther King, Jr.) during the "Jim Crow" and civil rights eras often sacrificed their time and, in some cases, their lives to help improve the economic, educational and social status of African Americans.

Scholars such as Williams, Wesley, Woodson, and DuBois researched and created knowledge about African Americans that could be integrated into the school and college curriculum. Educators Woodson and Wesley (1922) worked to integrate the school and college curriculum with content about African Americans during the early decades of the 20th century.

American social science and certainly American artworlds adopted a live-and-let-live position toward racial discrimination. African American artists during the Harlem Renaissance were permitted to entertain in establishments occupied by Whites, but they were not allowed to enter those establishments as guests or patrons. The same situation was true in national museums, but the situation was likely to be worse, African Americans and other multicultural groups were permitted to work to maintain and build art institutions but, were not represented in them as artists until much later in the 20th century. And even worse was the situation with schools in America. In 1896 the Supreme Court upheld segregation in its "separate but equal" doctrine set forth in *Plessy v. Ferguson* (Franklin and Moss, 1994). Separate but so-called equal schools and discrimination were common and existed throughout America in the 19th century and its impressions were apparent throughout the 20th century. Traces of these problems currently still exist and in some communities today the conditions are blatantly impoverished. The problem of developing the best education for minorities was usually placed back on the shoulders of the various minorities groups. This was also coupled with insufficient financial funds to foster the best education and even fewer political rights to support what minorities would see as important.

Historians and art historians also should hold some responsibility for the repression of the study of race and culture in education and art. During the early part of the 20th century academia assured itself of ignorance by excluding eminent minority scholars from White university faculties. W. E. B. Du Bois a graduate of Harvard University, was one of the most prolific scholars of Negro education and produced a doctoral dissertation on the slave trade, which became the first volume of the Harvard Historical Series. Although he lived to be 95 years old and became one of, if not the most important African American scholar of the 20th century, he was never invited to give a single lecture at his alma mater. In 1915 Carter G. Woodson, another pioneer and African American recipient of a doctorate in history from Harvard wrote, *The Education of the Negro Prior to 1861*. This is a historical document that depends on primary sources directly from African Americans and correspondence during his time. Today qualitative researchers would salute these primary rather than secondary research methods as important research. No later historian has covered the same ground. He was also discriminated against and ignored by White American historians. In 1934, Horace Mann Bond wrote a pioneer work, *The Education of the Negro in the American Social Order.* He took up his research at the point where Woodson stopped, covering the years since the Civil War. He was a master of his craft and wrote about the theory and practice of the Negro in education. He was also ignored by White scholars and universities until very recently.

The mainstream White universities until very recently ignored all three of these scholars and their important works. Similar discrimination occurred with other minority groups as well. It is very difficult to find a general history of the education of Mexican American and Puerto Rican, or other Latino children. During this period of time an excellent full-scale history of Indian education was written by Martha E. Layman (1942) but was never published (Weinberg, 1977, pp. 2-5).

In the field of art, the scholar Porter (1943, 1992) researched and wrote the text, *Modern Negro Art,* which is now the most quoted text in the field of African American art. As early as 1934, Porter had gathered a considerable mass of material on early African -American artists. In 1936, he completed a study of Negro contributions to the handicrafts and graphic and plastic arts from 1724 to 1900. Porter's meticulous research laid out a rich foundation for future researchers in African American studies. His colleague Alain Locke, the chair of the Department of Philosophy at Howard Unversity from 1917 to 1925 and again from 1928 to 1954, published the only two books that preceded Porter's accomplishments. Locke's two books, *Negro Art, Past and Present* (1936) *and The Negro in Art* (1940) were landmark publications because they were the first to survey the field. Neither book critically addressed the issue of race and identity as did Porter's *Modern Negro Art.* Locke's version of *The New Negro,* a standard publication during the Harlem Renaissance, emphasized African American cultural continuities with Africa. He affirmed what was positively valued as inferior by White culture; he affirmed positively an African identity even though Americanized in many ways; he applauded the folkways, rhythms, and rituals of African American life (Harris, 1989, p. 6). His views were very much different from those of Booker T. Washington, who held the leading accommodationists' views on African Americans and their education. In contrast, Locke and DuBois supported each other with advocacy views of the literature of African Americans that encouraged the self-conscious portrayal of Blacks in the struggle against racism and oppression.

Cedric Dover's 1960 text on *American Negro Art*, David Driskell's and Samella Lewis' books and studies of African American artists, and Eugene Grigsby's book and his development of curriculum materials on African American and multicultural artists, each have made major contributions to the literature of African American artists.

Even though a number of African American scholars were creating literature on and about African American artists, Grigsby and a few other art educators in the early 1970s wrote about the goals of teaching about multicultural artists to young people. He was one of the few African American art educators that wrote from his unique perspective on the goal of teaching art rather than training children to necessarily become artists. He offered experiences in his book that made a contribution to how children could use art to heighten their sensitivity to multicultural and multienvironmental views of the world. Much of the early movement in ethnic studies was born out of a need to directly influence and support the racial isolation that existed in the many segregated schools in America. One should keep in mind that it was not only the White American teachers who did not know about diversity in art and culture, but this was also a problem for African American children.

Those children who lived and attended racially isolated schools also lacked cultural diversity and global views of the world.

During the 1960s and 1970s and later an increasing number of art education publications focused on people of color but, few were written by people of color. Curriculum resources were written for the Getty by such art educators as Clover (2001), *Navajo Art: A Way of Life* and Erickson (2001), *Mexican American Murals: A Place in the World.* Art curriculums about Native Americans are very difficult to locate in part because the field of Native American Art history is young. According to K.C. Duncan (personal communication, February 8, 2001), a scholar of Native American art history, the field is young, and it is based strongly on structures of anthropological observation overlaid with the traditional formalist and connoisseurship concerns of art history. The study of Native American art is relatively new with a newly established literary history. For example it was not until an "Exposition of Indian Tribal Arts," was mounted in New York's Grand Central Galleries in 1931 that the first large exhibit in which Native American creations were called art and displayed as such. Ten years later in 1941 the Museum of Modern of Art opened the exhibit "Indian Art of the United States." The prestige and brilliant exhibit design lent cachet and validation, and further transformed the way Native American objects would be viewed thereafter. A limited number of Native Americans have advanced degrees in art history, although scholars such as Duncan believe the numbers are growing. Like contemporary artists they write most often about contemporary rather than earlier art. These contemporary artists are among the most articulate spokespeople on their art. A few examples of these Native authors included, Hill, 1992; McMaster and Martin, 1992; and Akwekon, 1994.

Beardsley and Livingston's (1987) book *Hispanic Art in the United States* as well as Simmen's (1997) book on an early Mexican American artist are loaded with important historical and contemporary artists though these authors are not Hispanics. The same is true for Gavin (1994), Pierce and Weigle (1996) on the arts of Spanish New Mexican art. A few examples of books on Chicano art written by Hispanic authors are: Del Castille, McKenna, and Yarbro-Bejarano (1991), Quirarte (1973), and Cockcroft, Barnet-Sanchez (1993). Insiders and/or people of color need to be encouraged to write more about themselves in art and art education. This is not to take away from the importance of what others are doing or have done in the literature, nonetheless self documentation, interpretation, and education are important and must move forward.

Mexican Americans and the Civil Rights Movement
It was common in the 1920s in many towns in Texas to refuse admittance of Mexican American youth to high schools. With the exception of a very limited group of wealthy Mexican Americans, educational opportunities did not exist. Mexican American children were segregated in California in the 1920s and 1930s. Segregation within formally desegregated schools was common. It was not uncommon to have graduation ceremonies for Anglo and Mexican American eighth-grade students on different days. During this period of time denigration of Spanish and Mexican culture was the rule in schools in the Southwest. In the 1920s and 1930s Mexican Americans were not subjected to discriminatory racial laws such as those related to African Americans, nor were they given the privileges of Whites. Mexican Americans have been in an unequal, unjust, discriminatory social position for years and many are still in this situation.

In the 1930s and 1940s, Mexican Americans in Los Angeles in their second generation started to become culturally adjusted. Immigrants and their children had made the United States their home throughout the 19th century, but it was not until the decade of the Mexican Revolution in 1910, and the mass immigration north that large numbers of Mexicans made Los Angeles their home. A massive movement of individuals and families crossed the Mexican border to the United States in the first three decades of the 20th century. Scholars estimate that one and a half million Mexicans migrated northward between 1900 and 1930 with most settling in the Southwest. Such a massive movement of people coming from one nation to another with unique values, traditions and cultures created enormous cultural transformations (Sanchez, 1993, p. 18, 254). The generation of the American-born Mexican Americans, did not become influential leaders in the Los Angeles area until their maturation during the period of the Depression. Meanwhile simultaneously, Mexican Americans were growing influential in establishing communities throughout the Southwest.

In the late 1960s pressure was put on the Federal Government from Mexican Americans in the Southwest and from Puerto Ricans in New York. Chicanos held school boycotts in California, Texas, and elsewhere, and demands were made for equality as well as for the enforcement of protective laws (Weinberg 1977, p. 286). One of the chief acts to be passed as a result of this pressure was the Civil Rights Act of 1964. In 1969 the Federal government made some progress in issuing documents to uphold and enforce laws (p. 287).

In 1975, Mexican Americans gained the status of an autonomous ethnic group, sharing special constitutional protection along with African Americans. Mexican and African Americans for years shared the common fate of deliberate, deprivation, and segregation. At this juncture in history these two groups and other minorities could use the law as legal weapons. How well these laws were practiced and are upheld today is a continuous story in American history (p. 287).

The saga and debate continues throughout the United States today. For example, in Arizona in the 2000 election voters passed proposition "203," which asked voters to vote either yes or no on teaching English only in all classrooms in the state. Essentially, this proposition does away with bilingual education in the public schools. It requires public school instruction to be in English, rather than in the existing bilingual programs. It also requires an intensive one-year English immersion program, to teach English as quickly as possible while teaching academic subjects. The language barrier was a problem for Mexican Americans in the 1900s and it is still a problem in the schools at the beginning of the new millennium. The new English-only policy also causes serious difficulties for the many Native American tribes in Arizona to keep their languages alive. There are certainly pros and cons on the English-only proposition. In any case, it presents old and new problems for Mexican Americans, Native Americans, and others.

According to Acuna (2000), Mexican Americans were very involved in pursing their own civil rights agenda during the 1950s. The U.S. Supreme Court ruling in the Brown decision of 1954 had little effect on schooling for Mexican Americans at the time. In 1970 in the *Cisneros et al v. Corpus Christi Independent School District et al* case, the U.S. Court for the Southern District of Texas ruled that Mexican Americans "constitute an identifiable ethnic minority with a past pattern of discrimination in Corpus Christi Texas." The court wrote, "We see no reason to believe that ethnic segregation is no less detrimental than racial segregation" (Joe Cisneros et. al, 1970). In the Keyes case of 1973, The U.S. Supreme Court held that "Negroes and Hispanos in Denver suffer identical discrimination in treatment when compared with the treatment afforded Angloamerican students" (Weinberg, 1977). It was and still is obvious that racism toward Mexicans and Mexican Americans is a historical fact, which can be demonstrated in our contemporary society today (Acuna, p. 319).

Art Education, Inequality, and Diversity
Multicultural issues should be studied with great attention in the United States and North America because they have increasingly influenced the culture we live in for a number of years and this trend is expected to continue for years to come. Likewise there are many reasons why diversity and multicultural studies especially in art education are important to study. Some of those issues are discussed in this chapter. When Grigsby wrote his ground breaking book in 1977 on *Art & Ethnics* he wrote about the importance of teachers providing information about artists of Black, Brown, and Red ethnic backgrounds. He encouraged teachers to become curious about the backgrounds of artists that were from diverse backgrounds and to teach their students to learn the art histories of these artists and their artworlds.

Grigsby championed the civil rights of African Americans, and other diverse populations and while doing so he insightfully realized through his experiences and demographic data that these populations may not be minorities in America forever. In some areas in the United States the groups that were once known as minorities are now the majorities. He didn't only speak of the artworlds of these groups but also of their social and educational worlds. He stated, "The Brown peoples, comprised of Mexican-American, Puerto-Rican, and other Spanish-speaking populations, followed by Native American Indians, had begun to be more vocal about their dissatisfaction with the lack of 'all deliberate speed' in implementing the 1954 Supreme Court decision or subsequent civil rights enactments passed by Congress to improve the quality of living for minority and poor people" (Grigsby, 1977, p.1). Grigsby's words were also ground breaking because he was the first nonwhite art educator to propose and write about issues of self-determination and teaching multicultural issues in art education. He also realized that the so-called "Brown people" would eventually become the largest or one of the largest minority groups in the United States. Diversity has always been a fact of life in America. The release of the Census 2000 (Census, 2001) data clearly paints a portrait of an increasingly diverse America. It shows explosive growth in the Asian and Hispanic population; especially in the biggest and fastest growing counties.

Americans cannot avoid diversity. According to Walker (1999), a noted professor of Sociology at Cornell University, we are a nation of many nations and we have been so since the days of the founders (p.53). Walker asserts the fundamental issue is whether, and how we can effectively manage our diversity. Some scholars are concerned about whether this country will become one that is deeply divided or fragmented or will learn to develop in a direction of racial harmony.

Immigration patterns and national immigration policy favored northwestern and central Europeans for close to two centuries, but since the 1960s, when immigration reforms were put into place, most of the immigrants have come from Asia and Latin America (Walker, p. 53). Americans have mixed views on what it means to have a national scene with a large changing complexion. Because many of these new immigrants are from underdeveloped countries, their arrival influences the competition for jobs and the composition of our schools and what society will determine to become culturally important. The current debate on diversity is netted in the combination diversity, inequality and an explosion in our population.

In the United States, African Americans, Hispanics, and Native Americans attend school fewer years, have poorer jobs, and have lower incomes than the White majority

(Walker, 1999; Alba, 1990). If the racial and multicultural issues in America could be all solved using the melting pot concept or by simply using diversification of our society, the national debates would not be so complicated. In this country the problems go back to the history of the nation, and involve the economics, social, and psychological foundations of our society. The authors of this book believe that by educating diverse cultural groups about the traditions of each other we may be able to contribute to a move closer to the long-term goals of racial and cultural understanding and harmony.

In 1965 McFee wrote about art education, cultural diversity and change in her paper "Society, Art, and Education" (McFee, 1998 pp. 1-23). Her paper was prepared for and read at The Penn State Seminar for research in art education. The purpose of her paper was to stimulate further inquiry into the relationships between intense social and cultural changes, art, and education, for possible directives for curriculum development in art. She wrote about the dynamic social changes occurring with the emergence of minority groups and their civil and education rights.

McFee states that one of the most serious problems in America is giving civil rights to minority groups without providing economic opportunity and meaningful education. The civil rights movement had a dynamic effect on many minority groups that range from those that still live in degrading situations, to those that made great benefits from the movement. It is imperative that the civil rights that improve the conditions for African Americans, Mexican Americans, American Indians, Whites and others be advocated to reach all groups that are deprived (p. 6). In 1990 in a Manuel Barken Memorial Award lecture, McFee warned that moving towards a multicultural educational system is not an easy task for American political and educational bodies to undertake. She compared this change with the difficulties the women's movement has met in efforts to change culture and achieve full participation in the society, including the arts and academia. It is not a easy task for those in the position of the majority to part with the conviction that one's own view of objective reality is the only genuine perspective. To part with such a conviction requires openness, study, and experience (p. 138). McFee's definition of a multicultural school setting is very open as she described it in a 1992, Getty sponsored, Discipline Based Art Education symposium. She purports that, a multicultural setting occurs when a teacher from one cultural background uses art or any subject to teach children from another culture. It could be a middle-class Mexican American born in the United States teaching immigrant Mexican children from different cultures in Mexico. According to McFee, "It happens when thousands of teachers try to reach children who have come to this country carrying other cultures, or who live in conclaves of people from their family's culture. Whenever the teacher's background culture differs from those of at least some of the students, a multicultural setting exists" (McFee, 1993, p. 74). Of course teachers must immerse themselves in learning cultures outside of their own culture in order to adequately teach other cultures. In many settings in American schools it may be impossible for the teacher to learn all of the diverse cultures in a single classroom because there may be as many different cultures in the class as there are students.

Hamblen (1987), cautioned, "Democratic pluralism in society and aesthetics should allow for elitism and populism, for the good and the not-so-good, for paradox and for nonsolutions. Through debate and contrast, the problematic, value-laden nature of our selections are revealed. There are dangers in education when choices are not available, but merely allowing for diversity is not sufficient without an ongoing critical, reflexive, stance toward what is chosen. Care must be taken to see the origins of any approach as being a matter of selection. Selection itself needs to be made meaningful by the knowledge that it is a choice and by the consciousness that what is chosen is politically embedded" (pp. 23-24). Multicultural art educators of color and those outside the mainstream may approach the opportunity of selection in a different way from those that align themselves with multicultural education for a host of other social and political reasons. Those that are politically embedded in the inner city or those in the rural areas on the reservations, or those in the Appalachian areas may have needs and aesthetics that have not been heretofore thought of by the majority in art education as being important. It is critical that all populations of our society become empowered to make conscious choices that will benefit their students and themselves. Democratic pluralism in this society and aesthetics should allow searches for equality and new solutions in underrepresented and nonrepresented areas. Some of those that are underrepresented have to mediate between two cultural heritages and two environments. Just as freedom and equal opportunity are politically embedded, multicultural art is politically, psychologically and emotionally embedded. As Hamblen points out, in a pluralistic democracy it may not be possible to raise above this debate or the selective nature of our choices.

In her book chapter "Masculine Bias and the Relationship Between Art and Democracy, " Collins (1987) analyzes the artworld and the relationships between art and democracy from a feminist point of view. She points out that women have historically been excluded from equal participation in the mainstream traditions of both of these spheres of cultural activity. She points to masculine bias of traditional art as the possible cause or at the very least a primary contributor to this problem. She points out a few definitions of mainstream and traditional art that have relevance for this book. She states (p. 27) "…mainstream art and mainstream tradition of art refer to the fine arts, as distinct from the folk, commercial domestic, popular, and applied arts of Western culture. The progress of mainstream art is recorded and defended by Western art history texts and courses presented and preserved by major European and American museums and galleries, critically monitored in journals such as *Art News, Art in America,* and *Art Forum.* The professionals and volunteers who produce, record, criticize teach about, buy and sell, and otherwise actively involve themselves in mainstream art and its institutions are collectively referred to as the artworld." Before improvements are made in this artworld Collins proposes a change in the attitude will be needed. It can be added that a change in practices in this artworld would also benefit the relationship of feminists and the mainstream artworld.

Sexual identity in the classroom is an issue that is being addressed in some art classrooms. The National Art Education Association (NAEA) published an advisory titled "Teaching More of the Story: Sexual and Cultural Diversity in Art and the Classroom" (Check & Lampela, 1999). The teacher's position, related research, and national organizational positions on this issue are serious topics that will yield further discussions in the years ahead. Lampela (2001) conducted a survey of art teachers on their knowledge and attitudes on this issue.

In 1990 the NAEA published Young's anthology titled, *Art, Culture and Ethnicity.* At the time of publication it claimed to offer new perspectives on the understanding of school, artistic growth, aesthetic cultural and historical achievements about people of color. The text was described by Thomas A. Hatfield, the Executive Director of the NAEA, as a groundbreaking experience to have art educators write a complete text on the educational problems, future problems and suggestions of potential initiatives that would deal with multicultural art education issues. Chalmers (1992) clearly states the book is important as a text that included writing from art educators of color that spoke for themselves about the Eurocentric, culture-bound, elitist, or even racist content in our current art curricula. Parts of the book criticized the current ethonocentric practices and thought that still dominate much of the literature in art education (p. 134).

A very important question that was raised by Grigsby, in the pages of the book was, where will the next generation of minority art educators come from? It is well documented today that the number of minority art educators in America is still decreasing and there is a shortage of general educators. This issue was discussed on the front page of the February issue of the *NAEANews* (2001). This is an ongoing problem that will indefinitely remain a problem (which we discuss later in this chapter).

Depillars (1990) in Young's text wrote a chapter asking in the title of his chapter if, "Multiculturalism in Visual Arts Education: Are American's Educational Institutions Ready for Multiculturalism?" Depillars claims that art historians like Janson, Gardner and others are misinforming, and miseducating themselves and their readers by promoting miseducation in regard to Black Africa and its descendants in the diaspora (p. 121). He states that these art historians and others like them contributed to the dis-Africanization of history and culture and further this dis-Africanization is the antithesis of multiculturalism. Dis-Africanization has resulted in Black people throughout the world that have little understanding of their history, culture, and artworld. In a larger schema of history Africans, Native Americans, Mexican Americans, and others have long been depicted as natives, with no culture, skills or formal social organization. Depillars goes further to claim that educators must accept new challenges to encompass a more inclusive curriculum to develop multicultural realities and artworlds. Spruill-Fleming (1990, p. 135), in the same text, asserts the historical perspectives of the African legacy have been misrepresented and in order to link the African legacy to the traditional textbooks, the vestiges of institutional racism in America must be faced squarely. As pointed out earlier, one of the most important distinctions of Young's text from others is the fact that art educators of color and others discussed multicultural issues for themselves. Empowerment and self-direction is an essential part of multiculturalism.

Chalmers (1996) asserts that not only is it important for art educators and artists of color to speak for themselves but also that other art educators join them. Duncum, Hamblen, Wasson, McFee, Stokrocki, Stuhr and others have pointed out that some of the so called "notions of good art" in North American schools and some art education scholarship are European, culture-bound, elitist, and even racist (p. 14). Chalmers summarizes the importance of multiculturalism in his monograph *Celebrating Pluralism* (1996) by stating that cultural diversity is a fact of daily life for most of North Americans. We live daily with combinations of multiple cultures and subcultures.

A Need for a Multiethnic Curriculum
In 1974, Banks, an educator, wrote in *The Crisis* magazine, an article about the need for a multiethnic curriculum. He stated that nothing less than a "radical reconstruction" of the curricula of our nation's public schools is required to bring truth, integrity, and reality to blacks in a multiethnic curriculum" (p. 125). While we have made many changes in our curriculum since the 1970s we still have not reach the level of change in the 21st century that can be characterized as making a "radical reconstruction." He went further to state, "the curriculum and social science specialists and teachers have a clear and compelling obligation to develop teaching and learning configurations that represent the ethnic and racial diversity of American history and culture. Failure to do this will result in a distorted, biased, and fallacious portrayal of American history in the nation's public schools" (Banks, 1974, p. 125).

Banks points out that a multiethnic curriculum, which today could be called a multicultural curriculum, is associated with another problem. A problem some would claim as the teaching of Black history or Chicano, or Puerto Rican or Women's history, etc., is as the teaching of a separate history. In today's literature most writers realize that Black history, like other multiethnic histories, is inevitably interwoven with the history of our nation. If Black American history is not taught and written within the contents of our total history, a distorted and inaccurate history will continue to exist. The role Black Americans and other multicultural groups have played in American history has been important in building this nation. When Banks wrote these sentiments he also believed the future outlook of developing a multiethnic curriculum in this nation did not present much hope.

While much work still needs to be done now and in the future, teachers can find evidence of some improvement in the representation of multicultural people in the curriculum. Banks believed that people of color should be positively represented in the literature. They should be included in textbooks with positive self-concepts and a body of literature by multicultural people should be created to counter balance the negative literature that has been produced over the years about multiethnic people. The prospects for the future are promising and complicated.

Multicultural Teacher Shortages and Urban Schools
To paint a picture of some of the students that are considered multicultural, here are a few facts supplied by three partner organizations that have studied the nation's largest urban centers. The three organizations are the Urban Teacher Collaborative, Recruiting New Teachers, Inc. (RNT), the Council of the Great City Schools (CGCS), and the Council of the Great City Colleges of Education (CGCCE). The survey was conducted in 1998-99 and has significant and useful information on urban schools at the beginning of the millennium. The schools in the report serve 6.5 million students, 40% are African American, 30% are Hispanic, 21% are White, 6.4% are Asian/Pacific Islander, and 6% are Alaskan/Native American.

Urban schools nationwide have unique challenges as they face the immediate future with teacher shortages. These schools educate between 40% and 50% of the students who are not proficient in English, approximately 50% are minority students, and 40% of the nation's low-income students. These urban schools have the lowest levels of student achievement, the highest dropout rates, and a disproportionate percentage of students with special needs. To complicate matters more urban schools are more likely to fill vacancies with teachers who have less than full credentials required for doing their jobs (The Urban Teacher Challenge, 2000, p. 6). Their report, which provides a

concise view of the demand and preparation for teachers in Great City School districts and Great City Colleges of Education, stated "Without improved teacher recruitment and development practices, this nation will fail to build the qualified, diverse, and culturally sensitive teacher workforce that today's and tomorrow's classrooms demand." (p. 7).

Generally the public, universities, and parents believe the improvement of teacher quality is essential in confronting the problems in our nation's schools. The study further points to a specific need for teachers of color. Almost three-quarters of the responding Great City School districts indicated they have an immediate need for teachers of color and 55% of these districts reported an anticipated demand for teachers of color over the next five years. In summary, it is a fact that the nation's Great City School districts have a real teacher shortage in specific fields, across grade levels and in the ranks of minority teachers. While art programs may not consistently be among the subject areas with extreme shortages of teachers, art education remains a small area compared to other subjects that does not have students oversubscribing to its programs. We hope that the concept and examples used in this text on Artworlds and multicultural issues will enrich the preparation of teachers of art and classroom teachers teaching art.

Artworlds
We deliberately chose artworlds as the central concept in order to develop an approach to learning about cultures. Our approach makes use of artworks as resources for instruction about the cultures of multitudes of people, places, activities, and ideas. The text describes artworlds, subcultures, cultures, and sub-sub-variations of mainstream museum artworld and also artworlds that would never be considered part of any mainstream. An attempt was made to cover a variety of perspectives that we hope will shed some light on artworlds about which many readers may have little prior familiarity. Erickson in her chapter on "What are Artworlds and Why are They Important" describes many simultaneous sometimes overlapping artworlds or systems. We urge readers to keep in mind that the concept of artworld is central to this book as the reader explores and attempts to gain a clearer understanding. Some readers may not consider all artworlds presented in this book multicultural or diverse in nature. If any artworld in this book does not represent what all readers consider an artworld of diversity we hope, we at least will open up new worlds, different worlds, and worlds of new categorizations, tolerances that can assist readers in the challenges of multicultural and artworld understanding.

Influences within Artworlds
We close this chapter with an example of the richness that can be achieved when multicultural artworlds overlap. In most artworlds the elements that make them unique are the historical time periods and the way individuals respond to

and are influenced by their cultures. For instance, there was mutual sympathy that existed between African American modernists and the painters, sculptors, and printmakers of the Mexican School of the 1930s. David Alfaro Siqueros pointed out the Mexican school was not a strict school of thought nor a single cluster of buildings, and for that matter it was not an actual school building at all. Rather, it was a group of artists that were all inspired by the same revolutionary social processes. They sought to solve problems of their time that would oppose dictatorships, discrimination, racism, exploitation of the poor, the scorned, the oppressed, and the pursued and also worked with purpose and unity. This line of thought was adopted and identified by many African American artists (LeFalle-Collins, 1996, p. 6). The influences of the Mexican and African American artworlds were also physical and geographical, since artists of both groups often settled in some of the same cities in the United States. The African American artists who were most directly affected by the Mexican school artists were Charles Alston (1907-1977), John Biggers (1924-2001), Elizabeth Catlett (b.1915), Sargent Claude Johnson (1888-1967), Jacob Lawrence (1917-2000), Charles White (1918- 1979), John Wilson (b. 1922), and Hale Woodruff (1909-1980). The works of these artists generally maintain several or all of the following four characteristics: the aesthetic theories of Alain Locke (one of the primary intellectual promoters of the concept of the New Negro); the social realist movement in the United States; the use of American socialism and communism; and the work of the Mexican School artists themselves, many of whom were actively working in the United States (p. 29).

The Mexican School artists that most influenced the figurative art of these African American artists were the Mexican muralists Diego Rivera (1886-1957), David Alfaro Siqueiros (1896-1974), and José Clemente Orozco (1883-1999). These artists provided images and a philosophy that directly expressed social, economic and political conditions of common people. These artists further expressed the shared goals of fighting oppression and a celebration of their cultural heritage. These efforts, modeling the conditions of Mexican life and work, became a model for some African American artists and the large-scale production of the mural became a standard form of expression. A similar influence can be found among Mexican Americans who also used the Mexican muralists as inspiration for their work.

Charles Alston created one of the first murals to suggest the heroic acts of the Mexican work. The mural was Alston's two part mural "Magic and Medicine" (1936), commissioned by the WPA for the Harlem Hospital in New York (The mural is no longer at the Hospital). It was common for African American artists like Alston to learn about the Mexican School through readings, lectures at WPA centers, or visits to the United States by Mexican artists. Some of these artists made visits to Mexico to study with the Mexican muralists. They studied original murals on location, sometimes with the assistance of the artists. They also made trips to the graphic artists at the Taller de Gráfica Popular (see Afredo Zalce's work presented in Part Four: Multicultural Resources in this volume). All of these influences assisted in forging the commitment of African American artists to this type of depiction and thinking about their art. Artworlds are important and often, as this example illustrates, the combination of multiple worlds, or influences from several artworlds can yield extraordinary work.

References

Acuna, R. (2000). *Occupied America, a history of Chicanos.* (4th ed.) New York: Longman Publisher.

Akwekon. (1994). Native American Expressive Culture. *National Museum of the American Indian.* XI, 3 & 4.

Alba, R. (1990). *Ethnic identity: Transformation of White America.* New Haven: Yale.

Anderson, F. (1991, Feburary/April). News from Native California. In R. Jorgen, (Ed.). (1992). *Columbus and beyond: view from Native Americans*, p. 57. Tucson, AZ. Southwest Parks and Monuments Association.

Bigelow, B., Miner, B. & Peterson, B. (Eds.) (1991). *Rethinking Columbus: teaching about the 500th anniversary of Columbus's arrival in America.* Milwaukee, WI: Rethinking Schools Publisher. p. 3.

Banks, J. A. (Ed.) (1996). *Multicultural education, transformative knowledge, and action: Historical and contemporary perspectives.* New York: Teachers College Press.

Banks, J.A. & Banks, C. A. M. (Eds.) (1995*). Handbook of research on multicultural education*: NY: Macmillan.

Banks, J.A. (1994). *Multicultural education: theory and practice.* (3rd ed.). Boston: Allyn & Bacon.

Banks, J.A. & Banks, C. A. M. (Eds.) (1993*). Multicultural education: issues and perspectives*. (2nd ed.). Boston: Allyn & Bacon.

Banks, J.A. (1993). Multicultural education: Historical development, dimensions, and practice. In L. Darling-Hammond (Ed.), *Review of Research in Education*, pp.3-49. Washington, D. C.: American Educational Research Association Publisher.

Banks, W.C. (1992). The theoretical and methodological crisis of the Africentric conception. *The Journal of Negro Education, 61*, (3), 262-272.

Banks, S.L. (1974, April). The need for a multiethnic curriculum. *The Crisis, 81*, (4), 125-128.

Beardsley, J. & Livingston, J. (1987). *Hispanic Art in the United States.* Houston & New York: Houston Museum of Fine Art & Abbeville Press.

Benjamin, M. (1996). *Cultural diversity, educational equity and the transformation of higher education.* Westport: Praeger.

Bolin, P.E. (1987). Historical participation: Toward an understanding of the historian in art education. In D.

Blandy & K. G. Congdon (Eds.) *Art in a democracy*. pp. 26-43. New York: Teachers College Press, Columbia University.

Bond, H.M. (1966). *The education of the Negro in the American social order.* (Reprint). New York: Octagon.

Census shows a more diversified U.S. (2001, March 9). *East Valley Tribune*, p. A13.

Chalmers, F.G. (1996). *Celebrating Pluralism, Art, Education, and Cultural Diversity.* Occasional Paper 5, Los Angeles: The Getty Education Institute for the Arts.

Chalmers, F.G. (1992). The orgins of racism in the public school art curriculum. *Studies in Art Education,* 33(3), 134-143.

Chase-Riboud, B. (1979, 1994). *Sally Hemings.* New York: Ballantine Books.

Check, E., & Lampela, L. (1999, Summer). Teaching more of the story: Sexual and cultural diversity in art and the classroom. NAEA *Advisory,* Reston, VA: National Art Education Association.

Cisneros et. al. v. Corpus Christi Independent School District et al., U.S.District Court for the Southern District of Texas, Houston Division, 324 F. Supp. 599; U.S. Dist. Lexis 11469. (1970).

Cockcroft, E. S. & Barnet-Sánchez, H. (1993*). Signs from the heart: California Chicano murals.* Venice, CA & Albuquerque: Social and Public Art Resource Center & University of New Mexico Press.

Collins, G.C. (1987). Masculine Bias and the relationship between art and democracy. In D. Blandy & K. G. Congdon (Eds.) *Art in a democracy.* pp. 26-43. Teachers College Press, New York. Columbia University.

Del Castille, R.G., McKenna, T., & Yarbro-Bejarano, Y. (1991*). Chicano art: resistance and affirmation, 1965-1985.* Los Angeles: Wight Art Gallery & University of California, Los Angeles.

DePillars, N.M. (1990). Multiculturalism in visual arts education: Are Americans educational institutions ready for multiculturalism? In B.Young (Ed*.) Art, culture, and ethnicity.* Reston, VA: National Art Education Association.

Dover, C. (1960). *American Negro art.* Greenwich Connecticut: New York Graphic Society.

DuBois, W.E.B. (1935). *Black reconstruction* New York: Harcourt Brace.

DuBois, W.E.B. (1973). *The education of Black people: Ten critiques, 1906-1960.* New York: Monthly Review Press.

Ezorsky, G. (1991). *Racism and justice: the case for affirmative action.* Ithaca, New York: Cornell University Press.

Franklin, J.H. and Moss, A.A. Jr. (1994). *From Slavery to freedom. A History of African Americans.* (7th ed.) New York: Alfred A.Knopf.

Gavin, R. F. (1994). *Traditional arts of Spanish New Mexico.* Santa Fe: Museum of New Mexico Press.

Gay, G. (1993). Ethnic minorities and educational equality. In J.A. Banks & C. A. McGee- Banks (Eds.), *Multicultural education issues and perspectives,* pp. 171-194. Needham Heights, MA: Allyn & Bacon.

Gollnick, D.M., & Chinn, P. C. (1986). *Multicultural education in a pluralistic society* (2nd ed.). Columbus: Charles E. Merrill.

Grant, C., Sleeter, C., & Anderson, J. (1986). The literature on multicultural education: Review and analysis. *Educational Studies, 12*(1), 47-71.

Grant, C. A. (1977). *Multicultural education: Commitments, issues, and applications.* Washington, DC: Association for Supervision and Curriculum Development.

Grigsby, E. J. (1977*). Art & ethnics: Background for teaching youth in a pluralistic society.* Dubuque, IA: Wm. C. Brown Company. (2000, reprinted by National Art Education Association).

Hacker, A. (1995). *Two Nations: Black and White, separate hostile, unequal.* New York: Ballantine Books.

Hamblen, K. A. (1987). Qualifications and contradictions of art museum education in a pluralistic democracy. In D. Blandy & K. G. Congdon (Eds.) *Art in a democracy* (pp.13-23). New York: Teachers College, Columbia University.

Harris, L. (Ed.) (1989). *The philosophy of Alain Locke.* Harlem Renaissance and beyond. Philadelphia: Temple University Press.

Hill, R. (1992). *Creativity is our tradition: Three decades of contemporary Indian Art at the Institute of American Indian Art.* Santa Fe: IAIA.

Jorgen, R. (Ed.). (1992). *Columbus and beyond: View from Native Americans.* Tucson, AZ: Southwest Parks and Monuments Association.

Keyes. (1973). School district No. 1 Denver, Colorado et al. V. Keyes et al. Supreme Court of the United States, No. 71-507 413 U.S. 189; 1973 U.S. Lexis 43.

Lampela, L. (2001). Lesbian and gay artists in the curriculum: A survey of art teachers' knowledge and attitudes. *Studies in Art Education. 42* (2), 146-162.

Layman, M.E. (1942). *A history of Indian education in the United States.* Unpublished doctoral dissertation, University of Minnesota.

LeFalle-Collins, L. & Goldman, S. M.(1996). *In the spirit of resistance African American modernists and the Mexican mural school.* New York: The American Federation of Arts.

Lewis, S. (1990). *African American art and artists.* Berkeley: University of California Press.

Locke, A. (Ed.). (1925). *The new Negro.* New York: Albert and Charles Boni Inc.

Locke, A. (1936). *Negro art, past and present.* Washington, DC: Associates in Negro Folk Education.

Locke, A. (1940). *The Negro in art: A pictorial record of the Negro and artist and of the Negro theme in art.* Washington, DC: Associates in Negro Folk Education.

Merriam-Webster Collegiate Dictionary (1999). 10th Edition. Springfield, MA.

McFee, J.K. (1961). *Preparation for art*. Belmont, CA: Wadsworth Publishing Co.,

McFee, J.K. (1993). DBAE and cultural diversity: Some perspectives from the social sciences. In *Disciplined based art education and cultural diversity: Seminar Proceedings, August 6-9, 1992* (pp. 64-67). Austin, TX: The Getty Center for Education in the Arts.

McFee, J.K. (1998). *Cultural diversity and the structure and practice of art education*. Reston, VA: The National Art Education Association.

McCarthy, C. (1994). Multicultural discourses and curriculum reform: A critical perspective. *Educational Theory*, Winter, 44, no. (1), 81-82.

McMaster, G. and Martin, L.A. (1992). (eds.). *Indigena: Contemporary Native perspectives*. Hill, Quebec: Canadian Museum of Civilization.

Pierce, D. & Weigle, M. (1996). *The arts of Spanish New Mexico, volumes I and II*. Santa Fe: Museum of New Mexico Press.

Quirarte, J. (1973). *Mexican American artists*. Austin: University of Texas Press.

Porter, J. A. (1992). *Modern Negro Art*. Washington DC: Howard University Press. (Original work published 1943)

Royal, R. (1992). 1492 And all that, political manipulations of history. Washington, DC: Ethics and Public Policy Center. Lanham, Md. National Book Network. 89-94.

Sánchez, G.J. (1993). *Becoming Mexican American*. New York: Oxford University Press.

Simmen, E. (1997). *With bold strokes: Boyer Gonzales, 1864-1943*. College Station, Texas: Texas A&M University Press.

Spruill-Fleming, P. (1990). Linking the legacy: Approaches to the teaching of African and American art. In B. Young (ed.) *Art, culture, and ethnicity*. Reston, VA: National Art Education Association.

Stokrocki, M. (1990). Issues in multicultural art education. In E.W. King and S.D. La Pierre (Eds.) *Using the arts as an educational model for high-risk individuals*. Denver: University of Denver, School of Art.

The Getty Center for Education in Arts Symposium, "DBAE and Cultural Diversity" 1992.

The Need for More Ethnic Teachers. Addressing the Critical Shortage in American Public Schools. (2001, February). *NAEA News, 43*(1), p1.

The Urban teacher challenge report. (January, 2000). Belmont, MA.: Recruiting New Teachers, Inc. (www.cgcs.org)

Villeneuve, P. (March, 2001) They learn what we [don't] teach. Editorial, *Art Education 54* (2), 4. Reston, VA: The National Art Education Association.

Walker, H.A. (1999). Two faces of diversity: Recreating the stranger next door? In A nation divided, diversity, inequality and community in American society. P.Moen, D. Dempster- McClain, and H. A. Walker, (Eds) Ithaca, NY: Cornell University Press.

Weinberg, M. (1977*). A chance to learn , the history of race and education in the United States*. London: Cambridge University Press.

Weinberg, M. (1977). Minority students: A research appraisal. pp. 286-287. Washington, DC: U.S. Department of Health, Education and Welfare.

Wesley, C.H. (1927). *Negro labor in the United States, 1850-1925; A study in American economic history*. New York: Vanguard Press.

White Deer of Autumn. (1992). *The native American book of knowledge*. Hillsboro, OR: Beyond Words Publisher.

White Deer of Autumn. (1992). *The native American book of life*. Hillsboro, OR: Beyond Words Publisher.

Williams, G. W. (1882-1883). *History of the Negro race in America from 1619 to 1880: Negroes as slaves, as soldiers, and as citizens* (2 vols.) New York: G.P. Putnam's Sons.

Woodson, C.G. (1977). *The miseducation of the Negro*. (2nd ed.) New York: AMS Press. (Original work published 1933)

Woodson, C.G. & Wesley, C. H. (1922). *The Negro in our history*. Washington, DC: The Associate Publishers.

Woodson, C.G. (1919). *The education of the Negro prior to 1861*. 2nd edition. Washington, DC: The Associate Publishers.

Young, B. (Ed.). (1990). *Art, culture, and ethnicity*. Reston, VA: National Art Education Association.

Website References

Arizona Secretary of State. (2000). Proposition 203 [On Line] Available: http://www.sosaz.com/election/2000/info/pubpamphlet/english/prop203.htm.

AT&T, (n. d.) Cybercampus [On line] Available: http://www.hsf.net/cybercampus/collegeguide/09.html.

Clover, Faith. (2001). Navajo art: A way of life, ArtsEdnet [On Line] Available: http://www.getty.edu/artsednet/resources/Navajo/index.html.

Erickson, Mary, (2001). Mexican American murals: Making a place in the world, ArtsEdNet, [On Line] Available: http://www.getty.edu/artsednet/resources/Murals/index.html.

Walker, H. (2001). African American art: A Los Angeles legacy, ArtsEdNet [On Line] Available: http://www.getty.edu/artsednet/resources/African/index.html.

15

Chapter 2

What Are Artworlds and Why Are They Important?

by Mary Erickson

The first chapter, "Multicultural Challenges in Art Education," describes how the United States, like many other 21st century nations, is profoundly multicultural. Educators in a constantly evolving multicultural society face the challenge of organizing instruction that, on the one hand, is meaningful to students who identify with distinct ethnic groups and, on the other hand, provides a structure within which students can understand people from other cultures (both within and outside the nation). At the same time, communities expect schools to provide instruction that allows students to gain a sense of membership in the larger culture.

A culture is maintained by people who invest meaning in, and center all or part of their identity on understandings and values that come from shared experience. Traditionally people have formed cultures around such shared values as ethnic heritage, political boundaries, language, and religion. A broad range of cultures make up the nations of North America. Hundreds of Native American cultures have thrived on the continent for millennia. Some, like the Iroquois, developed alliances or federations. European conquerors and colonists attempted to shape cultural diversity into formally structured, often hierarchical, societies. Some religious groups set out to establish utopian societies. Voluntary immigrants sought identities as members of new nations while enriching those nations with their diversity. Involuntary minority cultures that developed out of slavery and colonialism sought to preserve their cultural heritage in the face of domination and to seek their rights as citizens in a society in transition.

Teachers across the curriculum, especially in history and social studies, have the opportunity and responsibility to introduce the multicultural nature of North American nations to their students. A history teacher can guide students in comparing and contrasting characteristics of indigenous, colonial, imperial, agricultural, slave, peasant,

revolutionary, industrial, immigrant, democratic, and global cultures as they evolve through history. A social science teacher can guide students' investigation of characteristics that help define some of the many ethnic subcultures within a nation, such as Native American, African America, Latina/o, or Asian America.

In addition to identifying with traditional cultures, individuals also have built important associations around other more specific interests or experiences, such as a passion for sports, food, fashion, cars, popular music, business, politics, and the arts. If people invest meaning in and center all or part of their identities on understandings and values that come from shared experiences involving these (and many more) interests, these groups can also be understood as cultures. Interest groups, especially those with which students are familiar, provide students with prior knowledge of how cultures work. Many elementary and secondary students, even many adults, are largely unaware of the cultural structures that surround them. Teachers can exploit students' prior knowledge of the everyday cultures in which they participate as a means to introduce important cultures with which students may be less familiar. For example, analyzing key people, places, activities, and ideas of the skateboarding culture or pop music culture can help students construct a sense of culture as being defined by its people, places, activities, and ideas. They can then apply that sense of culture to their investigation of other cultures, such as Inuit, African American, or Latina/o cultures.

Artworlds are Cultures Within Cultures.
Throughout time and across the globe subcultures focused on art have developed within the larger cultures of various ethnic groups. Working with the support of these art subcultures, or artworlds, people have made and continue to make extraordinary objects, or artworks, that carry special meaning for the larger culture. Understanding these artworks

can be a key to understanding the ideas and values of the cultures in which they were made. As Smith (1995) has proposed "our understanding of what art is and how we should experience it must take into account more than its directly perceptible features; it is not enough just to look and see" (p. 69). Artworks are potent resources for instruction about one's own culture and about the culture of others. For example, the spiritualism of liturgical artworks produced in the 18th century in the territory now known as New Mexico mirrors the spiritual interests of the larger culture, Colonial New Spain, of which that territory was a part. Similarly the focus on consumerism that drives the advertising artworld mirrors the consumerism upon which modern capitalist, industrial cultures are built. Learning about a culture's artworld offers an approach to understanding these cultures.

A variety of distinct, yet interrelated artworlds make up the United States artworld (and also the Canadian and Mexican artworlds) today. Among those artworlds are the mainstream museum artworld, folk artworlds, commercial artworlds, ceremonial artworlds, and the artworlds of various ethnic groups. Similarly, within the artworld of any particular ethnic group (such as those of the Inuit, African American, or Chicana/o cultures) are diverse, evolving, overlapping artworlds. For example, Sam Coronado, a key figure in the Chicano artworld of Austin, Texas, recently identified three distinct artworlds in which he works: commercial, fine art, and technical artworlds (Coronado, 2000). In addition his work draws imagery from the mass media and popular arts of both the United States and Mexico, as well as from the artworlds of Pre-Hispanic Mesoamerica. Other artists deliberately set about to learn and use the traditions of more than one artworld. For example Roger Shimomura, the Japanese American artist, draws from both the mainstream contemporary artworld and the artworld of traditional Japanese woodblock printing. He borrows visual conventions from the latter and exhibits his work in museums associated with the former.

To art educators who assume that there is only one, global artworld, it makes sense to build curriculum around the knowledge and skills shared within that artworld. Teachers can pass on traditions and conventions without placing them within the artworld context within which they came to be. For example, teachers can teach students how to use two-point perspective or to value originality without any artworld context, thereby leading students to believe that these ideas are shared in all artworlds, which, of course, they are not.

In his recent book advocating art as intellect, Dorn (1999) sets forth a curriculum centered on "the creative act," apparently with the assumption that this act is universal for all art makers. He describes art educators who use the artworld as a basis for curriculum development as taking an overly sociological viewpoint. He proposes that were it the case that the artworld is a necessary precondition to art, there "would not be a single art world, but rather many simultaneous art worlds or systems" (1999, p. 183). This is precisely the belief that undergirds this book. In fact the model instructional unit introduced in the third chapter, "How Can an Artworld-Centered Online Curriculum be Used?" and assembled lesson plans presented in the second part of this volume are intended to illustrate the richness of those "many simultaneous art worlds or systems."

The concept of artworld may be a new idea for many teachers, even art teachers. Chalmers (1999), a long-time champion for multicultural art education, claims that there is now considerable support for the notion that "artists produce and perform their works within a matrix of shared under-standings and understood purposes. . . But curriculum has not kept pace with changes in theory" (p. 16). The concept of artworld can be invaluable to teachers both as a curriculum organizer and also as an important source of group identity. The concept of artworld as a curriculum organizer can help students and teachers seek meaningful connections among artworks from the diverse cultures that make up a multicultural society. Understanding artworlds also can help students and teachers gain the support that comes from being members of an important group.

The first chapter, "Multicultural Challenges in Art Educa-tion," makes a case for why art instruction (as well as education and scholarship) should be multicultural. Sabol (2000) identifies a barrier "that [often] prevents [art teachers] from putting the 'theory into practice'" (p. 13). He proposes that "one underlying cause of the problem is the lack of a curriculum model or structure in which to successfully organize and blend content of art history and multicultural education" (Sabol, 2000, p. 13). This book proposes that the notion artworld can be a central concept around which art teachers can build multicultural curriculum that integrates content from art history, and also from aesthetics, art criticism, and art making.

Key People, Places, Activities, and Ideas Characterize Artworlds.

An artworld is a culture maintained by people a significant portion of whose identity is drawn in some way from art. A person who is a member of an artworld is loosely or formally associated with other members of that artworld. Members of an artworld are familiar with some of the same art values and art ideas, and engage in, or are familiar with, some of the same art activities. Around the world and through the ages there have been many diverse artworlds, such as the Italian Renaissance artworld; the 16th century Incan artworld; the court artworld of Sung Dynasty China; the ceremonial artworld of the Kuba people of West Africa; and the contem-porary gallery artworlds in New York City, Chicago, and Los Angeles. The shared information, values, and activities that define these artworlds vary tremendously. Values and criteria prized in one artworld may not be prized in another. Investigating an unfamiliar artworld is an excellent avenue for gaining insights into unfamiliar, otherwise seemingly incomprehensible, or not easily appreciated artworks made within that artworld.

One can investigate particular artworlds by asking four questions about each:

1) Who are the *people* whom members of the artworld judge to be important in that artworld?
2) What are the *places* where members of the artworld meet to share activities and ideas?
3) What are the *activities* that are essential to maintaining the culture?
4) With what important art *ideas* are most members of the artworld familiar?

The heart of understanding any culture is understanding its activities and ideas. Identifying key people and places within a culture provides concrete entry points for the introduction of the distinctive activities and ideas of a culture. Concrete information is particularly important as a basis for introducing abstract ideas for elementary and secondary students. Let us consider each of these characteristics of artworld cultures in turn, beginning with the most concrete.

People

Individuals who identify with a particular artworld are very likely to be familiar with many of the same key people in that artworld. For example, individuals who identify with the contemporary Hopi silversmithing artworld are likely to be familiar with such prominent silversmiths as Gene Nuvahoyouma, Bernard Dawahoya, and Charles Loloma. They may be familiar with Paul Saufkie, who in the 1940s demonstrated Hopi silverwork as part of the Hopi Silver Project at the Museum of Northern Arizona (Mangum, 1995, p. 19). They may also recognize the name of Richard A. Mehagian, a non-Indian who owns Kopai International gallery and commissions Hopi silverwork (Wright, 1998). On the other hand, members of the European American Modernist artworld are likely to be familiar with prominent painters of the Modernist era, such as Jackson Pollack, Stuart Davis, and Georgia O'Keeffe and such prominent Modernist thinkers and patrons as Clement Greenberg, Monroe Beardsley, and Solomon Guggenheim.

Places

In addition to familiarity with prominent people, individuals who identify with a particular artworld are also likely to be familiar with many of the key places where members of the artworld meet to share activities and ideas. For example members of the early twentieth century African-American artworld were likely to be familiar with the Harlem Art Workshop, the Art Department and Gallery of Art at Howard University, the 135th Street Branch of the New York Public Library (now the Schomberg Center for Research in Black Culture), and the Carl van Vechten Gallery at Fisk University (Campbell, 1987; Reynolds & Wright, 1989, and Perry, 1992). Whereas members of the early 20th century Mexican artworld were likely to be familiar with the Workshop of People's Graphics, the School of Painting and Sculpture (founded by Siqueiros), and the National Museum of Art and the Academy of San Carlos in Mexico City (O'Neill, 1990).

Activities

Shared familiarity with art activities, like familiarity with key people and places, also varies from artworld to artworld. For example, the making of *santeros* (images of holy figures) and offrendas (temporary shrines) is an activity shared by many Mexican American artists. Whereas making, giving, and receiving objects representing particular family crest animals are activities associated with traditional Northwest Coast Native American artworlds (Stewart, 1979).

Ideas

Finally, commitment to different art ideas can distinguish members of different artworlds. The documentation of family ties and reinforcement of status derived from one's occupation or property were ideas often associated with the itinerant artworld of nineteenth century rural America. Whereas community heritage and solidarity are ideas often associated with the African American and Chicana/o mural artworld (Crockcroft & Barnet-Sanchez, 1993; and Griswold del Castillo, McKenna, & Yarbro-Bejarano, 1991).

Teachers wishing to help their students appreciate and learn from the rich variety of art in North America can look to its multicultural artworlds for guidance in introducing unfamiliar or challenging art to their students. Studying the distinctive characteristics of multicultural artworlds is important because:

1) Understanding diverse artworlds helps students broaden and refine their definitions of art. This key idea is that artworlds define art.
2) Students gain a more accurate (less mysterious) understanding of art making when it is introduced within an artworld context. This key idea is that artworlds enable artmaking.
3) Students expand the range of artworks they can understand and appreciate when artworks are introduced within an artworld context. This key idea is that artworlds reveal meaning in art.
4) Students who understand artworlds develop a more accurate understanding of the role of art in society. This key idea is that artworlds function in society.
5) Students who understand artworlds gain access to support systems they can use to enhance their own artmaking and/or art understanding. This key idea is that artworlds offer support.

Let us consider each key idea in turn.

Key Idea #1: Artworlds Define Art.

That's not art. A five-year-old could make it.
Art should be beautiful.
Art is individual expression.
Everything is art.

These statements reflect just a few of many commonly held, though often-unexamined, definitions of art. Understanding artworlds can help teachers and students evaluate the adequacy of their own definitions of art. In the 1960s Danto (1964) introduced the concept of "artworld" in an effort to deal with the new European American art of that time. He writes "to see something as art requires something the eye cannot decry—an atmosphere of artistic theory, a knowledge of the history of art; an art world" (p. 580). Later he writes that the knowledge he wanted to refer to is "a knowledge of what other works the given work fits with, a knowledge of what other works makes a given work possible" (Danto, 1997, p. 165).

Dickie (1974) proposed that artifacts can be called artworks because of the response of members of the artworld. He writes that "a work of art in the classificatory sense is (1) an artifact [made by a person], (2) a set of the aspects of which has been conferred upon it the status of candidate for appreciation by some person or persons acting on behalf of a certain social institution (the artworld)" (1974, p. 34). Dickie, like Danto, used the singular form of the word "artworld." He referred to *the* artworld, not to multiple artworlds. Danto's and Dickie's artworld institutions are European and European American organizations such as museums, galleries, arts councils, art funding agencies, and art schools.

Even though Danto's and Dickie's thinking has focused on contemporary European American art, the concept of artworld can be useful in understanding other art as well. In later years Becker (1982) used the concept of artworld more broadly, applying it not only to professional historical and contemporary European and American art, but also to mavericks, folk artists, and naïve artists. He writes:

> Art worlds consist of all the people whose activities are necessary to the production of the characteristic works which that world, and perhaps others as well, define as art. Members of art worlds coordinate the activities by which work is produced by referring to a body of conventional understandings embodied in common practice and in frequently used artifacts. The same people often, cooperate repeatedly, even routinely, in similar ways to produce similar works, so that we can think of an art world as an established network of cooperative links among participants (Becker, 1982, pp. 34-5).

Becker (1982) proposes that because "integrated professional artists" depend on shared history of problems and solutions, they "can produce work that is recognizable and understandable to others without being so recognizable and understandable as to be uninteresting" (p. 230). At the same time he argues that artworlds change as they "incorporate at a later date works they originally rejected" (Becker, 1982, p. 227). People understand and appreciate particular artworks because they already have some familiarity with other somewhat similar artworks made in the same artworld.

The ever-evolving traditional European and European American artworlds have been structured around quite different definitions of art through the centuries. In the 4th century BCE, Aristotle argued that art is imitation. In the 19th century, Tolstoy proposed that art is an expression of emotion. Engels, also writing in the second half of the 19th century, contended that art is a means of revolutionary action (or, if not, a bourgeois idea). In the early 20th century Fry defined art as significant form. In the mid-20th century Weitz called art an open concept. For Foucault, writing later in the 20th century, the production of meaning, in artworks and elsewhere, is a way to produce power.

Artworlds through time and around the world have defined and judged art differently. For example a 5th century Chinese Buddhist scholar wrote that landscape painting "expands the spirit" (Bush, 1983, p. 146). Bharata, an Indian intellectual of the third century, wrote that "art gives pleasure to mortals, and at the same time it shows them how to better themselves" (Anderson, 1990, p. 162). In traditional Yoruba aesthetics carved figures should meet nine criteria (neither too real or too abstract, clarity of line and form, luminosity, proper proportions, fine details, roundness, bilateral symmetry to give a sense of dignity, carving skill, and an optimal depiction of age between youth and old age) (Anderson, 1990, pp. 127-128). One would be hard pressed to propose a set of defining characteristics of good art that would be agreed to in all artworlds.

In some cultures there is no special word for art. Dissanayake (1988) proposes that cultures that do not have a word for art, nonetheless make special objects. These special objects, which others might call art, are produced with great care in order to make sure that people in the culture recognize and remember important events, such as changes in seasons; weddings; funerals; or other mythological, historical and spiritual events. Many artworld subgroups have also developed their own subculture with their own definitions and standards of quality, for example the ceramics, cartooning, computer graphics, watercolor, or installation artworlds.

There are at least two alternatives teachers can use to introduce students to definition(s) of art. They can choose a definition that has been developed and accepted in one artworld (perhaps the one with which they are most familiar or one presented in the popular media) and apply that single definition to all artworks in all artworlds. Or they can seek to discover multiple definitions held by members of different artworlds. The first alternative is arbitrary, tends to restrict the range of artworks presented to students, and can misrepresent that which is most meaningful in art, especially in artworks made in other artworlds. The second alternative stimulates curiosity about artworks with which one is unfamiliar. At the same time it resists the temptation to give up entirely and either propose that everything is art or that any definition of art is as good as the next. When teachers introduce students to the people, places, activities, and ideas of diverse artworlds, they provide them with appropriate information to consider when developing a definition (or definitions) of art, which they can support and share with others.

Key Idea #2: Artworlds Enable Art Making.

I wish I could draw.
I can't draw a straight line.
She's so talented.
Some people just have it and others don't.
He's so creative.
He's good with his hands.
She's a born artist.

These statements tend to imply that art making is an attribute with which one either is or is not fortunate enough to have been born. If artmaking is solely a gift of nature, then it follows that efforts by individuals without the gift will be futile.

In art, as in other areas of human endeavor, people differ in their abilities. There are child prodigies, like Mozart, who excelled in music at a very early age. Similarly there are children who seem "naturally" to take to drawing more than others. It is difficult to know to what extent a youngster's ability is natural or the result of encouragement and early positive experiences. Certainly early experiences can affect one's motivation. In turn, motivation affects one's willingness to seek knowledge or to master skills on one's own, and also affects one's receptiveness to instruction. Regardless of differences in abilities, in art, as in other areas of human endeavor, a supportive environment and instruction can make a huge difference. The achievements of so-called "talented" people, left on their own, especially if they are not strongly motivated, will usually be surpassed by people who are provided with the advantages of systematic instruction and support.

Some artists developed their artmaking skills in spite of their families. For example, over the protestations of his father, who disowned him for his decision, Luis Jiménez chose to go to Mexico City to work with the sculptor Francisco Zúñiga and then to New York where he apprenticed with the sculptor Seymour Lipton. Today Jiménez is, perhaps, the best-known Mexican American artist in the United States. His sculpture, *Vaquero,* stands at the entrance of the Smithsonian's Museum of American Art in Washington, DC. Jésus Moroles, a prominent contemporary Chicano sculptor was, in turn, Jiménez's apprentice. Moroles has described his work as an apprentice with Jiménez: "I was working with him, and even at the time I hadn't really decided what direction my work was going to go. I feel like in that one year I was able to gain so much experience just by osmosis, by being around him, doing the same galleries, the same exhibitions, the same museums, the same gallery talks, museum talks, transporting, shipping, work ethic, everything that he did that translated into what I wanted to do" (Moroles, 1999, p. 29). In addition to the traditional master-apprentice relationship, a number of Chicana/o artists have established supportive working collaborations, for example The Chicano Royal Airforce, Los Four, and Mujeres Muralistas.

Ester Hernández's persistence sustained her as she sought a supportive artworld environment. As a child she learned from her mother, who made traditional Mexican embroideries, and from her father, who was a photographer and carpenter who made religious sculptures in his spare time (Hernández, 1998). Just out of high school, when the United Farmworkers marched in her hometown, Hernández began to think of art as a way to change things for the better. In the 1970s she studied mural making and silkscreen printing with Malaquias Montoya, before being recruited by the University of California at Berkeley. She reports that at Berkeley "the art department was hell for all of us colored girls. All the teachers were old white men who could barely deal with the younger generation. We were of another world, another time. They were like dinosaurs with power and tenure. Fran Valesco was a lecturer in the art department. She respected people of color, and white women. The professors didn't respect us. They basically stayed with the boys who they thought were going to emulate their style of work or who were already following what was going on in New York. Yet we put up with the abuse and disrespect, because we wanted to contribute to our communities" (Mesa-Bains, 1995, n.p.). Still later she found support when she exhibited at San Francisco's Galleria de la Raza and joined a group of Chicana artists who called themselves Mujeres Muralistas.

Of course the means of developing art knowledge and skills and the means of learning to meet the criteria generally agreed upon within an artworld vary from artworld to artworld. For example, in the 19th century United States, the Academy of Art and Design in New York City established standards for those it accepted in its ranks and assisted artists in learning how to meet those standards. Traditionally

Navajo medicine men teach and set standards for sandpainting. Nampeyo, a well-known Hopi potter of the late 19th and early 20th centuries, learned pottery making from her grandmother and was also influenced by prehistoric pots being unearthed in the Southwest where she lived. Today a number of female descendents continue pot-making traditions passed down in the Nampeyo family.

Still there are exceptions—people who are motivated and self-disciplined enough to persist in educating themselves. Occasionally, the achievements of artworld "outsiders" or "self-taught" art makers are recognized and shared through publications, exhibitions, and efforts to preserve their work. Today many self-taught artists benefit from seeing art (or reproductions of art) made by established artists. Some outsider artists have been discovered by the mainstream artworld. Rhodes (2000) writes "Paradoxically, for living artists, problems relating to the quality of Outsider Art arise only when the work becomes visible to national and international audiences…. Except in cases of extreme indifference to their surroundings, the new status… will almost inevitably alter the aspirations of the maker (without necessarily altering the *look* of the work)" (p. 20). More often than not the achievements of self-taught artists are personal, or limited to the sphere of friends and relatives, and disappear with the passing of the art maker.

Becker (1982) sums up the importance of artworld support of artmaking when he argues that: "all artistic work, like all human activity, involves the joint activity of a number… of people. Through their cooperation, the art work we eventually see or hear comes to be and continues to be. The work always shows signs of that cooperation" (p. 1). If teachers attribute the success of art making predominately to inborn "talent," they may deprive students of the opportunity to acquire the knowledge and skills developed, maintained, and passed on in diverse artworlds.

Key Idea #3: Artworlds Reveal Meaning in Art.
I just don't get it. It just looks weird to me.
It looks so real. You can almost feel the fur on the dog.
Wow. It must have taken a long time to make that.
It doesn't look like anything to me. What's it supposed to be?
It's pretty. It would look nice in my living room.

These expressions are indications of many individuals' assumptions or confusions about what to make of the art they see. Without an introduction to art, people can reach adulthood without understanding that artworks can convey meaning. Many adults in North America assume without question that artworks should be realistic, beautiful, and well crafted (Parsons, 1987). They may never even have considered that artworks can express ideas and feelings, that is, that they can be meaningful.

Things derive much of their meaning from their contexts. The Dow Jones Industrial average is meaningless without some knowledge of the world of finance. Even though one can appreciate Michael Jordan's athleticism by simply watching tapes of his performance, the significance of his basketball achievements is enriched by an understanding of the game and rules of the National Basketball Association.

The context required to understand some visual images, at least on the surface, requires no special training. Marketers, the mass media, and advertisers are expert at tailoring their products to particular groups. People who are in the target audience for particular images and products require no special education to understand those images and products. For example growing up in the United States in itself prepares one to recognize Mickey Mouse, Uncle Sam, Snoopy, and the Stars and Stripes. However growing up in the United States does not necessarily prepare one to appreciate many of the achievements of people in other cultures, including achievements in multicultural artworlds.

Artworks, like achievement in other domains, depend for much of their meaning on prior understanding of particular images and ideas. Just as today's writers depend on their readers' understanding of certain verbal references, such as Shakespeare's phase "a pound of flesh" or Mark Twain's fence-whitewashing story, art makers draw upon their viewers' prior visual experience. Without some grasp of traditional or conventional visual references, viewers can only access a limited portion of the rich meanings that artworks can convey. Robert Colescott's *George Washington Carver Crossing the Delaware* loses its bite if the viewer is unfamiliar with Emanuel Gottlieb Leutze's mid-19th century painting, *George Washington Crossing the Delaware*. Viewers gain a fuller appreciation of Mark Rothko's color field paintings from prior acquaintance with Joseph Albers's *Homage to the Square* series. Similarly, viewers familiar with North American quilts bring certain visual understandings to their appreciation of the quilts of Faith Ringgold.

Many people in North America have little or no prior knowledge to draw upon as they attempt to appreciate art made in their own or others' cultures. Teachers interested in helping their students broaden and deepen their appreciation of a wide range of artworks might want to be sure to consider artworks made in traditionally under-represented artworlds in North America, such as Native American, African American, Latina/o, and Asian American artworlds.

When teachers present their students with artworks isolated from any artworld context, students appreciate those artworks only superficially, or do not appreciate them at all. Of course students may enjoy some visual qualities or perhaps respect the craftsmanship of an unfamiliar artwork. However without knowledge of an artwork's artworld context, students' understanding of unfamiliar or challenging art-works is limited and may even be erroneous. As Chapman (1982) argued two decades go, neither art making nor art understanding are "instant." If teachers look for and share information about features found in any artworld (people, places, activities, and ideas), they can build a bridge from students' prior understanding of any culture or interest group, to otherwise unfamiliar cultures and artworlds. Sharing artworld information provides students with appropriate bases for seeking meaning in a wide range of artworks, both those made in the students' own culture and those made in the cultures of others.

Key Idea #4: Artworlds Function in Society.

Art is a frill.
Art isn't practical. It doesn't really do anything.
I wouldn't want that in my house.
Art is mostly for rich people.
If that's good taste, I must not have any.

These statements reveal a limited understanding of the power of art within society. Parsons (1987) proposes that many people who have had little sustained experience with art either respond unreflectively to artworks or judge all art against the standards of beauty, realism, and skill. To these people statements such as those above make a lot of sense. On the other hand, if one sees artworks as functional cultural artifacts, these statements are inadequate to explain the role of art in society.

Some viewers understand that artworks can express meaning, though they may be confused about where meaning resides. Parsons (1987) contends that for many people, the sole arbiter of meaning in an artwork is the art maker. Whatever the art maker's intentions are must surely be the meaning of the artwork. For others, an artwork means whatever any sincere viewer thinks it means.

Only when viewers understand that artworks derive much of their meaning from their contexts, do they begin to grasp two ideas: (1) art reflects its culture and (2) art affects its culture (Erickson, 1995). As one learns about the cultural context within which artworks are made, one begins to understand how art reflects differences in those cultures. Currier and Ives prints, and the paintings of American Regionalists, like Thomas Hart Benton and Grant Wood, clearly reflect more agrarian cultures than those in which many people live today. Similarly examination of Aztec Codices, Navajo sandpaintings, 18th century American portraits, and modern sculptures yield a good deal of information about the cultures in which they were made.

For many, cultural understanding of art stops with the idea that art *reflects* culture and does not extend to the idea that art can *affect* culture. When one begins to focus on the many functions that artworks have served through time and across cultures, one begins to comprehend how powerful art has been and still can be. When one asks not only the question "What does it express?" but also "What does it do?" (Tagg, 1988), one opens up a whole new vista for understanding.

H. W. Janson, a prominent art historian, condemned Grant Wood's midwestern country paintings as fascist propaganda. The New York artworld claimed that Wood's paintings satirized up-tight midwestern values (Corn, 1983). Meanwhile midwesterners, who flocked in record numbers to view Wood's *American Gothic* in Chicago's Art Institute, may well have found that Wood's paintings celebrated their own traditional values. If one wishes to discover the role of particular artworks within their cultures, one might ask, for example: What did Aztec codices do for priests, aristocracy, rulers, peasants, and slaves? What do Navajo sandpaintings do for medicine men, clan members, and individuals who are ill or dealing with imbalance in their lives? What did eighteenth century portraits do for the sitters, for visitors to homes where the portraits were displayed, for workers in those homes, for others in early American society? What do modern sculptors do for museum patrons, corporations, or individuals who own them, and for the general public?

In recent years some elected officials and members of the public have raised questions about sexually explicit photography, artworks that appropriate traditional religious or patriotic symbols, music and movies with violent subject matter, and media ads that employ visual references to implicitly sway voters or consumers. Radio and television talk shows and Internet chat rooms present evidence that many people today believe that the arts not only have an impact on society, but may even be dangerous. That is, some individuals have perceived certain controversial artworks as contributing to such societal ills as religious intolerance, violence, ethnic or gender prejudice, general incivility, or inappropriate sexual behavior.

Investigating the artworlds within which diverse artworks are made can shed light on the many ways that art functions within various cultures. As teachers prepare to present artworks, they can seek information about the key *people* in the artworlds (for example, art makers, patrons, intended viewers and users, critics, and collectors). They can attempt to identify key *places* in those artworlds (for example ceremonial centers, places accessible only to the privileged or initiated, government buildings, private homes, galleries, and museums). They can investigate key *activities* associated with the making, viewing, and using the artwork (for example, working within a guild systems; serving as an apprentice; training at an art school or academy; using art in prayer, sacrifice, or ritual; museum going as a tourist activity; buying art as an investment; attending art receptions to make contacts; and studying art as a scholarly career).

Finally, they can begin to reflect on the key *ideas* and beliefs that undergird the artworks (for example, status, religious devotion, capitalism, and social harmony). Readers are invited to use the Artworld Analysis worksheets in the Resources part of this book to guide their study of whatever artworlds they believe are important enough to include in their curriculum.

When one is unaware of the existence of artworlds one may confuse a learned or conditioned response to art with a "natural" or biological response. Parsons and Blocker (1992) explain that what may seem to be a direct response to an artwork may in fact be misleading or overstated. They propose:

> The directness of our response rests on a set of expectations and conventions that we share with artists and their audience and that lie beneath our conscious awareness… .All art… rests on expectations about its functions and how the audience should respond to it, and all art uses conventions that give shape to its structure and meaning. But in many cases these expectations and conventions have become habitual to us and have faded into transparency. . . . The unconscious assimilation of ideas accounts for the immediate appeal of art from our own culture (Parsons and Blocker p. 41).

People who are unaware of the existence of, or role played by diverse artworlds within their cultures and who believe that understanding art happens without context can develop interesting explanations for their appreciation (or lack of appreciation) of particular artworks. For example, if they don't care for artworks that others seem to think are great, they may conclude that they lack some attribute like "taste" or "a good eye." Or if they discover that they seem to appreciate the same sorts of artworks as others in their social class, they may conclude that they do indeed have "taste" or "a good eye," when in fact what they share may be similar family and social expectations and conditioning. When they don't immediately appreciate unfamiliar artworks, they may close off any opportunity to increase their appreciation by accepting the idea that individuals' responses to artworks are ultimately and unavoidably idiosyncratic. For such individuals there is little point in discussing artworks.

When teachers help students understand the many diverse artworlds within which artworks are made, they not only help them understand the many functions of art in society, but also provide students with a foundation for discussing artworks with others who are not already of a like mind, and the means to make informed decisions about the role of art in their own lives and within their own cultures.

Key Idea #5: Artworlds Offer Support.
I don't know anything about art, but I know what I like.
Artists are eccentric (weird, isolated, unappreciated, etc).
I'm just not an art-kind-of person.

These statements reveal no awareness of the artworld cultures that support art activity within a community or culture. Artworlds offer a great deal to people who are interested both in making art and also in understanding the art of others. While some self-taught artists have achieved some success largely on their own, the vast majority of art makers and other art specialists have benefited from crucial artworld support. Pervasive romantic ideas about starving artists struggling in isolation perpetuate mystical notions about artmaking. In addition although one can enjoy some aspects of artworks through direct examination, many people who appreciate art do so in large part because of the conditioning and/or education they have received through contact with artworld systems.

Teachers can introduce their students to a system of support that students can use throughout their lives as they pursue their own interests both in artmaking and also in art understanding. Teachers can help their students understand that there are key *people* in their community (art makers, critics, art historians, art teachers, community art leaders, museum personnel, etc.) who can help them pursue their interests. They can introduce their students to key artworld *places* in their community (art schools, colleges and universities, art galleries and museums, community art centers, libraries, art supply stores, art fairs, etc.). They can introduce their students to some of the many *activities* through which they can pursue an interest in art (for example participating in gallery talks and artist workshops, taking classes, reading reviews and criticism, visiting exhibitions, reading popular and scholarly publications, and of course, making artworks and constructing their own interpretations). Finally teachers can guide students in thinking more broadly and deeply about *ideas* associated with art (for example, about its nature, value, and role in society) and thereby help them reflect on themselves, their culture, and the art and cultures of others.

To sum up, the concept of artworld provides teachers with a powerful idea around which to construct multicultural art curricula that draw on the overlapping disciplines of aesthetics, artmaking, art criticism, and art history. Studying how artworlds define art (Key Idea #1) offers an entry point for multicultural aesthetics. Examining how artworlds enable art making (Key Idea #2) opens new approaches to multicultural art production. Investigating how artworlds reveal meaning in art (Key Idea #3) broadens avenues for multicultural art criticism. Considering how artworks function in society (Key Idea #4) suggests a way to integrate multicultural art history. Exploring how artworlds offer support (Key Idea #5) gives teachers a tool to help students discover the artworld of their own community as a basis for understanding and building connections to that artworld and to the many other artworlds that exist in North America.

References

Anderson, R. (1990). *Calliope's sisters: A comparative study of philosophies of art*. Engelwood Cliffs, NJ: Prentice Hall, Inc..

Becker, H.S. (1982) *Art worlds*. Berkeley, CA: University of California Press.

Bush, S. (1983) Tsung Ping's essay on painting landscape and "Landscape Buddhism" of Mount Lu. In S. Bush & Murick, C. (Eds), *Theories of the arts in China* (pp. 132-164). Princeton, NJ: Princeton University Press.

Campbell, M.S. (1987). *Harlem renaissance art in black America*. New York: Harry N. Abrams.

Chalmers, G. (1999). Why focus on the common ground? *Journal of Multicultural and Cross-Cultural Research in Art Education, 17,* 16-19.

Chapman, L.H. (1982). *Instant art, instant culture: The unspoken policy for American schools*. New York: Teachers College Press.

Corn, W. M. (1983). *Grant Wood: The regionalist vision*. New Haven, CT: Yale University Press.

Coronado, S. (2000). Notes taken by Mary Erickson at presentation at Arizona State University's Hispanic Research Center on September 15.

Crockcroft, E.S. & Barnet-Sanchez, H. (1993). *Signs from the heart: California Chicano murals*. Venice, CA: Social and Public Art Resource Center.

Danto, A.C. (1964). The art world. *Journal of Philosophy, 61* (19), 571-84.

Danto, A.C. (1997). *After the end of art: Contemporary art and the pale of history*. Princeton, NJ: Princeton University Press.

Dickie, G. (1974). *Art and aesthetics: An institutional analysis*. Ithaca, NY: Cornell University Press.

Dissanayake, E. (1988). *What is art for?* Seattle: University of Washington Press.

Dorn, C. (1999). *Mind in art: Cognitive foundations in art education*. Lawrence Erlbaum Associates, Inc.

Erickson, M. (1995). A sequence of developing art historical understandings: Merging teaching, service, research, and curriculum development, *Art Education, 48,* (6), 23-37.

Griswold del Castillo, R.,McKenna, T. & Yarbro-Bejarano, Y. (1991). *Chicano art: Resistance and affirmation*. Los Angeles: Wight Art Gallery, University of California.

Hernández, E. (1998). Latina/Latino artists discussing their works: I, 1848/1898@1998, Transhistorical Thresholds, Arizona State University, December 10, 1998.

Mangum, R. & S. (1995). *The Hopi silver project of the Museum of Northern Arizona*. Flagstaff, AZ: Museum of Northern Arizona.

Mesa-Bains, A. (1995). *The art of provocation: Works of Ester Hernández,* Gorman, Museum, UC Davis: Davis, CA.

Moroles, J. (1999. March-April). Fourth General Session, *In Keynote Addresses* (pp. 28-34). Washington, DC: National Art Education Association Convention

O'Neill, J.P. (1990). *Mexico: Splendors of thirty centuries*. New York: Metropolitan Museum of Art.

Parsons, M.J. (1987). *How we understand art: A cognitive account of the development of aesthetic understanding*. New York: Cambridge University Press.

Parsons, M.J. & Blocker, H. G. (1993). *Aesthetics and education*. Urbana and Chicago: University of Illinois Press.

Perry, R.A. (1992). *Free within ourselves: African-American artists in the collection of the National Museum of American Art*. Washington, DC: National Museum of American Art.

Reynolds, G.A. & Wright, B. J. (1989*). Against the odds: African-American artists and the Harmon Foundation*. Newark, NJ: The Newark Museum.

Rhodes, C. (2000). Outsider art: Spontaneous alternatives. London: Thames & Hudson.

Sabol, R.F. (2000). Studying art history through the multicultural education looking-glass. *Art Education, 53* (3), pp. 12-17.

Smith, R.S. (1995). *Excellence II: The continuing quest in art education*. Reston, VA: National Art Education Association.

Stewart, H. (1979). *Looking at Indian art of the northwest coast*. Vancouver, British Columbia: Douglas and McIntyre.

Tagg, J. (1988). Art history and difference. In A. L. Rees & F. Borzello (Eds), *The new history of art* (pp. 164-171). Atlantic Highlands, NJ: Humanities Press International.

Wright, M.N. (1998). *Hopi silver: The history and hallmarks of Hopi silversmithing*. 5th ed. Flagstaff, AZ: Northland Publishing.

Chapter 3

How Can an Artworld-Centered Online Curriculum Be Used?

by Faith Clover

Six art teachers, collaborating with university professors Young, Erickson, and Clover, made up the team that participated in preparation for and teaching of an artworld-centered curriculum unit. Research findings on the effectiveness of the unit on students' understanding of their own artworlds are in the next chapter. This chapter focuses on curriculum and instruction. The team identified several online curriculum resources that had the potential to become the basis of an artworld-centered unit of instruction called "Protest and Persuasion." As all good teachers do, these teachers adapted and augmented the available online resources and developed teaching strategies that would best help their students to achieve the objectives of the unit. This chapter introduces the online resources and describes how teachers used and augmented these resources.

Who are the Teachers and Students Involved in this Research?

Six experienced art teachers participated in this study. One high school art teacher taught two sections of Art 1-2 and one section of Art and Cultures at an urban high school that is predominantly Hispanic in population. Two Navajo art teachers at a high school on the Navajo Nation in northeastern Arizona taught the unit to one class of ceramics students and one class of design students. Two middle school art teachers participated. Both teach in greater urban settings where the majority of students are on free or reduced lunch and over 50% of the students are Hispanic. One elementary art teacher taught two sections of fourth graders in a large suburban school that is predominantly white and middle-class through upper middle-class.

This group of teachers, along with the three university professors[1][2], collaborated in the design of the procedure for teaching "Protest and Persuasion." While the basis of the unit they taught was an online resource, they made selections of activities and augmented instruction with additional materials they designed individually or together.

What Artworld-Centered Resources Did the Teachers Use?

Because teaching the concept of artworld was central to the unit, students were introduced or reintroduced to this concept as a foundation for studying "Protest and Persuasion." For this purpose the teachers drew from components of a lesson called "Places in the LA Artworld." This lesson is part of a larger unit called *Understanding Art* (Erickson and Clover, 1998), which is one of a series of units designed to introduce students to a variety of artworlds posted in a larger curriculum resource called *Worlds of Art* (Erickson, 1998). "Places in the LA Artworld" introduces students to the idea that an artworld is a culture within a culture and that there are special people, places, activities, and ideas associated with each particular artworld. This lesson uses Self-Help Graphics as an example of an important place in the Los Angeles artworld. Self-Help Graphics provides a showcase for Chicana/o art and artists within that community in Los Angeles. Its printmaking workshop is a place where artists can produce their prints. They provide a rich array of programming that serves both the Chicana/o community and the broader art community of Los Angeles. The lesson lists people, places, activities, and ideas representative of that artworld. The lesson also includes discussion questions that can be used to examine any artworld. All these resources could be used as they appear online. However, the teachers who participated in this study chose to adapt, supplement, and extend the lessons.

The core of the unit is "Protest and Persuasion" (Erickson, 1997). This thematic, inquiry-based unit appears on *Chicana and Chicano Space* (Erickson & Keller Cárdenas, 1997-1999), a site posted by Arizona State University's Hispanic Research Center. The theme of this unit is expressed in two statements:

- We all choose which traditions to follow and which to challenge.
- Art can protest, propose, and provoke ideas.

A general introduction to the theme is as follows:
> When people are not satisfied with things the way they are, they sometimes protest or try to persuade others to change their ideas. They work to change things by criticizing or protesting the old ways and replacing them with new ways. Some protests lead to revolutions. There are various kinds of revolutions. In political revolutions the old powers are overthrown and new people take over the government. In social revolutions the relationships between social classes change, or the population experiences the rise of new social classes or the expansion of existing classes. In economic revolutions wealth changes hands. There are also scientific, industrial, agricultural, artistic, and religious revolutions when old ideas are replaced by new ideas.

This online unit has two strands that address these theme statements. One is on murals; the other is on printmaking. The team used only the printmaking strand.

An inquiry-based approach uses questions to help students learn. This approach helps focus student research and makes students active seekers of knowledge, rather than passive listeners. As an inquiry-based unit "Protest and Persuasion" draws from a set of eighteen inquiry questions accessible in the onlineunit. The unit addresses just three of these questions. Asking "What can I learn about the tools, materials, and processes the artmaker chose?" leads students to an exploration of the printmaking processes used by artists whose artwork is used as exemplars, as well as guiding their own printmaking choices. Asking "What visual elements do I see?" (in this case, the element of shape) students develop an understanding of how printmakers have used positive and negative shapes to create symbols of protest and persuasion that communicate a message to the viewer. Finally, investigating "What can I learn about how the patron, user, or viewer understood the artwork?" helps students to understand the artworld in which the artists live (or lived) and work (or worked). This question is one that directly addresses the concept of artworld as incorporated into the "Protest and Persuasion" unit.

Once students have been introduced to the concept of artworld it is a thread that can run through the teaching of any inquiry-based or thematic unit in which the art of one or more artworlds is being studied. Over the course of a semester or school year, students may be introduced to a number of artworlds from different times, places, and cultures. In this way they come to understand both the similarities and the differences of the people, places, activities, and ideas among different artworlds.

"Protest and Persuasion" includes eight lessons. The team drew from five for their unit. The first lesson is an "Introduction to Protest and Persuasion," in which students begin to think about using art for the purposes of protesting to improve situations and of persuasion to influence people's opinions. They look for evidence of subject matter or symbolism used by Mexican and Chicano/a artists to protest or persuade. In the second lesson students examine a number of prints that represent "Art for Protest and Persuasion." A total of eleven prints are posted with the unit. A total of 32 images are posted on this site. Each of these images is accompanied by well-researched answers to the eighteen inquiry questions. The third lesson, "Shaping Ideas," aids students in looking for the use of shape in an effective composition and to express ideas of protest and persuasion through symbolism and choice of subject matter. In the fourth lesson students discuss the question of "Who Sees Art?" This lesson is about the characteristics of the overlapping Chicana/o and Mexican artworlds. Finally, the students are "Making Art that Matters." Here they express their own opinions about issues making linoprint images of protest and persuasion. Readers are invited to examine the online lessons introduced above using the Website addresses provided in the Reference list.

What Basic Structure Did the Teachers Agree to Use?
First, the research team agreed to limit the number of primary Mexican and Chicana/o prints to four and to add four prints by African American artists. The four Mexican and Chicana/o artworks are Carlos Cortez Koyokuilatl's *Untitled Linocut*, José Guadalupe Posada's *Calavera Revolucionaria*, Alfredo Zalce's *Untitled Woodcut* and Lisza Juarigue's print *Divide and Conquer*. Four prints by African American artists were selected to introduce the African American artworld. These prints were not available online, but were chosen by Young, who also provided the artworld inquiry information on these artworks. The four prints are Elizabeth Catlett's *Harriet*, John C. Scott's *Saint George*, William E, *Smith's Bill Johnson as Emperor*, and Charles White's *Solid as a Rock*. (These four artworks, as well as the four Chicana/o prints, are reproduced in the Resources part of this book.)

The team agreed to a basic structure of lessons for their unit. Two pre-assessment activities preceded instruction and these activities were repeated as a post-assessment. Details of these activities appear in the next chapter.

In Lesson Two, "Art for Protest and Persuasion" teachers presented printmaking techniques. Students made sketches of shapes and symbols that might be used in their own protest and persuasion prints. Some students used ideas from their pre-assessment in these sketches. Ultimately, they created a relief print in black ink on white paper.

The teachers introduced the concept of shape, using examples of how a number of artists use shape. The classes examined the use of positive and negative shape and the contrast of black and white. Teachers stressed seeing shapes as symbols that have the ability to communicate ideas about protest and persuasion. The concept of shape is outlined in Lesson Three: "Shaping Ideas."

Teachers next presented the idea of artworld. Some teachers introduced or reviewed the concept of artworld, using ideas and activities based on "Places in the LA Artworld." The primary instructional focus, however, was drawn from Lesson Four: "Who Sees the Art?" In this lesson students were asked to think about the viewer, user, or patron for whom an artwork might be intended. Students were asked to show their preliminary plans and tell the class for which specific viewers their artwork was intended. Students discussed the art making decisions they were making in order to communicate effectively with their intended viewers.

The Mexican and Chicana/o printmaking artworld was introduced and the people, places, activities, and ideas of that artworld were discussed using the four primary prints as a focus for the discussion. The African American artworld was introduced and the four prints were used as the basis of the instruction. During this time students continued to refine their plans for their own protest and persuasion relief prints.

Following the post-assessment activities, students completed their final protest and persuasion relief prints based on their plans. Each class engaged in Lesson Five: "Making Art that Matters."

How Did Teachers Adapt the Online Resources?
The research team met often and agreed on selections from and/or adaptations to the online unit. Several of the teachers met to develop packets of supplementary materials to aid in teaching the various concepts of the unit. From that point on, teachers developed specific teaching strategies that would be most effective with their own students.

Introducing the Theme of Protest and Persuasion
Together the teachers created 22" x 36" laminated poster reproductions of the eight prints accompanied by basic information about each print. The teachers displayed these reproductions of the eight prints and basic information about each in their classrooms for the duration of the unit. This gave students repeated opportunities to examine the prints and become more familiar with them.

One of the middle school teachers created a handout "What is Protest and Persuasion?" that she used with students. Another developed a one-page handout for each print. These handouts included an outline of the protest or persuasion purpose of the print.

One of the high school teachers introduced the theme using the online curriculum. She followed with a brainstorming session in which students gave examples of protest with which they were familiar. They listed a variety of protest issues such as world hunger and school food. They went on to discuss the ways that people protest, such as marches, speeches, petitions, and editorials. Each student then determined an issue that was of concern to himself or herself and wrote a persuasive statement outlining his or her position on that issue.

Learning About Shapes and Symbols
Teaching about shape required teachers to develop strategies for their particular levels. The first task was to teach or review the concept of positive and negative space. Elementary teachers gave their students a copy of one of the prints. They asked them to trim away the entire area that was not part of the image itself. Next they gave students each one sheet of 12" x 18" colored construction paper that they folded in half. Then students were to cut out the positive or black shapes in the print. This was a difficult task for many students as they tried to decide how to cut the black shapes out in as close to one whole piece as possible. Some students found that they had four or more pieces. A great deal of artmaking decision-making was involved. Students then placed the leftover negative or white pieces down on one half of the construction paper and traced around the empty positive spaces. These spaces became the area where they glued down the black shapes to the construction paper. On the other side of the folded construction paper the students glued the white shapes. The end result was two compositions: one from the original positive shapes and one from the negative shapes.

One middle school teacher had the students make a mirror image composition in which the students cut a shape from black paper and glued it onto a white paper in the same position in which it was cut from the black. Then the remaining black negative shape was backed with white paper. The other middle school teacher taught the concept of positive and negative shape through a tracing activity. The teachers found that cutting shapes from paper was more effective in teaching about positive and negative shape than was any kind of drawing activity.

For the high school students, one teacher developed a packet of additional relief prints found in art books. These prints were ones in which positive and negative shape was very prominent. Teachers gave students these packets to examine and analyze.

The concept of symbols also proved difficult to teach. The elementary teacher took each print and cut out the symbols in each one. Students could recognize some symbols easily. They found others quite difficult to identify. Teachers divided students into small teams. Each team selected a recorder and, as each team tried to identify the meaning of each of the symbols, the recorder wrote down their group answer. Each team reported their results and discussed the similarities and differences in interpretations of the symbols.

One middle school teacher led a discussion of symbols based on the set of prints. She kept notes on butcher paper for future reference. The high school teachers helped students to identify the use of symbols in the prints and to think about what they could use to symbolize the issue they wished to illustrate. The idea of using symbols to convey an idea seemed easier for the high school students to understand.

Presenting Information about the Artworks and Artworlds

For the elementary classes the teacher rewrote the online information about the artworks in language appropriate for fourth grade readers. In addition, she gave each student a copy of one of the prints. Both middle school teachers created short, edited versions of the information about the artworks. They highlighted the key points on the handouts. In one classroom, teams of three students selected one of the prints and completed a worksheet covering information about the artwork.

At the high school on the Navajo Nation, the teacher gave the teams of students the information about the Mexican and Chicana/o prints from the website and print-based information about the African-American prints. Each team divided responsibility for summarizing sections of information and then reported out to the whole class.

Developing Technical Skills in Printmaking

Several of the teachers collaborated to develop a packet of technical information on relief printmaking. They selected a number of artworks to illustrate the studio processes involved. They selected other artworks to illustrate concepts of center of interest, texture, value, composition choices, and the use of various tools and strokes to create various effects. One handout emphasized the criteria that students should consider in order to make a successful print. Having these criteria available to them helped students to self assess their progress toward a successful relief print.

Learning about Artworlds

To review the concept of artworlds the teachers developed a handout that they used in concert with the online lessons. This handout gives examples of artworld places, activities, people and ideas associated with art and provides students with an opportunity to tell about the artworld places they have visited and activities in which they have participated.

The elementary classes wrote information they learned about artworlds on 8.5" x 11" enlarged poster copies of the artworld icons. The teacher designed artworld icons (an artworld activity icon, an artworld person icon, an artworld place icon, and an artworld idea icon) to reinforce features of artworlds. As the teacher presented information and as students discovered it on handouts they recorded information about artworld people on the people icon poster, about artworld places on the places icon poster, and so on. Then these posters, along with the large size posters of the primary prints, became part of the classroom environment for the duration of the unit.

At the Navajo high school the teacher used overhead transparencies of Navajo artists and patrons, art festivals, trading posts, and other art places and activities. The teacher asked students to identify the people, places, activities, and the ideas that are associated with the Navajo artworld. The teacher recorded their ideas on butcher paper. Then she asked the students to look again at the Mexican Chicana/o prints and recall what they had learned about the artists and artworld. The teacher recorded their responses on another piece of butcher paper. She repeated the same process with the African American prints. Finally, using a map of North America, the students defined the geographic outlines of the three distinct artworlds. They discussed how the differing geographic locations might influence aspects of these artworlds.

Creating Prints and Seeing a Printmaker in Action

Learning about the process of printmaking and planning for their own prints took place simultaneously with the other components of the unit. Now the focus of instruction moved to the studio process. Students began the process of carving their relief print. For the students in the Phoenix area, local Chicana artist Lisza Juarigue visited each classroom and demonstrated the printmaking process. She made an original print of *Divide and Conquer*, the print that is part of the primary set of artworks in this unit.

At the Navajo high school Navajo artist Ed Singer did a 2-week residency with the students. In addition to teaching the printmaking process, Singer shared with students the skills that artists require to be successful, beyond the artmaking skills. This component was added to meet the school's goals relating to the School to Work initiative. Singer left a framed print of his work for the school to exhibit.

Assessing Outcomes

One teacher who participated in this study reported three major outcomes of instruction during the unit "Protest and

Persuasion." The students could use art as an effective, non-violent way to express their views on issues important to them. They began to look for more visual clues or symbols in artworks as a strategy for understanding the meaning of the work. And they were able to personalize their ideas and take ownership and pride in the ideas incorporated in their artwork.

Several teachers stated that they use the concept of artworld as a primary organizer for each unit of instruction. When students understand more about the people, places, activities and ideas associated with artwork by artists from different times, places, and cultures, they understand more about the artwork itself and the significance of the artwork. Using artworlds as a central concept for instruction and adapting available online resources such as "Protest and Persuasion" can be a powerful tool for improving students' understanding of art at the same time that they improve their art making skills.

References
Erickson, M. (1998). Worlds of Art. [On Line]. Available: http://www.getty.edu/artsednet/resources/Worlds/index.html.
Erickson, M. (1997). Protest and Persuasion. [On Line]. Available: http://mati.eas.asu.edu:8421/ChicanArte/unit1.html.
Erickson, M., & Clover, F. (1998). Understanding Artworlds. [On Line]. Available: http://www.getty.edu/artsednet/resources/Artworlds/index.html.
Erickson, M. & Keller Cárdenas, G. (1997-9). Chicana and Chicano Space. [On Line]. Available: http://mati.eas.asu.edu:8421/ChicanArte.

[1]In addition to contributing to the group discussion regarding the best ways to present material and in which general order, the three university professors made the following specific contributions to the classroom instruction of the unit. Bernard Young chose the four African American prints that were added to the original online "Protest and Persuasion" unit and prepared the information that accompanied the prints. Mary Erickson co-authored the "Protest and Persuasion" unit and the "Understanding Artworlds" unit, which provided most of the content for instruction. Faith Clover assisted in teaching parts of the unit to the Navajo students and co-authored the "Understanding Artworlds" unit. She also recorded the teachers' reports of adaptations to the unit before, during, and upon completion of the regular meetings.

Chapter 4

Teaching about Artworlds: A Collaborative Research Project

By Mary Erickson

This chapter reports on a study designed to determine whether elementary and secondary students who receive instruction focused on the concept of artworlds, as described in Chapter Three, increase their understanding of their own artworlds. This study is not the first to address how the concept of artworld contributes to one's understanding of art. Parsons (1987) interviewed 300 individuals of various ages with various art backgrounds and used the idea of artworld to help explain more advanced stages of art understanding. Parsons' early study lacks the multicultural diversity among participants and artworks that many art educators see as paramount today.

In his later writings Parsons with Blocker takes a broader view of the concept of artworld. When tempered with a multicultural perspective, insights Parsons draws from his extensive series of interviews provide a useful explanation of how one's understanding of the concept of artworld affects one's general understanding of art. He describes teachers as welcoming "the opening of the art world and of art education to disenfranchised traditions and groups and the richness they bring" (Parsons & Blocker, 1993, p. 62). He goes on to write that "art traditions have often been too elitist, too exclusive, and too remote from students' experience" (Parsons & Blocker, 1993, p. 62). On the other hand he is not prepared to abandon the notion of making value judgments in the selection of artworks to be included in curricula. He contends that most cultural pluralists want artworks in the curriculum that "are valuable as artworks and are therefore worthy of study. They do not want trivial or worthless pieces to be chosen just because they are from a particular culture" (Parsons & Blocker, 1993, p.37). Parsons concludes that:

> We should learn from postmodernists a measure of modesty about our claims and a sense of the historical character of understanding. They can help us be more aware of power and political relations than we

were. At the same time we should be sceptical of the more extreme claims.... Art traditions and conventions have elements of continuity as well as change, and it is the former that allows us to make sense of the latter (Parsons & Blocker, 1993, p. 65).

Educators can look to the judgments of people of the artworld within which an artwork was made for guidance in selecting works to present to their students.

Clover and Erickson (1998) propose a series of five viewpoints for art understanding. These five viewpoints draw substantially on Parsons's theory. However, they differ at the higher levels of achievement by accommodating alternative artworlds.

In Parsons's five-stage theory the concept of artworld plays a role in one's understanding of art only when one uses ideas associated with later stages. Among his interviewees he found some correlation between age and stage, but only for the first stages. After stage three he found that "circumstances become more important than age" (Parsons 1987, p. 12). He argues that older people do not learn to use ideas associated with later stages on their own, but "reach later stages of aesthetic understanding only with an education in which [they] encounter works of art often and think about them seriously" (Parsons 1987, p. 27).

Stokrocki (1994) employs the idea of artworld to describe the art experiences of Navajo students living on the Navajo Reservation and attending public school there. These students acquired knowledge and skills drawn from at least two different complex and evolving artworlds: the Navajo artworld and the mainstream European American artworld. They gained their knowledge and skills both in school art classes and also through family and community activities outside school. In addition, these students, like so many others, may have learned knowledge and skills drawn neither primarily from the mainstream European American nor from the Navajo artworld, but instead from decades-old activities and projects perpetuated in school art classes. Efland (1976) referred to the results of these activities (such as coloring in photocopied line drawings and making step-by-step holiday art) as products of "the School Art style." The mass media provide another source of information about art that, as often as not, promulgates popular myths and stereotypes rather than conveying information shared by members of any artworld.

According to Parsons (1987), people who use ideas associated with his stage four understand that an artwork "exists not between the two individual poles of the artist and the viewer but in … a community of viewers" (p. 85). They understand that there are art traditions that people within an artworld share. They understand that viewers can more fully understand an artwork if they understand the ideas of the artworld in which that artwork was made (Parsons 1987, p. 116). They also understand that people "take [certain] standards for granted because [those standards] are so familiar and are an accepted part of [their] artworld" (Parsons 1987, p. 139).

The concept of artworld is not commonly included in elementary and secondary art curricula, and few individuals, either children or adults, use the idea to help them understand the art they see. Not all students in North America have the opportunity to learn knowledge and skills from even one artworld, let alone from several. If they have a teacher with some education in art, they may be introduced to artworks that were made within the mainstream European American artworld, and increasingly also within other artworlds. When students are provided with some information about the artworld contexts within which diverse art ideas develop, they can begin to understand and appreciate the richness of multicultural art. Erickson (1994) reports finding some evidence of artworld understanding among a few adolescents, though she found no evidence of such understanding among younger students. Many teachers provide some cultural information to help students understand the many roles that artworks play in diverse artworlds. However, some teachers introduce artworks made in cultures other than their students' without providing any cultural context-often as a means to illustrate visual qualities or to stimulate ideas for student art making. Even fewer teachers provide students with information about the artworlds that nurture, stimulate, and value these artworks.

Without some understanding of the artworlds that maintain, support, stimulate, and value the wide range of art knowledge and skills that exist in today's multicultural societies, students are left to their own devices to choose among, prioritize, or reconcile sometimes conflicting beliefs about art. If students have no prior knowledge of the qualities and ideas prized by specialists in diverse artworlds, they are likely to inappropriately apply dominant, usually Modernist, European American art standards to all unfamiliar artworks that they encounter. Or if they lack any artworld understanding at all, they have little choice but to resort to personal preferences, popular stereotypes, fame, financial value, or the like as their sole bases for appreciating unfamiliar artworks.

A major goal of the instructional unit outlined in Chapter Three, which constitutes the intervention reported in this chapter, is for students to develop a rudimentary understanding of the concept of artworld upon which they can build more sophisticated understandings. Activities in the unit present the concept of artworld as a subculture that is centered on art. Instruction focuses students' attention on people, places, activities, and ideas that are important in several different multicultural artworlds in North America. Teachers draw parallels to students' own art experience as a basis for introducing these multicultural artworlds. The hypothesis of the study is that after engaging in instruction that is focused on multicultural artworlds, elementary and middle school students will be able to more accurately identify people, places, activities, and ideas in their own artworlds.

Background of the Study

Various members of a team of art teachers and researchers have worked together on a series of projects for a period of 10 years. Bergman and Fiering (1997) describe how the collaboration evolved over time to reflect an agenda less dominated by the primary researcher's interest and reflecting more of the interests and priorities of the teachers. The team began to focus on the concept of artworld after 5 years of more broad ranging research.

In the first collaborative study that addressed artworlds[1], the team identified people, places, activities, and ideas as four characteristics they could use in a concrete way to introduce their students to diverse artworlds. The four characteristics identified in that study served as the framework for a regional, day-long forum for teachers of art, called Overlapping Artworlds, presented at the Phoenix Art Museum.

In turn, the Overlapping Artworlds forum provided the conceptual structure for the development of an online unit called *Understanding Artworlds* (Erickson and Clover, 1997). In this unit students identify people, places, activities, and ideas that are important within an artworld. *Places in the LA Artworld*, a lesson within the *Understanding Artworlds* unit, includes activities and resources for introducing the idea of artworld to young people. Photographs documenting urban elementary children's investigation of their local artworld[2], statements by Navajo youngsters about their artworld, and worksheets developed by members of the collaborating team appear with the lesson.

Members of the team convinced a downtown cooperative art gallery[3] to mount its first-ever student art exhibition. Teachers exhibited elementary and secondary artwork made by their students after the students had studied the people, places, activities, and ideas of other artworlds. Exhibition brochures, signage, an interactive game for visitors, and a reception for parents, administrators, and school board members focused on the concept of multicultural artworlds. Meanwhile *Understanding Artworlds* (Erickson & Clover, 1997), together with units focused on African-American art (Walker, 1999), Mexican American art (Erickson, 1999), and Navajo art (Clover, 1999) grew to become a multicultural curriculum resource called *Worlds of Art* (Erickson, 1998).

Using what they had discovered in these prior endeavors, over the period of another two years the collaborating team met together to plan, refine, monitor, and score the research study[4] presented in this chapter. They negotiated together until they agreed on an instructional intervention that draws content from several units posted on the Internet. The instructional plan integrated an introduction of artworlds with a printmaking project. With one teacher taking the lead on developing and refining a reliable assessment rubric[5], the group met repeatedly to discuss, refine, and pilot test a series of assessment rubrics.

Methodology

Participants

Three art teachers participated in the study[6]. There were 122 student participants: 61 females and 61 males. One teacher taught 55 students in two intact fourth-grade art classes. Two teachers taught a total of 67 students in an intact seventh-grade art class and in an intact eighth-grade class. Teachers scored only the work of students for whom they had both pre- and post tests. Among the 122 students in the study, 10 were African American; 24 were Hispanic; 2 were Asian American; 1 was Middle Eastern American; and 85 were European American (including one Bosnian immigrant). There were ESL students and learning disabled students among students who participated.

Figure 1: Percentages of Students by Ethnicity

	N	%
Asian	2	1.6
African American	10	8.2
Hispanic	24	19.7
Middle Eastern	1	0.8
Bosnia	1	0.8
European American	84	68.9

Three university researchers worked with the art teachers on various aspects of the multi-facet project.[7] Three high school art teachers also taught the instructional unit in their classes.

Reports of adaptations made by these high school teachers for their inner-city and Navajo Reservation students appear in Chapter Three. The inner-city high school art teacher who took the lead with assessment aspects of the project is reporting high school student data in her master's thesis, which addresses not only students' artworld understanding, but also several aspects of their learning in art making.

Design and Intervention

The design of the study was quasi-experimental with a written pre-test, an instructional intervention, and a written post-test. Because elementary classes met only once a week and middle school classes met daily, the instructional time varied, though it occupied the majority of a semester at both levels. Here is an outline of the testing and instructional schedule.

1) Administer Pre-Assessment.
2) Introduce theme and ask students to begin planning their artwork.
3) Introduce multicultural prints.
4) Introduce linoleum block printing processes and help students think about how to adapt their plans for that process.
5) Introduce the concept of artworlds.
6) Administer Post-Assessment.
7) Work with students as they execute their final prints.

Chapter Three describes in detail the instructional unit, which was drawn from *Protest and Persuasion* (Erickson, 1997) and *Understanding Artworlds* (Erickson & Clover, 1997). Samples prints made in classes taught prior to this study by participating middle and high school teachers accompany the online unit, *Protest and Persuasion* (Erickson, 1997).

As described in Chapter Three, teachers adapted the instruction in various ways to suit their students, teaching style, resources, and teaching environment. In order to ensure some consistency all teachers used the eight key artworks reproduced in this book and worked toward the following objectives:

- Students use positive shapes in artwork.
- Students use negative shapes in artwork.
- Students state in words their position on a specific issue, problem, or concern.
- Students express in their artwork their position on a specific issue, problem, or concern.
- Students identify people, places, activities, and ideas within several North American cultures.
- Students identify people, places, activities, and ideas within several North American artworlds.
- Students describe their own artworld.

Assessment

Two participating teachers scored pre- and post-tests written by students in other teachers' classes. They used scoring rubrics describing five levels of achievement (0-4) for responses about artworld activities, people, places, and ideas. Students' written responses to the following four paired items constituted the pre- and post-test.

Scoring rubrics follow each pair of items that made up the eight-item assessment instrument, which was called My Artworld.

MY ARTWORLD

A. ARTWORLD ACTIVITIES

1) There are many ways to get involved with art. Describe an art making activity that you've enjoyed or learned a lot doing.

2) Not counting artmaking activities, describe some other art activity you've enjoyed or learned a lot from.

SCORING RUBRIC:

0   no response or responses not about (visual) art
1   names any artmaking activity (or art medium or art project) or non-making (visual) art activity
2   names any artmaking activity and any non-making art activity OR describes (more than naming) an art making activity
3   describes an artmaking activity and names a non-making art activity
4   describes *both* an artmaking and a non-making art activity

B. PEOPLE OF THE ARTWORLD

3) Many different kinds of people are involved with art. Name a person you know about who is involved with a art. Describe what that person does.

4) Name another person you know about who is involved with art. Describe what that person does.

SCORING RUBRIC

0   no response or identifies any person whose connection with art is not clear (The connection can be clear either because the name is well known, such as Van Gogh, or because the student describes the connection with art.)
1   identifies one person clearly connected with art
2   identifies two people clearly connected with art
3   identifies two people clearly connected with art and describes what *at least one artmaker does*
4   identifies two people clearly connected with art and describes what *at least one non artmaker does*

C. ARTWORLD PLACES

5) People go to different places to get involved with art. Name an artworld place. How do you know about this place?

6) Name another artworld place. How do you know about this place?

SCORING RUBRIC

0   no response or any place not clearly connected with art (The connection can be clear either because the place is well known, such as Phoenix Art Museum, or because the student describes the connection with art.)
1   names one place clearly connected with art
2   names two places clearly connected with art OR names one place clearly connected with art and tells how s/he knows about the place
3   names two places clearly connected with art and tells how he/she knows about *at least one* of those places
4   names two places clearly connected with art and tells how s/he knows about *both*

D. ARTWORLD IDEAS

7) People of the artworld have some very different ideas about why art is important. Explain why you think that art is important. (If you do not think art is important, explain why not.)

8) Think of someone who you think has (had) a different idea about why art is important. Explain why you think that person believes (believed) that art is (was) important.

SCORING RUBRIC

0   no response, or identifies an idea not about why art is (or is not) important, or statement of preference
1   identifies his/her, or someone else's, idea about why art is (or is not) important
2   identifies his/her own idea about why art is (or is not) important, as well as someone else's different idea about why art is (or is not) important OR identifies his/her idea and explains (elaborates in some way) why art is (or is not) important
3   identifies his/her own idea about why art is (or is not) important, as well as someone else's different idea about why art is (or is not) important and explains (elaborates in some way) *either* his/her own or someone else's ideas about why art is (or is not) important
4   identifies his/her own idea about why art is (or is not) important, as well as someone else's different idea about why art is (or is not) important and explains (elaborates in some way) *both* his/her own and someone else's ideas

Two teachers produced eight scores for each student: a pre- and a post-test score for artworld activities, people, places, and ideas. Two teachers scored each student's tests. Teachers did not score work by their own students. A Pearson r correlation analysis reveals that teachers' scores were highly reliable with a p-value .01 on all four measures of artworld understanding. Significant inter-rater reliability correlations provide support for the reliability of the measure.

Figure 2: Inter-Rater Reliability Correlations (N = 122)		
Measure	Pre	Post
Activity	0.851	0.886
People	0.908	0.849
Place	0.913	0.660
Idea	0.927	0.783

Teachers scored lack of response to either item or irrelevant responses at the 0 level. Below are sample responses by both fourth grade and seventh/eighth grade students scored by teachers at level 1 and at level 4 on measures of understanding of all four artworld characteristics. Each pair of responses in quotation marks is the precise response written by one student, complete with grammatical errors and misspellings. Readers may wish to refer back to "My Artworld" (above) to review the two text items responses to which appear below:

Sample Pairs of High- and Low-Scoring Fourth-Grade Student Responses

Level 1 Artworld Activity Response:
- Item #1: "clay models in school"
- Item #2: "?"

Level 4 Artworld Activity Response:
- Item #1: "I really like clay making because it is fun and I learned a lot."
- Item #2: "I liked studing Egyption art because the Egption art was cool to look at and to study."

Level 1 Artworld People Response:
- Item #3: "[Classmate's name] is good at drawing."
- Item #4: "?"

Level 4 Artworld People Response:
- Item #3: "Mrs. Corlett because she teaches us about art stuff."
- Item #4: "Van Gogh he does a lot of art stuff and painting."

Level 1 Artworld Places Response:
- Item #5: "a art museum"
- Item #6: "I don't know."

Level 4 Artworld Places Response:
- Item #5: "Art museum. I see it there in the newspaper and on TV."
- Item #6: "Art room. I've been in a art room for a long time and I've seen art."

Level 1 Artworld Ideas Response:
- Item #7: "I think art is important, because everything is art."
- Item #8: "I don't know?"

Level 4 Artworld Ideas Response:
- Item #7: "It is important because if we don't have we wouldn't paint or draw."
- Item #8: "[Classmate's name] thinks art is important because people see it in other way."

Sample Pairs of High- and Low-Scoring Seventh/Eighth Grade Student Responses

Level 1 Artworld Activity Response:
- Item #1: "making a portrait"
- Item #2: "I don't know."

Level 4 Artworld Activity Response:
- Item #1: "An art making activity I've enjoyed is made a shading drawing of a animal. I've also made linoleum print with a linoleum block to protest things, I think we should do or change."
- Item #2: "I have [been] to the Phx Art Museum and saw art and learned about it. I've also been to Desert Sage Library and read about art in books to see how to make stuff such as clay pots."

Level 1 Artworld People Response:
- Item #3: "My Grandma because she paints rocks."
- Item #4: "My Grandma she paints shirts."

Level 4 Artworld People Response:
- Item #3: "Elizabeth Catlett. She's an artist who makes prints, for example she made an print of Harriet Tubman taking the slaves to freedom."
- Item #4: "Mrs. Bergman. She's an art teachers over at Estrelle mid school she teaches student about art."

Level 1 Artworld Places Response:
- Item #5: "the art museum"
- Item #6: "no comment"

Level 4 Artworld Places Response:
- Item #5: "A museum. I know about it because I had experiance."
- Item #6: "Print shop. I know about it because I heard about it."

Level 1 Artworld Ideas Response:
- Item #7: "Because I can draw me something."
- Item #8: "?"

Level 4 Artworld Ideas Response:
- Item #7: "Museum curators, because they want to save it for the future."
- Item #8: "My grandpa thought it was important because he used it for money."

Findings

A Tukey HSD analysis of the students' pre- and post-test scores reveals that there was a significant improvement between the pre- and post-tests by both elementary and middle school students' scores for all four artworld characteristics.

Figure 3: Significance of Improvement by Middle School Students

	Activity	People	Place	Idea
Pre	2.10	2.37	1.76	2.49
Post	2.89	3.40	3.69	3.55
df	66	66	66	66
t-value	4.91	6.24	10.04	6.24
p-value	0.000	0.000	0.000	0.000

Figure 4: Significance of Improvement by Elementary School Students

	Activity	People	Place	Idea
Pre	2.30	2.70	2.55	1.95
Post	2.79	3.46	3.45	3.25
df	54	54	54	54
t-value	3.17	4.64	4.95	7.52
p-value	0.003	0.000	0.000	0.000

Figures 3 and 4 reveal p-values of 0.000 on all scores except the elementary students' improvement on their responses about artworld activities, which were significant at a p-value of 0.003.

Discussion and Implications

This study suggests that with focused instruction, children as young as the fourth grade can increase their rudimentary understanding of their own artworlds. The following are a few specific artworld learning objectives teachers might consider integrating into their teaching:

1) *Students identify artmaking activities and also non-artmaking art activities.* Building on students' prior experience with artmaking and with viewing and talking about art in class, teachers can introduce additional art activities such as reading about art, browsing for art on the Internet, writing about art, collecting or commissioning art, visiting museums, etc.

2) *Students identify several artists and also people (or roles of people) who are art specialists but who do not make art.* Building on students' prior knowledge of a few famous artists and their own teacher of art, teachers can introduce other art specialists, such as apprentices, collectors, critics, teachers, patrons, art historians, curators, conservators, aestheticians, etc.

3) *Students identify places people go to share ideas and get involved with art.* Building on students' prior knowledge of art classrooms and museums, teachers can introduce artists' workshops, art centers, galleries, libraries and archives, community centers, universities, Internet sites, etc.

4) *Students identify ideas about art that reflect viewpoints other than their own.* Building on students' prior familiarity with various ideas about art held by family members and classmates, teachers can introduce not only beliefs about art and art standards held within the dominant artworld but also beliefs and art standards held in multicultural artworlds.

Teachers will only choose to include instruction focused on artworlds if they are convinced that the concept is important and if they have the resources to do so. Chapter Two, "What are Multicultural Artworlds and Why are They Important?", presents arguments for the following benefits of learning about artworlds:

1) Understanding diverse artworlds helps students broaden and refine their definitions of art.
2) Students gain a more accurate (less mysterious) understanding of artmaking when it is introduced within an artworld context.
3) Students expand the range of artworks they can appreciate when artworks are introduced within an artworld context.
4) Students who understand artworlds develop a more accurate understanding of the role of art in society.
5) Students who understand artworlds gain access to support systems they can use to enhance their own artmaking and/or art understanding.

If these, or other arguments, prove to be convincing, the reproductions, lessons, and information identified in this book provide rich resources for integrating artworld information into a balanced art curriculum.

Readers are invited to:
- adapt and teach the model unit presented in Chapter Three using the eight prints reproduced in part three of this book,

- select, adapt, and teach one of the 15 lesson plans that constitute part two of this book using the artworld information and reproduction sources provided with each, or
- identify an artwork (or several artworks) from an artworld that is important for their students to under stand, use the "Artworld Analysis" worksheet in part three as a guide to investigate key characteristics of the artworld from which that artwork sprang, and develop and teach their own artworld-oriented lesson.

Readers with an interest in assessment or research are invited to use the assessment survey (See "My Artworld") and scoring rubric introduced in this chapter (or adaptations of them) to assess their students' prior knowledge of their artworld or the effectiveness of an artworld-oriented lesson.

Endnotes

[1] This study was supported in part by funding from the National Art Education Foundation and by the Arizona Arts Education Research Institute.

[2] Fourth grade bilingual students in Marissa Vidrio-Nadbornik's art classes at Starlight Park Elementary School in the Cartwright School District completed a bulletin board as part of their study of artworlds.

[3] MARS (Movimiento Artístico Río Salado) is a cooperative gallery in Phoenix, Arizona.

[4] The College of Fine Arts at Arizona State University provided a grant to help support this study.

[5] Roxanna May-Thayer, an art teacher in the Phoenix Union School District, is completing a Master's thesis that focuses on scorer reliability and transfer between art making and art understanding.

[6] Lorna Corlett taught two fourth grade art classes at Liberty Elementary School in the Paradise Valley School District. Liza Bergman taught one seventh grade art class at Estrella Middle School in the Cartwright School District. Susan Raymond taught one eighth grade art class at Greenway Middle School in the Paradise Valley School District.

[7] Mary Erickson, a professor at Arizona State University, was project leader. Bernard Young, also a professor at Arizona State University, focused much of his advice on data collection techniques. Faith Clover, at the time of the study a visiting assistant professor also at Arizona State University, focused her attention largely on how teachers adapted online lessons for different students and teaching situations.

References

Bergman, L.M. and Feiring, N.C. (1997). Bridging the gap between university researcher and the classroom teacher. *Art Education, 50* (5), 51-56.

Clover, F. (1999). *Navajo art: A way of life.* [On Line]. Available: http://www.getty.edu/artsednet/resources/Navajo/index.html.

Clover, F. & Erickson, M. (1998). *Viewpoints: Exploring how you understand art.* [On Line]. Available: http://www.getty.edu/artsednet/resources/Viewpoints/index.html.

Efland, A. D. (1976). The school art style: A functional analysis. *Studies in Art Education, 17* (2), 37-44.

Erickson, M. (1994). Evidence for art historical interpretation referred to by young people and adults, *Studies in Art Education, 35* (2). 71-8.

Erickson, M. (1999). *Mexican American murals: Making a place in the world.* [On Line]. Available: http://www.getty.edu/artsednet/resources/Murals/index.html.

Erickson, M. (1997). *Protest and persuasion.* [On Line]. Available: http://mati.eas.asu.edu:8421/ChicanArte/unit1.html.

Erickson, M. (1998). *Worlds of Art.* [On Line]. Available: http://www.getty.edu/artsednet/resources/Worlds/index.html.

Erickson, M. & Clover, F. (1997). Using and understanding art from other cultures. In *Understanding Artworlds.* [On Line]. Available: http://www.getty.edu/artsednet/resources/Artworlds/Using/index.html.

Parsons, M.J. (1987). *How we understand art: A cognitive account of the development of aesthetic understanding.* New York: Cambridge University Press.

Parsons, M.J. & H. G. Blocker. (1993). *Aesthetics and education.* Urbana and Chicago: University of Illinois Press.

Stokrocki, M. (1994). Expanding the artworld of Navajo students. *Journal of the Australiam Institute of Art Education, 17* (3), 39-49.

Walker, H. (1999). *African American art: A Los Angeles legacy.* [On Line]. Available: http://www..getty.edu/artsednet/Resources/African/index.html.

Part Two: Lessons

Our aim in this book.

Our aim in this book is to use the artworld as a vehicle both for art learning and for greater multicultural understanding. Part Two presents fifteen lessons that focus, at least in part, on aspects of many different artworlds in North America. Needless to say, no set of fifteen lessons selected from submissions after a call for papers can represent all important artworlds in North America.

Among artworlds represented are many that spring from distinct ethnic groups, such as:

- African American,
- Mexican American,
- Native American, and
- Appalachian art traditions.

Several lessons in Part Two also center on overlapping artworlds. Bernard Young concluded the first chapter by describing the richness achieved in the early and middle 20th century at the intersection of African American and Mexican artworlds. In this section example lessons focus on:

- a painting by Jean Michelle Basquiat, whose work crosses boundaries between the mainstream New York artworld and the world of street graffiti;
- the 19th century painting of Edward Hicks, whose artworld influences came both from coach-decoration traditions and from established mainstream engravers;
- masks by Zarco Guerrero, who builds on traditional Mexican Day of the Dead mask-making and also on mask-making traditions in Japan, Indonesia, China, and Alaska;
- drawings of Art Spiegelman, whose work crosses the borders between the mainstream New York artworld and the artworlds of children's book and comic book illustration; and
- a Tibetan sand mandorla, made by exiled monks following ancient Tibetan art traditions under the patronage of mainstream North American art museums.

As introduced in Chapter Two, an artworld is a culture maintained by people a significant portion of whose identity is drawn in some way from art. A person who is a member of an artworld is loosely or formally associated with other members of that artworld. Members of an artworld are familiar with some of the same art values and art ideas, and engage in, or are familiar with, some of the same art activities. Part Two presents 15 lessons that, at least in part, focus on the people, places, activities, and ideas of under-represented artworlds in North America.

People

Individuals who identify with a particular artworld are very likely to be familiar with many of the same key people in that artworld. Among key artworld people identified as important to artists in the lessons that follow are earlier artists, family members who are art makers, traditional craftspeople, community activists, auto show judges, museum directors, a philosopher, collectors from one culture commissioning art made in another, teachers, collaborating art makers, members of a government agency, and members of cultural and arts organizations.

Places

In addition to familiarity with prominent people, individuals who identify with a particular artworld are also likely to be familiar with many of the key places where members of the artworld meet to share activities and ideas. Authors of the lessons in Part Two refer to a great range of places that are important within different artworlds. For example they mention universities and professional art schools; art museums and galleries; artists', craftspeople, and tradespersons' workshops; local art and cultural centers; auto shows; a car museum; monasteries; and local, regional arts and cultural fairs and festivals.

Activities

Shared familiarity with art activities, like familiarity with key people and places, also varies from artworld to artworld. Information accompanying key artworks for each lesson indicate a great number of art-associated activities. Just a few are giving and receiving awards and prizes, giving and receiving commissions, collaborating with other art makers, political activism, borrowing ideas from the vernacular, focusing on special viewers, working as apprentices, learning traditional technical processes, making objects for ceremonial purposes, borrowing ideas from earlier art makers, attending art classes, pioneering new techniques, joining art-associated clubs and organizations, praying and meditating, following ancient texts and rituals, memorizing exact details, teaching art, publishing, showing work in exhibitions, "tagging," following gender-specific art making traditions, serving as artist in residence, giving away artwork, using personal imagery, and using traditional symbols.

Ideas

Finally commitment to different art ideas can distinguish members of different artworlds. Artists whose work is featured in the following lessons hold some very different ideas about art. Some of those ideas include understanding art: as storytelling or narrative; as a manifestation of one's cultural, social, or tribal heritage or identity; as a message; as a challenge to viewers; as a means of instruction; as an expression of individuality; as a temporary form; as a commodity for outsiders; as a way to understand oneself; and as a form for healing. Other ideas include commitment to building a global community; defining art as a tool for social change; belief in high standards; and commitment to complex, well-established symbol systems.

The Dove

Art Maker
Romare Bearden

**Access
Information**
Color prints of *The Dove*
are in *Romare Bearden,* by
Lowery Stokes Sims,
(1993). New York: Rizzoli
International Publications.

Date of Artwork
1964

**Location of
Artwork**
The Museum of Modern
Art, New York

Medium
Paste, paper, gouache,
pencil, and colored pencils
on cardboard

Size
13 3/8" x 18 3/4"

Subject Matter
This is a crowded street scene, possibly depicting Bearden's memories of Harlem. It
shows many people sitting on stoops, looking out of windows and doorways, and
walking along the sidewalk. The viewer witnesses the ritual, popular in many
communities, of spending leisure time greeting and watching neighbors and passers-
by.

Visual Organization
The main areas of color are the background of red brick apartment buildings. The
street is a patterned area suggesting an uneven surface of patched potholes. Two
cats are present and a white dove perches above a doorway. The scene is busy,
implying movement and energy, but it also conveys a sense of cohesiveness,
community, and a certain peace represented by the dove. People appear comfortable
with each other, but there is an air of tension. Most human and animal figures are
depicted in black and white, their bodies, abstracted and distorted, are composites
constructed from commercially printed reproductions from magazines, postcards,
and books. Their faces resemble African masks often incorporated by Bearden into
his works. The dense composition has top-heavy balance in that most of the lines,
patterns, and colors are located in the upper three-quarters of the piece, while the
lower one-third contains the more open area of pavement and one lone cat. This
arrangement might suggest the crowded nature of tenement life within the vastness
of urban sprawl. It also seems to suggest individual anonymity in the midst of the
throng of people inhabiting this place.

Short Biography of Art Maker
Romare Bearden was born in Charlotte, North Carolina, on September 2, 1912, and
spent his early boyhood in Harlem. His father was a New York city employee and
his mother was New York correspondent for the *Chicago Defender,* a founder of the
Negro Women's Democratic Association, and a friend of Eleanor Roosevelt.
Bearden attended Boston University, then transferred to New York University, where
he graduated in 1935. Bearden was drawing political cartoons for the *Baltimore
Afro-American* when he began to study at the Art Students League in New York
City, which led to his decision to paint. To support himself, he became a welfare
caseworker. After serving in the U.S. Army, Bearden tried cartooning and song-
writing to support himself. Many of his songs were recorded. In 1963 he helped
found Spiral, an association which supported the work of African-American artists
who sought to depict the civil rights movement and other aspects of their heritage.
Bearden coauthored *A Painter's Mind* with Carl Holty in 1969, *Six Black Masters of
American Art* with Harry Henderson in 1972, and *A History of African-American
Artists From 1792 to the Present* with Harry Henderson in 1993. He died on March
12, 1988, in New York after a long illness.

Artworld Information
In his art, Bearden used specific regional and personal memories and his iconogra-
phy assimilated traditional, classical, and religious symbols. He linked his work to
the mainstream of art history. His work sought to make connections; depicting
meaning through many layers of interpretation. Despite his work to support the work
of artists who chose to use Black subject matter, in an article written in 1946 called
"The Negro Artist's Dilemma" he challenged the assumption that the Black artist
should be limited to doing so.

Bearden's revolutionary use of collage led to his recognition as a modern master.
His first show, at the Kootz Gallery, was bought out by collector Samuel Lewisohn.
In 1950 he went to Paris, where he devoted his time to studying literature, philosophy,

and the work of old and modern masters. In 1971 he was given a major show at the Museum of Modern Art in New York. Exhibiting in Europe, Japan, and throughout the United States, he was awarded an honorary degree by Carnegie University in 1980, and that same year he was honored by President Jimmy Carter along with nine other African-American artists. In 1987 he was awarded the National Medal of Arts by President Ronald Reagan.

Bearden's struggle was to reconcile historical tradition, personal content, and modernist forms and techniques. In his work he incorporated collage methods and styles used by Picasso, Braque, and Matisse, combining these with the "bite of photography" to enhance his particular expressive distortions and narrative subject matter.

References
Anderson-Spivy, A. (1991). *Romare Bearden*: The human condition. New York: ACA Galleries.

Bearden, R. & Henderson, H. (1993). *A history of African-American artists from 1792 to the present.* New York: Pantheon Books.

Greene, C. (1971). *Romare Bearden: The prevalence of ritual.* New York: The Museum of Modern Art.

Perry, R. (1992). *Free within ourselves: African-American artists* in the collection of the National Museum of Art. Washington, DC: Smithsonian Museum.

Sims, L. S. (1993). *Romare Bearden.* New York: Rizzoli.

Washington, M. B. (1973) *The art of Romare Bearden: The prevalence of ritual.* New York: Harry N. Abrams.

Romare Bearden: Collaged Memories

Objectives

Students:
1) investigate art-related ideas, values, and activities within the culture and times of Romare Bearden.
2) identify influences of modern masters on Bearden.
3) demonstrate how memories of rituals can be depicted in collage form using a variety of materials.
4) identify and discuss design elements of Romare Bearden's work (including composite figures, distortion, symbolism, and interior-exterior views), as well as concepts of line, color, shape, space, proportion, perspective, and texture as used by Bearden.
5) incorporate some of Bearden's design elements in a collage they create.

Activities

Day One

Display and discuss a reproduction of Bearden's *The Dove*, and possibly others of his works. Formulate a list of observable design aspects found in the artwork. These include composite figures, distortion, symbolism, and interior-exterior views, as well as line, color, shape, space, proportion, perspective, and texture as used by Bearden. Use questions such as the following to guide discussion: What do you notice about the size of the figure's hands? Are they in proportion with the rest of his body? What might Bearden be suggesting in making them so large? Describe what you see in the man's face. What do you think Bearden used to achieve this effect? What does the technique of creating figures that are composites of cut-up and sometimes enlarged photographs imply? Are the images different from how they would be if they were made of matching parts? How many levels of interest are contained in the scene? Describe the environment in terms of the multiple areas we can see. What effect does this create? Are there elements that you would characterize as being symbolic? What is their significance? What mood does this artwork convey? What aspects create that mood? How would you describe the colors? The lines? The use of space? The use of perspective? What is the scene depicting? We know Bearden painted many types of rituals. Do you see any in this image? Why do we have rituals? What examples can you think of? Why do you think it would it be important to him to create works showing various rituals? Do you like this work? Why or why not?

Day Two and Three

Ask students to think of a ritual practiced by themselves, their families, or their friends. It should be one that is significant because of its meaning in their lives or its importance for other reasons. They should plan to incorporate the design aspects used by Bearden (composite figures, distortion, interior-exterior views, and symbolism) and use them to illustrate ideas in their collages. Consult Artworld Information and share selected information with students. Ask students to explain the influences of modern masters they see in Bearden's work.

Ask individual students to work alone to create collages using the prescribed criteria and materials listed below. Ask students to create visual images by cutting and gluing collage materials to heavy cardboard. Enhancements can be done with oil pastels, markers, and paints. Students will work at their own pace over two or more class periods of about 50 minutes each.

After blocking in the scene's composition on heavy cardboard, ask students to fill it in using various papers, photos, magazines, fabrics, and other glueable materials.

Day Four

Ask each student to describe the scene in his or her collage in terms of its historical context, location, date, people, personal significance, and symbolism. Ask them to explain their use of Bearden's design aspects (composite figures, distortion, symbolism, and interior-exterior views) and their use of line, color, shape, space, proportion, perspective, and texture.

Ask students to answer the following questions in the oral reports: 1. Describe the scene you created in your collage. What is the historical context? Location? Year? People? Significance to you? Symbolism? 2. Explain your use of Bearden's design aspects (composite figures, distortion, interior-exterior views, and symbolism). Explain how you used these and tell about their significance in your work? 3. Discuss line, color scheme, proportion, and perspective as you used them in your artwork.

Assessment

Use the following questions as part of your assessment:
What aspects of this creative process did you like?
What aspects did you dislike?
What modern master influenced Bearden's art? How?
What problems did you have making the collage?
What would you do differently if you were to do this again?
How was your collage influenced by Bearden's artworks?
Write a brief description about how your collage looks and your feelings about it. Include any insights you gained.

Use the following evaluation checklist to assess students' artworks:
Uses a variety of collage materials
Depicts a scene based on personal memory and ritual
Includes composite figures
Includes distortion
Includes symbolism
Includes interior-exterior view
Includes use of line, shape, and color scheme appropriate to mood and meaning
Includes perspective, space, and texture appropriate to mood and meaning
Demonstrates neat execution

Art Supplies and Other Resources
scrap papers
fabrics
yarn
ribbon
magazines
miscellaneous
materials

scissors
white glue
cups (paper, plastic, etc.) for diluting glue
glue
brushes
water
oil pastels
markers
watercolor or tempera paints
slides or prints of Romare Bearden's art

Calacas Mask

Art Maker
Zarco Guerrero

**Access
Information**
The mask is pictured with
a larger skeleton puppet
and a smaller skull mask at
http://www.azcentral.com/
ent/dead/photos/calacas.
shtml. The calacas mask is
in the lower left corner.
For other masks, designed
by Zarco, see http://
members.aol.com/
zarkmask/masks.htm.

Date of Artwork
Circa 1980's

**Location of
Artwork**
On display in the artist's
home studio and gallery.

Medium
Fiberglass, acrylics paint,
and fur.

Size
A natural-sized face mask
approximately 12" high
including hair fur.

Subject Matter
Calacas are enchanting skull masks that represent rejuvenation and rebirth. The mask has
yellow-rimmed eyes, lilac decorative shapes on his head, and an inviting smile. Notice the
lightning symbols on its forehead that represent re-birth. Calacas are figures of Death for the
Dia de Los Muertos, Day of the Dead Festival, which occurs on November 2. The mask
allows us to marvel at the power of death and its omnipresence.

Visual Organization
The *Calacas Mask* is three-dimensional, symmetrical, and painted with contrasting
colors. Although the lightning represents rebirth, other designs on the smooth
surfaces are mere decorations meant to please the eye and solicit a positive response.

Short Biography of Art Maker
Zarco Guerrero was born in 1952 in Mesa, Arizona. He was the only boy and
youngest of four children of Mexican American heritage. Eventually he assumed
the nickname "Zarco," meaning "clear-eyed one." (His eyes are more of a gray-
green than brown.) Zarco's early childhood influences can be traced back to his
mother and father. His mother was a seamstress who made clothes for his flamenco-
dancing sisters. Zarco says that he is keenly aware of fabric and costumes because
of her influence. His dad was a commercial artist and formally-trained portrait
painter. Zarco intently watched him draw and followed his dad to painting classes.
Zarco first painted his classmates' portraits. He remembers, "I found that capturing
the likeness of an individual is very difficult." Elementary school formally offered
few art experiences, except making school posters. In high school, he took the
regular art courses, but was more interested in wrestling at that time. However, he
soon became the class artist. People always told him that "he would become an
artist, like his dad." These constant reminders reinforced his interests in art.
Despite little formal art training, he considered himself a sculptor.

Artworld Information
Zarco wanted to learn how to make sculpture, three-dimensional images. After he
graduated from high school, he visited Mexico City's famous sculptor, Francisco
Zúñiga, who felt that too many people imitated his style. Consequently, he sent
Zarco to work in the De Aguila bronze foundry from age 20-25. Zarco worked there
as an apprentice, alongside other artists and learned how to make molds and casts.

In 1975-76, Zarco won a prestigious Japanese Fellowship from the National
Endowment for the Arts. With this support, he studied master mask makers in
Kyoto for a year. To learn more about mask making traditions, he traveled to
Indonesia, China, and Alaska. Zarco explains, "My initial inspiration was my
cultural heritage. Now I interpret the world. I thank my teachers in Mexico, Japan,
and Alaska for their advice and I give back to children what I have learned."

Zarco teaches plaster mask-making workshops for the Phoenix Boys and Girls Club
of Metropolitan Phoenix after school in predominately Chicana/o areas. The
children love to work in teams, cast their faces to make relief masks, and paint them.
The primary objective of the workshop is for youth to acquire knowledge about
Meso-American myths, rituals, and symbols and their significance in contemporary
Chicana/o culture. Ancient Aztecs used the jaguar symbol because they believed the
jaguar controlled rain. Every year in Acatlan, Mexico, they sacrificed someone to
call forth rain for the growing season. Today men perform in jaguar costumes and
masks, but when a player spills some blood on the ground, symbolizing fertility, the

ritual ends. Judy Butzine, Coordinator of the Art Web component of the Boys and Girls Club, contracts Zarco to conduct mask making workshops and praises his efforts, "These inner-city kids, many who are at-risk, need a positive relationship with at least one adult."

The *Calacas* Mask is used to celebrate The Day of the Dead Festival on November 2 each year. On this occasion families honor their ancestors with *ofrendas* (homemade altars), offerings of spicy and sweet foods, colorful flowers, fragrant incense, and lively music. Death is embraced not feared. Roots of this festival go back to Aztec and Mayan seasonal times of sacrifice to guarantee fertility. Aztec aesthetics is based on "flower and song" (Anderson, 1990). Zarco's sculptural style is usually figurative and full of both human and animal symbols. The mask continues to dominate Zarco's work. He explains, "There's a mysticism and spirituality about masks. Their power and attraction comes from the linkage with the ancient past and the animal kingdom." Zarco also works as an actor who dramatizes Chicana/o community concerns. One of his recent plays is called, "Face-to-Face in a Frenzy" in which he uses exaggerated human wooden masks that he carved to portray an old man, a drunk, and a rapper.

Zarco loves to collaborate with other people in the Chicana/o community. "He provides a mission for our disenfranchised family, whose problems are not alleviated. He reaffirms traditional cultural values that are lacking in society" L. Jaurigue, personal communication, January 27, 1998). Zarco summarizes, "I want to make art that affects people's lives, which is a reward in itself. It's a tool for social change and sharing cultural experiences." He feels that "art is an expression of the self in relation to the world around us." He uses the term "humanizarte" to refer to this idea. He believes that we are those whose hearts hunger and whose souls sing out the desperate need for an effective art of the people. He believes in: ART inspired by hope and sensitivity whose message gives itself totally to the struggle of mankind towards respect for the earth and humanization; ART as a means to create compassion and to stimulate collective expression of liberation with our lives; ART that acts to educate the masses of the abused and oppressed to experience dignity, fulfillment and pride; ART as self-sacrifice, a commitment to nurture social consciousness that ceases to exploit, ravage and victimize; ART as a revolutionary armament that speaks out in defiant protest against poverty, racism and pollution; ART determined to overcome apathy and injustice; and ART as spiritual ceremony and celebration!

References
Anderson, J. (1990). *Calliope's sisters: Comparative aesthetics.* Englewood Cliffs, NJ: Prentice Hall.

Video
Portillo, L. & Munoz, S. (1989). *La Ofrenda: The days of the dead.* (50 min.VHS). Santa Monica, CA: Direct Cinema Ltd.

Website
ChicanoArte, http://mati.eas.asu.edu:8421/ChicanArte

Calacas Mask: Plaster-Wrap Sculpture Relief Modeling Lesson

Objectives
Students:
  1) describe, analyze, interpret and judge a calacas mask.
  2) explain the Mexican and the Chicana/o artworlds.
  3) make sketches, build a model on another's face, smooth and prime, and paint with acrylics.
  4) develop a symmetrical design.
  5) paint two different personally meaningful symbols and explain their importance.
  6) self-evaluate their own masks by describing, analyzing, interpreting, and judging them.

Activities

List the following definitions on the board or handout and refer to them throughout the lesson: Sculpture is an art form that is three dimensional; the form must have length, width, and thickness. Some sculpture is in the round. It can be seen from all sides. Other sculpture is relief, and protrudes from a flat background. Modeling is a sculpture process of adding parts to build up a form. Symmetry is a form of balance in which the same lines and shapes are used on both sides of a design. Symbol is a visual image that stands for something else; e.g., jaguar symbolizing control of rain and lightning symbolizing rebirth in Zarco's mask.

Art Criticism

Make copies of the calacas (skull) mask from the Internet. Ask students to describe and analyze the artwork by exploring the internal clues about its meaning hidden in the artwork: What subject matter is used in the mask? How did Zarco design the mask (symmetrically or asymmetrically? What is the major shape of the mask? (circle, square, triangle, other). Are his shapes organic or geometric or both? Are the colors monochromatic (one color with different lights and darks), contrasting (opposite colors on the color wheel), analogous (neighboring colors on the color wheel) or , other? How did he make the mask? (carved, modeled, cast, assembled pieces, other). What material did he use? (clay, paper maché, plaster, plastic, other).

Next ask students to interpret the artwork: What style of mask did Zarco make? (human, animal, spiritual, other). What symbols did he use? Then ask students to judge the artwork. Encourage them to choose more than one answer from the following list and to explain their choices. The mask is important because:
- a) the artist experiments with unusual shapes, colors or materials (formalistic);
- b) the mask has unique symbolic qualities (expressive);
- c) the mask has different functions (for protection, for praying, for education, other);
- d) the mask is realistic and represents a particular person or thing (representational).

Art History and Aesthetics

Prepare an art history handout that presents information about the key artwork, especially the Short Biography of the Art Maker and the Artworld Information sections. Give students external clues as to the cultural meaning and importance of the mask. Ask students to explain the Mexican and the Chicana/o artworld by completing an Art History worksheet with the following guiding questions: What is relief sculpture? Where did Zarco learn how to make molds and to cast? Who taught him? What kind of learning is this? What mask makers from other cultures does he admire? What other jobs does Zarco have? What is the objective for his workshops? Why does he teach children? Who is a Chicano/Chicana? Why does Zarco collaborate with Chicano people? How have Zarco's masks and style changed? What is art? Why is it important?

Art Making

List mask-making steps on another handout, distribute to students, and demonstrate the process of art making. Direct students to work in teams to model a mask on each other's face. The following is a list of suggested steps: Make three sketches, using a symmetrical design. Include two different personally meaningful symbols in your design. You may want to sketch on a paper plate. Grease your face with Vaseline or liquid soap so that the plaster won't stick to your face or hair. Wear a hair band to keep hair off your face. Cut plaster-modeling tape into sections and place on a classmate's face beginning on the nose ridge for strength. Cross pieces of plaster gauze at right angles for reinforcement. Model or build up the form by covering the face with two or three layers. As soon as the bottom pieces get heated, remove the mask and set aside to dry. To add parts, such as horns, wings, fins, cut out pieces of foam core cardboard (which is light) and attach with pieces of plaster modeling tape. Be sure to crisscross pieces at the joints for strength. Prime the mask (paint with gesso first), then sand it for smoothness. Paint the background and large areas first, using a large brush. Paint in the next largest areas. Use a small brush for final details. Make the mask stronger and waterproof by spraying outdoors with fixitif or by brushing with polyurethane. Clean brush with related solvent. Add attachments or decorations, such as ribbons, hair, fur, glitter, rings. Cleanup by placing excess plaster in a plastic bag in regular trash when it sets. Do not put any plaster in a sink because it will clog the pipes. It is best to have a trap under the sink.

Display the students' masks. Ask each student to describe his/her use of symmetry and identify two different symbols in his/her mask. Lead a discussion focussed on questions you asked earlier about Zarco's mask in the art history and aesthetics activity.

Safety Tips
Some students may be allergic to plaster, so use paper maché over a balloon or clay base instead. Never cover a person's nostrils with plaster. The plaster will become hot with changing chemical reaction.

Assessment
Use students' participation in the art criticism activity as evidence of their ability to describe, analyze, interpret and judge Zarco's calacas mask.

Assess students' completed art history and aesthetics worksheets as evidence of their ability to explain the influences in the Mexican and the Chicana/o artworlds on Zarco's work.

Assess the students' masks for their ability to model in plaster and paint, and for their ability to develop a symmetrical design.

Assess students' individual comments and group discussion of their masks as evidence of their ability to describe, analyze, interpret, and judge them, as well as evidence of their ability to use symbols in their masks.

Art Supplies and Other Resources
- Printouts of Zarco's calacas mask for each small group
- Handout on key artwork
- Art history and aesthetics worksheet
- Step-by-step mask-making handout
- Definitions handout (optional)
- Plaster modeling tape (precut gauze strips covered with plaster called Paris craft) or make your own with cheesecloth strips and plaster of Paris. To mix plaster: sift plaster into a deep bowl until an island appears in the middle of a bowl; wait a few seconds; then stir, when plaster starts to set, dip in strips; finally, apply to face and smooth.

Extension Ideas
Hold a Dia de los Muertos celebration in school for social studies instead of Halloween celebrations. Watch and discuss the video, *La Ofrenda: The days of the dead* (Portillo & Munoz, 1989).

Photograph courtesy of Judy Butzine, Coordinator of ArtsWeb, Boys & Girls Club of Metropolitan Phoenix.

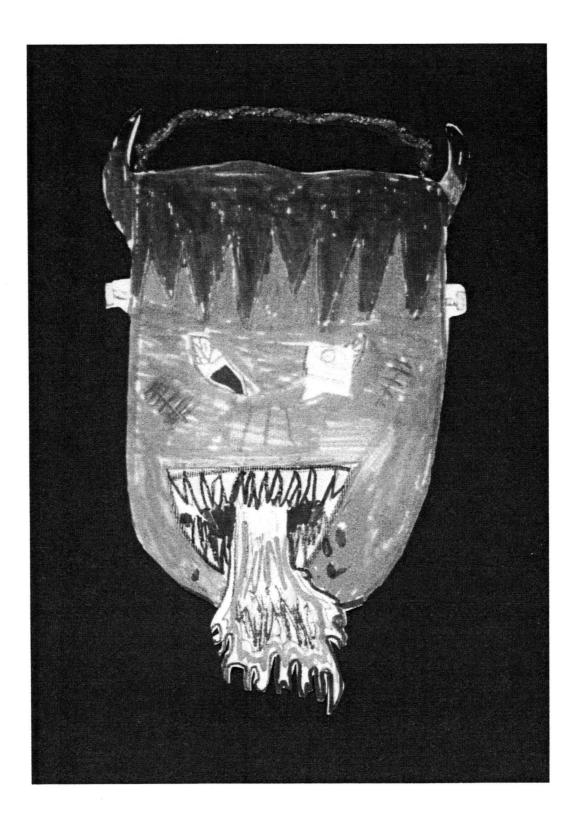

Photograph courtesy of Judy Butzine, Coordinator of ArtsWeb, Boys & Girls Club of Metropolitan Phoenix.

Exodus: Cherokee Trail of Tears

Art Maker
Willard Stone

Access Information
A poster reproduction and a postcard reproduction are available from the gift shop at the Cherokee National Historical Society, P. O. Box 515, Willis Road, Tahlequeh, OK 74465 918-456-6007, FAX 918/456-6165, http://www.powersource.com/powersource/heritage/

Date of Artwork
1967

Location of Artwork
Cherokee Heritage Center, Tahlequah, Oklahoma

Medium
Walnut

Size
36" x 36" x 12"

Subject Matter

In 1838 the Cherokee people were forcibly removed from their homeland in the southeastern United States by the federal government. Hundreds of thousands of Cherokee people of all ages traveled to Indian Territory, now the state of Oklahoma, many on foot without adequate clothing, shelter, food, or medical care. Thousands of people died. The suffering and deaths caused this removal to be called the Trail of Tears. Those who survived established the Cherokee Nation of Oklahoma.

Exodus: Cherokee Trail of Tears, created by Willard Stone, portrays a Cherokee mother, seeming to struggle against a stiff wind or storm, as she walks the Trail of Tears. Her hair is blowing back over her hunched shoulders and a tear slips from her eye as she carries her infant in a large carrying cloth or bag. The baby's face is turned to the side and is resting on its small fists. The closed eyes and miserable expression on the baby's face suggest suffering from exposure and hardship. This sculpture was commissioned for the opening of the Cherokee Cultural Center (Wade & Strickland, 1981). *Exodus,* which expresses not only the suffering of the Trail of Tears but the courage and determination of all humankind, has become a symbol of the Cherokee Nation of Oklahoma.

Visual Organization

Stone used two counterbalanced teardrops to visually organize this piece. One teardrop curves around the face of the mother; the other tear drop curves around the form of the baby in the carrying cloth. "The design is composed of two large teardrops—one balancing the other—on a base representing the contour of the earth for each man's individual trail as he carries his load through his lifetime. One teardrop is composed of his courage and determination to survive in his search for happiness; the other is representative of the heavy load of love in his heart and on his back that he willingly carries in his short lifetime on his long trail." (Stone, quoted in Wade & Strickland, 1981, p. 49)

Short Biography of Art Maker

Willard Stone (Cherokee) was born in 1916 on a sharecropping farm in Oktaha, Oklahoma. He was the youngest of eight children. Shortly after his birth, his father abandoned the family. When he was 13, a dynamite cap exploded in his hands, ripping away the thumb and parts of the first two fingers of his right hand. He stopped attending school but was determined to find a way to continue creating artworks. He taught himself to use his right hand again to draw and sculpt. Soon after the accident he entered several small clay figures in the Muskogee Free Fair, held in Muskogee, Oklahoma, and won several blue ribbons. This brought Stone to the attention of Oklahoma historian Grant Foreman, who persuaded Stone to continue his education. Although Stone never finished high school, through Foreman's influence he was able to receive art instruction at Bacone Indian College, Muskegee OK. Two artists influential in the Native American Fine Arts Movement, Acee Blue Eagle and Woodrow Crumbo, were both faculty members at Bacone Indian College at this time. Both encouraged Stone in his wood carving and sculpting (Culp, 1992).

In the early 1940s Stone was not yet able to totally earn his living from the sale of his artwork, so he worked at odd jobs. After his marriage to Sophie, they moved to a small farm in Locust Grove, Oklahoma, where Stone had his workshop. Today a small museum of Stone's work is located there as well. Shortly after moving to Locust Grove, Stone served as an artist-in-residence at the Thomas Gilcrease Institute for three years. When the residency was over, Stone worked as a dye finisher and tool designer for Douglas Aircraft in Tulsa. He carved small figures during the travel time from Locust Grove to Tulsa. He finished about 20 sculptures per year during this time, which sold readily. Eventually Stone was able to support his family of 10 children from the sale of artworks alone (Culp, 1992). Although Stone would occasionally turn to alcohol, according to his wife, alcohol never interfered with his art production (Culp, 1992). Twelve years before his death in 1985 he suffered a stroke from which he never fully recovered. Stone is remembered today as an influential Native American artist and a humble man.

Artworld Information

In the 1890s the United States government began the practice of sending Indian children, often coerced, to government boarding schools. Upon arrival the students were stripped of their culture. Speaking their Native language or practicing their religions often brought severe physical punishment. Students were discouraged from making visual expressions of their culture as well.

In 1921, the Bureau of Indian Affairs issued Circular 1665, which ordered Indian agents to suppress tribal dances. The arts community that gathered around Mabel Dodge Luan in Taos, New Mexico, fought Circular 1665. Other groups fought government attempts at allotment of Indian lands. In 1926 the Board of Indian Commissioners requested a comprehensive review of federal policy toward Native Americans. Dr. Lewis Meriam directed the research. The findings of the Meriam Report stated that Native Americans were living in tragic poverty, ill health, and malnourishment as a result of allotment. The Meriam Report recommended increased funding for Indian education and health management. Official change came about in 1934 when the Indian Reorganization Act (IRA) ended allotment. The IRA lifted the ban on teaching art in boarding schools, which had profound implications for Native American artists (Archuleta, Meyers, Nahmias, Woodsum, & Yorba, 1994). Art educators such as Oscar Brousse Jacobson at the University of Oklahoma and Dorothy Dunn at the Santa Fe Indian School displayed the artworks created by their Native students to a wide public, helping to create a market for Native American art. Jacobson's student, Acee Blue Eagle, established the art department at Bacone College in 1935. Bacone soon became a nationally recognized center for educating Native American artists. Stone was a student at Bacone College.

During the early 1900s Native American artists began incorporating non-Native art materials and visual languages into their art. This marked the beginning of the Native American Fine Art Movement (Archuleta, et. al., 1994). Moving beyond ceremonial and useful objects, Native artists in the first half of the 20th century produced a significant number of paintings in a flat, linear "traditional" style which emphasized depiction of ceremonies and ways of life that were thought to have disappeared or were on the verge of being lost through change and time. The second half of the century witnessed the continuation of this style as well as social, political, and cultural statements produced in a wide array of modern and post-modern styles (Archuleta, et al., 1994). Stone, whose artworks express his sensitivity to humans and nature, wit, and cultural pride, is considered a member of the Native American Fine Art Movement. Stone is known primarily for his sculptures, but he also worked occasionally in other media. Stone's fluid, Art Deco-influenced style has itself been influential among other Native American sculptors.

Stone was the recipient of many awards, including Outstanding Indian Award from the Council of American Indians, Waite Phillips Outstanding Artist Award from the Philbrook Art Center, an honorary doctorate from Oklahoma Christian College, and a posthumous retrospective at the Cherokee National Museum at Tahlequah, Oklahoma.

References
Bigelow, B., & Peterson, B. (Eds.), (1998). Rethinking Columbus: The next five hundred years. Minneapolis, MN: Rethinking Schools.
Bruchac, J. (1999). *The trail of tears.* New York: Random House.
Cohlene, T. (1990). *Dancing drum: A Cherokee legend.* Watermill Press.
Perdue, T. (1989). *The Cherokee.* New York: Chelsea House.
Wade, E., & Strickland, R. (1981). *Magic images: Contemporary Native American art.* Norman, OK: Philbrook Art Center and University of Oklahoma Press.
Video:
Culp, E. (Executive Producer). (1992).*Willard Stone: Against the odds* (Available from Cherokee Language and Culture Center, 4158 East 48th Place, Tulsa, OK 74135-4739).

Websites:
Archuleta, M., Meyers, M., Nahmias, S., Woodsum, J., & Yorba, J. (1994). *The Native American fine art movement: A resource guide.* [On-line]. Available: http://www.heard.org/education/resource/resource/index.html.
The Cherokee Observer, http://www.geocities.com/Heartland/Prairie/5918.
The Heard Museum, http://www.heard.org.
Native People's Magazine Online, http://www.nativepeoples.com.
NMAI Conexus (The National Museum of the American Indian), http://www.conexus.si.edu/mainie.htm.
The Official Site of the Cherokee Nation based in Oklahoma, http://www.cherokee.org.

Collections:
Cherokee Heritage Center, P.O. Box 515, Tahlequah, OK 74465-0515
Gilcrease Museum, 1400 Gilcrease Museum Road, Tulsa, OK 74127-2100
Willard Stone Family Museum and Gallery, HC 67, Box 110, Locust Grove, OK 74352.

Exodus: Cherokee Trail of Tears

Teacher Statement

A fourth-grade student once asked me, "If we live in Indiana, and in the city of Indianapolis, why are there no Indians?" This lesson was created as a response to that question. I feel that one artwork in particular, *Exodus: Cherokee Trail of Tears* by Willard Stone, can help students to find answers to this question. The Native peoples who historically reside in Indiana have suffered from being displaced from their homeland. However, I decided to teach students in depth about the events that caused the removal of the Cherokee people from the southeastern United States. I am an enrolled tribal member of the Cherokee Nation of Oklahoma. My ancestors were among those who walked the Trail of Tears.

My father was a friend of Stone. They both attended classes on the campus of Bacone College in Muskogee, Oklahoma; my father as a resident of the Murrow Indian Orphanage located on the grounds; Stone as a student in art classes taught by the college faculty. I can remember going with my father on a visit to Stone when I was a child. While they talked I played in the wood shavings on the floor of Stone's studio and stared in awe at his many works in progress.

Objectives

Students:
1) understand that artworks can provide insights into different artworlds, an artist's   personal vision, culture, and the human condition.
2) learn about the history of the Cherokee people, and that Native American cultures and artworlds are currently alive and changing.
3) conduct an in-depth analysis of the Cherokee sculpture, *Exodus.*
4) use a symbolic shape to organize a composition.
5) interpret a sculpture through writing creatively.
6) create drawings in which they express their own ideas and feelings about an issue that is important to them that is happening in their school, community, or world.

Activities

Begin by asking students to volunteer what they know about Cherokee people and the Trail of Tears. Either briefly overview the events or identify a reading assignment from one of the references to help students gain a grasp of Cherokee history and the events that surrounded the Trail of Tears. Ask students to define the word "exodus." Have a student look up the word in the dictionary if needed. Ask students for examples of contemporary exodus, such as the forced removal of ethnic Albanians from Kosovo, or of an exodus that happened historically, such as the exodus of the Jewish people from Egypt.

Display a reproduction of Stone's sculpture, *Exodus: Cherokee Trail of Tears.* Ask students to look at it, silently and intently for one minute, noting all the details they can see. Ask them to decide what the sculpture makes them think or feel. Ask students to share their reactions, then to describe the artwork in detail. Ask them if they can see the teardrops Stone used to visually organize the work. Why do the students think he used teardrops? What do the students think Stone was trying to communicate with this sculpture? What do they think were his thoughts and feelings about the Trail of Tears? What do they think might have been Stone's ideas about how people should react to adversity? Have students discuss whether they think Stone created a work that expressed the suffering of the Trail of Tears effectively and ask them to explain why or why not.

Review the Short Biography of the Art Maker and Artworld Information. Discuss important events in Stone's life, such as his accident, his reactions to those events, what he found inspirational, how he showed his love and pride of his culture through his artworks, and if he thought his people's exodus on the Trail of Tears was just. Ask students to draw parallels between Stone's reaction to the adversity in his own life and to what he portrayed in *Exodus*. Discuss Stone's artworld, where and from whom he learned about art and how his work can be considered part of the Native American Fine Arts Movement. *Willard Stone: Against the Odds* is a video that gives information about Stone and his place in the Native American Fine Art Movement. If possible, show excerpts from the video. Ask students to compare how they are learning about art in school with the way Stone learned about art. Be sure to note the role of government policies.

Ask students to become the voice of either the mother or the child in *Exodus* and write a short story that describes what she or her child sees, feels, tastes, hears, and what happens to them next. Ask students to write vividly and descriptively with great detail so that readers will feel what it's like to actually be that character. Ask students to interpret what they think is the meaning of the sculpture through their portrayals of the figures in *Exodus*.

Ask students to create charcoal drawings of a current or historical event that they have discussed in class that is important to them. The drawings can be of a personal experience or about something that happened in the school, community, nation, or world. Ask them to use a symbolic shape (such as, but not limited to, a tear-drop) as an organizational device in the composition. After they are finished with the drawing, ask the students to write a paragraph describing the intent of their drawings.

Assessment

Use students' participation in discussion to assess their understanding of Cherokee history and factors that influenced the Native American artworld.

Use state language arts standards to assess their creative interpretive writing about *Exodus*.
Ask students to assess their artworks from 4 (highest) to 1 (lowest) using the following criteria:

1) I used a symbolic shape to organize my drawing. My shape is _____. The shape really helps the meaning of the drawing come through to the viewer.

2) I wrote a paragraph that explains my drawing. I used vivid writing that really helps the viewer to understand my drawing.

3) I think my drawing has impact. I think that through my use of symbolic shape to organize the composition people will want to look at my artwork and think about what my artwork has to say.

Extension Ideas and Other Interdisciplinary Extensions

How have different artists expressed their thoughts and feelings about a problem? Examples fo discussion could be the AIDS quilt, Picasso's *Guernica,* and the Guerrilla Girls' happenings. Have students discuss actions they could take to bring awareness about a problem through art, such as create artworks and writings and then use them to create a website or hold an art exhibit and reading of their works. Have the students refine and implement a plan that they have agreed upon.

Use the Heard Museum's Native American Fine Arts Resource to integrate learning in art and social studies to teach further about Native American artworlds.

Art Supplies and Other Resources
charcoal
white drawing paper
a poster reproduction of *Willard Stone's Exodus: Cherokee Trail of Tears*

John Henry

Art Maker
S. L. Jones

Access Information
His work can be found in: Lampell, Ramona & Millard Lampell. 1989. *O'Appalachia.* New York: Stewart, Tabori & Chang, Inc. ISBN # 1-55670-098-9. Distributed in the United States by Workman Publishing, 708 Broadway, New York, New York 10003. In Canada by Canadian Manda Group, P.O. Box 920 Station U, Toronto, Ontario M8Z 5P9. Distributed in all other territories by Little, Brown and Company, International Division, 34 Beacon Street, Boston, Massachusetts 02108.

Date of Artwork
Circa 1970

Location of Artwork
This piece is owned by an anonymous collector.

Medium
Walnut wood and paint

Size
3' x 2'

Subject Matter
The story of John Henry takes place between 1869 and 1872, during the construction of the C&O Railroad's Great Bend Tunnel in Talcott (Talk-it), West Virginia. It is estimated that 1,000 men and boys of African and Irish descent died during the construction of the tunnel and were buried in makeshift pits at both ends of the tunnel including John Henry. His fame began when he challenged a drilling machine to a race.

There are many variations of the story, which is depicted in ballad form but the ending states that John Henry died. There are no official records of his birth or death and it is by way of the ballad that his story spread to labor camps across the United States and the world. Many scholars have explored the validity of the story, its transformation to folklore, and have attempted to trace John Henry's lineage and most agree that John Henry was a real person or a compilation of many men.

Visual Organization
Mr. Jones uses volume and scale to create tension and energy. The scale is large to symbolize Henry's heroism. The heaviness and the large size stress endurance and stability and directs the viewer to deal with it.

Short Biography of the Art Maker
S. L. Jones was born in 1900 as Shields Landon Jones and was one of 13 children of a farmer. He quit school after the eighth grade and worked for the Chesapeake & Ohio Railway Company. He worked for the C&O for 46 years. His family was grown and his wife passed away. He turned to an art form of his boyhood—whittling. He began to carve out figures from his childhood, neighbors, and railroad men. He never studied formal art. His community, Hinton, West Virginia, was full of community-based artists: quilters, whittlers, basketmakers, musicians, sculptors, candlemakers, and potters, to name a few. Community festivals such as the Railroad Festival occurred every year and S.L. Jones began to sell his work. He often would draw for someone and give it them. Although Mr. Jones work is sold internationally, he was known only as that nice man who plays the fiddle and carves wood. No one knew that he was famous outside of West Virginia. He died at home in 1997. His son, Ralph Jones, has followed in his father's footsteps. His sculptures illustrated his love for wood and an understanding of the nature around his area. It is stated that Mr. Jones could identify every tree by shape, leaf, and bark from a distance and which could be sculpted.

Artworld Information
As stated earlier, S. L. Jones was community minded and was a part of a community-based artworld. Ideas, support, and marketing their art were developed while participating at festivals in the West Virginia area known as Appalachia. The original people of this region were Cherokee and Choctaw. During the 1700s, people from Scotland and Ireland who were escaping the bonds of the English came into the region, as well as Africans seeking freedom from slavery. In many ways, these three ethnic groups infused and created Appalachian Culture(s). S. L. Jones was a member of this culture and practiced an artform called whittling. The art forms often reflect survival skills of the home and farm. Many of Jones's pieces deal with ordinary people who have done something significant in their lifetime but the world may not know about it. The community-based cultural pedagogy emphasizes the connection between traditions, heritage, and culture. The Mountain festival tradition is a model in the artworld of the Mountain Culture. The West

Virginia Mountain festivals are events where local and regional artists share stories, songs, spirituality, political views, visual arts, and food with their community. The tradition of festivals goes back to the early 1800s, beginning as community gatherings and expanding in the early 1900s with the coming of outsiders who saw the arts as a commodity and a festival as a market. Confusing commodity with the need to socialize has not been an issue for Mountain Cultural festivals. The arts are used as a tool for social change which is advocated today by some social and critical theorists as the way to develop social and cultural reformation. It is within the tradition of the Mountain Culture that the arts are used as a tool to re-establish social reconstruction, and the festival is the format of the people to celebrate community triumph, confirmation, and reaffirmation of their identity and voice. Tables with one's goods are displayed and sold. The festival usually lasts up to three days and includes a variety of arts. S. L. Jones attended these festivals as a young boy and participated in them until his death. His son continues the tradition and during some festivals, opens his home as a community museum displaying S. L. Jones's work and works of other family members.

References
Lester, J. (1994). *John Henry* New York: Penguin Books.
PBS Character Quest Porchlight Entertainment in association with KCET, Los Angeles and is available through PBS Video, 1-800-344-3337.
Morris, C. B. (1998). Cultural Ecology: Arts of the Mountain Culture. *Art Education, 51* (3), p. 14.

Website
www.carts.org

Self, Cultural, and Community Identity

Objectives
Students:
1) compare, and contrast S. L. Jones's sculpture of *John Henry* with cartoons, books, and ballads telling the same story taking into account the significance of John Henry's life on the community and world.
2) discuss, write, and reflect on the multiple identities one must possess to be a leader and identify leaders in their community based on students' criteria.
3) recognize that artists such as S. L. Jones use proportion, distortion, medium, color, and size to create meaning.
4) explore and discuss multiple signs and symbols that were utilized to illustrate *John Henry* and create a sculpture of a community leader(s).
5) reflect on the purpose and value of their own art work.
6) identify ways that Appalachian arts festivals support art and art makers within mountain cultures.

Activities
After students have viewed various media interpretations about John Henry, such as Julious Lester's book *John Henry*, videos that explore John Henry such as *Shelly Long's Folk Tales* or PBS Character Quest, listened to the ballad, *John Henry,* and read historic accounts such as *John Henry: A bio-bibliography* by Brett Williams (Greenwood Press, 1983), have them explore each interpretation of John Henry's life. Why is he considered a leader and a hero? Can a person be a leader and not a hero and visa versa? How and why? After the students have had an opportunity to explore the idea of hero/leader as a group, have them individually write their hero/leader criteria. Place them in small groups to discuss their criteria and develop a set of group criteria. Then repeat discussion as a class. Are the class criteria different from their individual response? How and why? Teachers may find that they will need to explore differences in what is a hero and a celebrity.

Using the class criteria have the students explore people in their community, past or present, that meet their standards as a leader and/or hero. Discuss their contributions to the community and the value placed by the community members. If the community/town has a historical society or elders who have lived a long time in that community, invite them to be a part of this portion of the lesson. Photographs, newspaper articles, etc. are also beneficial. Encourage students to find as much information as possible utilizing various means such as: library, Internet, museums, and community members. After their research is completed, discuss their findings and compile a list of community leaders/heroes with possible photographs and a story about their contributions including statistical information, what, where, when, and how.

Show the students S. L. Jones's *John Henry* sculpture. Talk about S. L. Jones and how his life paralleled John Henry's (see the Short Biography of art maker). They lived in the same area of West Virginia, worked for the railroad, and were viewed by others as a community leader. S. L. Jones sculpted people that were important to his life and that he felt should be remembered. Explain that different people have a variety of ideas about why art is important and what is art. After a minute of scanning, ask the students to explore Jones' idea of art and how that may or may not be their idea of why art is important and what is art.

Consult the Artworld Information, selecting information to share about the artworld of Mountain Culture, especially the role of arts festivals. Next ask the students to respond in writing to the question, "How does Mr. Jones use proportion, distortion, medium, color to portray his idea of hero/leader?" After they are done, have them discuss their ideas. Make sure that key components are mentioned and explored: 1.) John Henry was strong and big; therefore, Jones used heavy walnut wood; 2.) he made the size larger than humans to emphasize qualities of hero; 3.) the mouth open illustrates John's will to have a voice in this world; and 4.) no photographs were available of John Henry; so, Jones used the ballad, stories, and his personal feeling to create his sculpture. To S. L. Jones, likeness was not important. The story, his connection to the story, and the value he placed on it were much more important. Jones believed that his approach gave his sculptures life because it is more important what is inside than outside.

Using Jones's approach and artistic philosophy, have the students sketch ideas of anyone of the people on their community hero/leader list. Remind them that their choice should be carefully made by considering *their* relationship to the deed or person.

Once their sketches are complete, remind the students why Jones used walnut to represent the strength and rarity of this type of persona and Jones's admiration. Keeping this in mind, have the students collect their sculpture material and construct their assemblage sculpture. During this process, encourage students to question their material choices and have them write down their responses. Upon completion, ask students to use their process notes and research data to write an artist's statement. In an open space, arrange sculptures with statements and have students view each others' work.

Assessment

Discuss their process, learning about John Henry, developing hero/leader criteria, identifying a local hero/leader, researching, and creating. Did their idea of hero/leader change, how and why? Did their view of what it means to be a community member change, how and why or why not? What value do they place on community, leaders, and hero? Does living in a community make someone a member? In what way would it not? What ways could they be a community member and/ or leader? What reasons would they have to be one? How could they become one? In a journal have the students respond to the questions that they had discussed as a group: Did their idea of hero/leader change, how and why? Did their view of what it means to be a community member change, how and why or why not? What value do they place on community, leaders, and hero? How did art festivals affect Jones? What value does this piece have to the community? Region? Working people? To the student? Utilizing and reviewing their process notes, what did they find restricting with this project? Grading of the project includes:
    1) Written artist statement included their process and research;
    2) Generated research information;
    3) Writing style, grammar, and syntax;
    4) Participation in discussion;
    5) Chose material to help convey meaning.
    6) Completed all steps—research, criterion, group discussions, sculpture, and self evaluation.

Art Supples and Other Resources
Computer
Printer
Pencils
Paper
Journals
Junk for sculptures
Glue
Books,cartoons, music about John Henry
Historical society.

Extension Ideas or Interdisciplinary Connections

Researching and writing community leader and/or hero information are connected to language arts. The information could be developed into poetry, plays, and the music teacher could teach them how to write a ballad and or song. This lesson could also be connected to social studies by studying railroad history and labor union history in the United States.

The ballad of John Henry is considered a Bluegrass, Country, and Folk music standard and can be found recorded by various artists such as Johnny Cash, Bill Monroe, Harry Belafonte, David Morris, and Jim Costa. Because it is a folk ballad, there are many versions. The following is a traditional ballad, which requires no copyright permission to be used: As sung by David Morris (Morris, 1998, p.14).

When John Henry was a little bitty boy
Sittin on his daddy's knee
Well he picked up a hammer and a piece of steel
Said hammer's gonna be the death of me Lord Lord
Hammer's gonna be the death of me.

Well John Henry hammered in the mountain
With his pappy by his side
And the rock was so tall and little Johnny was so small
That he laid down his hammer and he cried Lord Lord
He laid down his hammer and he cried.

Well the captain he said to John Henry
Gonna bring that steam drill 'round
Gonna bring that steam drill out on the job
Gonna whop that steel on down Lord Lord
Gonna whop that steel on down.

Well John Henry said to his captain
Well a man ain't nothin but a man
But before I would let that steam drill beat me down
Die with a hammer in my hand Lord Lord
Die with a hammer in my hand.

Well John Henry said to his shaker
He said shaker you'd better sing
I'm a swinging 12 pounds from my hips on down
Listen to that cold steel ring Lord Lord
Listen to that cold steel ring.

Well John Henry said to his captain
Lord you think you're mighty fine
Well John Henry done drove 14 feet of steel
Steam drill only drove nine Lord Lord.
Steam drill only drove nine.

Well John Henry went out upon the mountain
And he looked out on the other side
And the only words that he did say
A cold drink of water 'fore I die Lord Lord
A cold drink of water 'fore I die.

Well John Henry had a little woman
And her name was Polly Ann
And when Johnny was sick and had to go to bed
Polly drove that steel like a man Lord Lord
Polly drove that steel like a man.

Well they took John Henry to the graveyard
And they buried him under the sand
And every locomotive that goes rumblin by
Yonder lies a steel drivin man Lord Lord
Yonder lies a steel drivin man.

Samples of Student Work

Dennis's Artist Statement

S. L. Jones was an artist from West Virginia. He worked with wood. His works were about himself and people from his town. He used wood that told about the people. The type of wood, how big it was and the shapes used tell me a lot about the people he carved. He used strong wood and rare wood to represent John Henry. My piece is about my mom. She works very hard. I used fabric, wire, and paper because my mom uses fabric to sew and wire to make flowers and she is my mom. She makes those things and made me too. I used paper because that is what we had. I asked what culture I was and mom doesn't know but I know that I am African American and the color green is important. I used green to be mom's garden and she tells me I am her weed so I am growing and I need lots of stuff to keep growing.

Jenny's Artist Statement

We studied S. L. Jones in our class. He was a famous artist from West Virginia who carved a famous person called John Henry. John Henry was a slave who became free. He took a job making a tunnel and died racing a machine. He raced the machine to make a point. The machine was going to replace him and he fought real hard to keep his job because a job is important. Although he won the race, he died but he represents hope to fight for one's right to work and make a living in this world. Mr. Jones thought John Henry was special and rare and used black walnut to symbolize the person and the event. Black walnut is a rare, hard wood. He also exaggerated features and made John Henry large to symbolize his hero. A hero is someone who is motivated to do something for the cause for others. They do not think of themselves as much as they do about other people. I chose my teachers as my heroes. I used a book to represent them and learning. The pages represent all of the knowledge they have and try to give to us as their students. Inside the book are small students who are not ready to come out yet because they are still learning.

Aunt Harriet's Underground Railroad in the Sky

Art Maker
Faith Ringgold

Access Information
Aunt Harriet's Underground Railroad in the Sky.
(1992). New York, NY. Dragonfly Books of Crown Publishers, Inc., Div. of Random House.
Website: *Aunt Harriet's* Website: http://www.artincontext.org/artist/ringgold/collect.htm.

Additional Resources
Hopkins- Bradford, S. (1886). *Harriet: The Moses of Her People.* NY: J.J. Little and Co.
McMullan, K. (1991). *The Story of Harriet Tubman, Conductor of the Underground Railroad.* NY: Dell Publishing.

Date of Artwork and Book*s*
1992

Location of Artwork
The illustrations for the book remain in the artist's private collection.

Medium
Ringgold's illustrations for the book were original paintings on canvas paper.

Size
Book size 9.25" x 12"

Subject Matter

The book is based on Harriet Tubman's adventures with the Underground Railroad. Born a slave about 1820, Tubman made her first journey on the Railroad in 1849 reaching freedom in Canada with the help of many "conductors." She returned to become a conductor herself and eventually escorted over 300 slaves to freedom without ever losing a passenger. Toward the end of her life, Tubman had dreams of flying to freedom aided by a circle of women dressed in white. Ringgold incorporated this imagery into her book, as well as the slave tradition of flinging a quilt over the roof of a house as a sign for good luck.

Ringgold's story begins as Cassie and her brother Be Be are flying high up among the stars when they come across an old train in the sky. The children watch as hundreds of people appear and begin to board the old train when a woman wearing a conductor's apron calls "all aboard." Cassie's adventure starts when Be Be jumps on without her and the train disappears to the sky, leaving behind an ominous message in the clouds: Go Free North or Die! As Cassie fearfully calls for her brother, the voice of the woman conductor whispers gently into her ear, introducing herself as Harriet Tubman, and telling Cassie of the story of slavery and the Underground Railroad. "Aunt" Harriet tells Cassie that every hundred years, as a commemoration, the old train will follow the same route that she traveled on the Underground Railroad so no one ever forgets the cost of freedom. Aunt Harriet tells Cassie that although Cassie missed this train, she can follow along until she reaches freedom in Canada where she will be reunited with Be Be. Aunt Harriet proceeds to advise Cassie on what to do, warning her that she will have to make this journey mostly on foot as her great-great grandparents did, relying on the help of other conductors who operate safe houses along the way.

With Aunt Harriet's voice as her guide, Cassie re-lives her ancestors' experience as she makes her way and avoids capture by learning to read visual images as signs and messages, such as quilts flung out on rooftops whose designs indicate a direction to be followed. The adventure ends when Cassie makes it to freedom, flying over Niagara Falls to the "Promised Land." There she finds Aunt Harriet, her brother and the other passengers on the Underground Railroad, all in the embrace of many women dressed all in white, flying in a large circle around them.

Visual Organization

Painted on canvas paper, the images Ringgold created to illustrate the book are not unlike those in her other children's books. Intense color, richly textured surfaces and bright patterns combine with dramatic subject matter and personal narrative to draw readers in as if they were following right along behind the children on this dangerous and exciting journey.

Short Biography of Art Maker

Faith Ringgold, whose career began as a painter over 30 years ago, was born in Harlem, New York in 1930. As a young child, Ringgold suffered from asthma, and art became a major pastime as she sketched in bed for hours while her mother, a fashion designer, sewed dresses nearby. Ringgold raised two daughters while pursuing her education and teaching art in New York City public schools until 1973 when she quit to pursue her artistic career full-time.

During the sixties, Ringgold developed her first mature painting style in a series of artworks that reflected the artist's social activism. Throughout the seventies, influences of family, African-American culture, feminism and memories of Harlem, where she lived most of her life, become intertwined with political statement as Ringgold's art began to chronicle her personal experience as a woman artist of color living in the United States. The artist's mother, Willi Posey, became a profound influence during this period and collaboration between mother and daughter set the stage for the creation of Ringgold's first story quilt, completed 2 years after Posey's death in 1981. Ringgold began to focus her creative energies on making story quilts, combining painting and sewing with complex narrative in ways that transform perceptions of African American people and challenge the dominant culture's view of reality (Gouma-Peterson, 1998).

In 1991, Ringgold published the award-winning *Tar Beach,* the first of her books for children. Today, Faith Ringgold is recognized as a major contributor to contemporary American art. Her work has been widely exhibited and she has received numerous awards and honorary degrees. She is currently professor of art at the University of California at San Diego, living half the year in California and the other at her home in New Jersey.

Artworld Information

Today, Faith Ringgold is well known for her story quilts, art that combines painting, sewn fabric and storytelling, which she began developing in the early 1980s. Since her career began in the 1960s, however, she has produced a wide-ranging and prolific body of work, including paintings, masks, dolls, costumes, and performance, all drawn from a broad reserve of intellectual, emotional and social concerns. She has traveled, exhibited and lectured across America and in Europe, received National Endowment for the Arts awards, fulfilled major commissions and remained steadfast in her activism. Faith Ringgold has been a prominent force in the endeavor to create a more global art community, bridging artworlds of Euro-American modernism, postmodernism, and African American artistic contribution to western culture.

Throughout her career, Faith Ringgold has entered many artworlds, some uninviting, others overlooking her uncommon gifts or misunderstanding the methods she used from early on, many of which, such as collaboration and use of the vernacular, are in artistic vogue today (Tucker, 1998). Her tenacity and courage have allowed her to successfully navigate these worlds in spite of whatever roadblocks she encountered. Much like one of her story quilts, Ringgold pieces these experiences together from a uniquely personal vantage point, transforming and reconstructing them through an alluring blend of fact, fiction and fable that offers an alternative view of life, history and culture. As Marcia Tucker, director of the New Museum of Contemporary Art in New York City, so aptly states, Ringgold's work constitutes an extraordinary visual chronology, including "the history of historical omission by virtue of race and gender" (1998, pp. ix).

The artist, Ringgold, as author, makes connections between her personal life and history. Cultural experience, art making and social activism resound in each story as the reader quickly recognizes the narrative voice in Ringgold's books as the artist's own. She masterfully invites young readers to explore an idea or issue through the eyes of an artist while imbuing each story with a sense of magic, wonderment and ultimately hope. Such ingenuity allows the greater message contained within each story to be more accessible and to impact the reader in a way that generates empathy for the important social concerns Ringgold is addressing through her characters and their adventures. Very much like her art, which she intended to be accessible to everyday people, Ringgold's storybooks touch the human spirit in a way that allows the reader to identify with the characters and their adventures, whether it be discovering the richness of one's cultural heritage, struggling against the odds, or daring to dream "what if..." The beautiful illustrations that fill Ringgold's books strike a similar cord in their ability to convey meaning and stir the reader's aesthetic sensibilities in a most compassionate manner.

References

Cameron, D. (1998). Living history: Faith Ringgold's rendezvous with the 20th century. In D. Cameron (Ed.), *Dancing at the Louvre: Faith Ringgold's French collection and other story quilts.* New York: The New Museum of Contemporary Art.

Gouma-Peterson, T. (1998). Faith Ringgold's jouney: From Greek busts to African American dilemma tales. In D. Cameron (Ed.) *Dancing at the Louvre: Faith Ringgold's French collection and other story quilts.* New York: The New Museum of Contemporary Art.

Tucker, M. (1998). Foreword, In D. Cameron (Ed.) *Dancing at the Louvre: Faith Ringgold's French collection and other story quilts.* New York: The New Museum of Contemporary Art.

Freedom Quilt of Safe House Signs for Elementary and Early Middle School Levels

Objectives

Students:

1) learn that artists often serve as conveyors and preservers of important cultural and historical information.
2) increase awareness of art as narrative and the artist as storyteller.
3) develop their understanding of the power and importance of visual imagery as a means to communicate important ideas.
4) develop greater appreciation for the accomplishments of people of color and their contributions to the complex contemporary artworld and culture.
5) develop a sense of social responsibility through awareness of the arts as vehicles for social change.
6) use line, color, shape, abstraction, repetition, and pattern to develop symbols.

Activities

This lesson can be easily adapted to elementary through high school grade levels. Begin by presenting the idea that many artists tell stories through their artwork, and some use their art to remind us about important times in our history that sometimes are overlooked or misunderstood. For older children, introduce the term, *social activism*, and the idea that some artists create art as a means to bring the public's attention to important issues such as discrimination.

Introduce the artist and storyteller, Faith Ringgold, an African American woman, much of whose life work has centered on revealing truths in the histories of accomplished women of color and the African-American cultural experience in America. The artist accomplishes this in two ways: through her story quilts for which she is renowned, and through her books for children to which she brings the same enthusiasm, purpose and aesthetic concern. Read through the short bibliography of the art maker and the artworld information selecting information about Ringgold and her artworld to share with your students. To create her story quilts, an art form that Ringgold developed in the early 1980s, the artist uses paint, sewn and quilted fabric, and words to tell a story about a certain topic. Faith Ringgold began to write and illustrate children's books in order to make her stories more available to people of all ages. In the story, *Aunt Harriet's Underground Railroad in the Sky*, the artist sends Cassie Louise Lightfoot on an adventure back in time to learn about Harriet Tubman and the Underground Railroad and how Cassie's great-great grandparents escaped from slavery.

Introduce Harriet Tubman and explain the Underground Railroad and the circumstances in American society that resulted in its establishment. What do you think it was like to be a slave, taken from your home against your will, and forced to work on someone else's land for no pay? How would you feel about staying in such a situation? Freedom is such a precious and important part of being human that many slaves were willing to risk their lives to escape. Many people of different colors and backgrounds, who were against slavery, helped them to do so. One such person was Harriet Tubman who brought over 300 slaves to freedom on the Underground Railroad without ever losing a passenger.

The students should proceed to hear/read the story and view the illustrations, making particular note of the painting that shows Cassie finding a colorful quilt flung out on the roof of a safe house as she makes her way through the woods. Point out to the students the way in which the artist has painted her colorful illustrations, noting the effective use of texture and pattern and how these help to make the story come alive.

The students should discuss what they have seen and read, using the following questions as a guide: What is a safe house and what did conductors who operated safehouses do for the people who were traveling on the Underground Railroad? How did these conductors use elements of art (lines, shapes, colors) to communicate a secret message to a slave who was hiding in the woods? Why did the message have to be secret? Why didn't the signs, quilts and other markers use words and sentences to give information? (Slaves were not allowed to learn reading and writing, so understanding lines, colors, and shapes was very important.) Why was Harriet Tubman called "Moses" by her people and why was Canada called the "Promised Land"? (Bible stories were an important part of slave life, and many slaves found comfort in the story of Moses who delivered his people out of slavery to freedom in the promised land.)

Freedom quilt of safe house signs activity (motivation)

Present idea that students can go back in time, like Cassie, by using their imaginations to explore what it was like to be a slave and what it was like to be a conductor who could help those trying to escape. To increase understanding of oppression and human rights, ask the students to imagine they are slaves trying to escape to freedom on the Underground Railroad and what this might be like. What is your journey like? What is difficult, scary, terrible? Is your family with you? How do you feel? To foster a sense of social responsibility for supporting tolerance and diversity, ask the students to then imagine themselves as conductors who operate safe houses offering respite to the weary travelers. What does your safe house have to offer? If you were escaping, what would you need to help you through? (For example, food, a bed for rest, new shoes.) A list of the students' responses should be made on a large display paper, one response per line, leaving room on the paper across from the response word. Remind the students to recall how they felt when they imagined themselves as escaping slaves, and encourage them to think of every-thing that might be needed by someone on such a journey (this can also include non-material things like comfort, love, spiritual activity). When the list is completed, recall the use of the quilt in Ringgold's book, and suggest that the students could make a sign to hang out that will let an escaping slave know what their safe house has to offer. Remind the students of two crucial factors: one, the "message" contained in their sign must not include words, and two, the message must be disguised so that slave catchers and bounty hunters cannot understand it. (Mention that the slave tradition of creating quilts filled with lines, shapes, colors, and patterns makes slaves more attuned to "read-ing" visual imagery.)

Creating a safe house sign

To reinforce the power and importance of visual imagery, using a cut-paper collage method, the students will use basic art elements and principles to create an abstract safe house sign containing a disguised message for those traveling on the Underground Railroad. Borders will be decorated with Adinkra prints echoing the use of African design by slave quilters and further protecting the message from spies and slave catchers since the meaning of this culture-specific imagery is not readily accessible to them. Explain that our "quilting" method has been inspired by Ringgold but that paper collage will be used to make our pieces. Working as a group and using the list of students' ideas displayed on the board, have each student decide what his/her safe house will offer. Then have students name an object that symbolizes the offering and chart this across from the corresponding word on the list. For example, the offering may be food, so objects to show this could be a bowl and spoon.

Because the next step presents a challenge to students, group work with the class as a whole should continue. Now the students must figure out a way to abstract the objects into their simplest shapes and lines. Select a listed object, demonstrate how to abstract it up on the board next to the list, and then ask a student(s) volunteer to come up and demonstrate again with another object. Now students will use their abstracted objects to create a design that commu-nicates its message in a disguised manner.

Have the children recall principles of repetition and pattern and explain/demonstrate how these, along with an arbitrary use of color, will help to convey the message without giving it away. Using the bowl and spoon example, the abstract bowl image might be repeated twice and placed in the middle of the black background paper with one bowl mirroring the other. The spoon symbol can then be repeated several times and placed around the center bowl image in a radiating fashion. Additional shapes and lines can be added to the design.

Remind students that to a slave catcher, these signs will simply look like pleasant designs often seen in quilts, while to escaping slaves, they will convey important messages. Students proceed to create their designs, cutting their shapes from colored paper and gluing them in the desired manner onto black paper backgrounds and within pre-drawn one inch borders around the outer edge of the background paper. Border lines can be drawn using a white or light-colored pencil. To complete their safe house signs, the students will then use white tempera paint and eraser stamps that have been pre-carved with African Adinkra symbols to print a design inside the pre-drawn border space surrounding their designs.

In the final step create a Freedom Quilt by piecing all the individual collages together and gluing them down to larger paper (taping two sections of mural-sized paper together works well for a large background). If the class is large, more than one quilt can be made. Students can also make two signs so that one can go home and the other can be contributed to the group quilt.

Until there is time for gluing the final Freedom Quilt together, a temporary version can be made by taping the individual pieces onto the board with edges touching. The students should discuss their Freedom Quilt and note the ways in which their classmates used the elements and principles of art to convey a disguised message.

Assessment

Use the following minimum criteria to determine beginner, competent and advanced levels of performance. Students can:

Name the artist/author and describe her cultural background and artworld.

Name two ways in which the artists tell stories (story quilts and children's books).

Describe a social and/or historical concern that influenced the artist to write and illustrate Aunt Harriet's Underground Railroad.

Define the Underground Railroad and describe Harriet Tubman's involvement.

Describe how visual imagery was used to help travelers on their journey.

Design and create an abstract cut-paper collage that visually communicates a safe house offering using elements of shape, line, color and principles of repetition and pattern.

Extension Ideas and Interdisciplinary Connections

The map provided at the end of the book, Aunt Harriet's Underground Railroad in the Sky, and a call to the local historical society can determine if students live in an area where there may be actual Underground Railroad sites that can be visited. Integrate this art lesson with a unit on American history. Language arts can also be incorporated as students might be asked to write the story of what would happen when an escaping slave sees the student's safe house sign and seeks refuge.

Art Supplies and Other Resources

Large display paper

Black marker

Colored construction paper

9" x 12" sheets of black construction paper for each student with a pre-drawn one inch border around perimeter scissors

Glue sticks or white school glue with dishes and brushes

Set of Adinkra symbols carved from erasers

White tempera paint and shallow dishes

Masking tape

African Adinkra symbols can be found in many books on African design and in the book, Brown Bag Ideas From Many Cultures by Irene Tejada (1993, Davis Publications, Worcester, MA).

Parfleche Case

Art Maker
Unknown Sioux woman

Access Information
Reproduction of Parfleche case available at http://www.getty.edu/artsednet/images/O/parfleche.html. Other parfleche cases are reproduced in *Indians of North America - Yankton Sioux* is available from Crizmac Arts & Cultural Educational Materials, P. O. Box 65728, Tucson, Arizona 85728-5928.

Date of Artwork
Circa 1880-90

Location of Artwork
Southwest Museum in Los Angeles

Medium
Cowhide and paint

Size
22" x 14"

Subject Matter
A *parfleche* is a leather carrier decorated with geometric designs, bound with red felt or leather lacing. It was used as a carrier for supplies. The parfleche was made in several shapes and forms to adapt to its use. Shapes on parfleche cases, such as this one, are sometimes symbolic and other times simply decorative. Women from different tribes painted different symbols on their parfleches. Sometimes the same shape had different meanings in different tribes. For example, the diamond shape could stand for a turtle, a person, a buffalo wallow, a hill, abundance, or the interior of a tent. Sioux women often used the diamond to symbolize the turtle, which was connected with women's sacred power. In contrast, Crow women used the diamond as a symbol for the sand lizard, connected with safety, health, and long life. The hourglass shape symbolized the buffalo. The four colors of the parfleche cases were usually associated with the four directions, with life forces, and with the four seasons.

Visual Organization
All the shapes are angular and defined with straight lines. The painter used many triangles and pure colors: red, orange, blue, and green. The parfleche case has a rectangular shape. The artist painted orange rectangles on the upper and lower flaps that echo the shape of the parfleche itself and frame the other shapes on the parfleche. In the center of each flap, she combined two triangles at the ends of a rectangle to form a modified diamond shape.

Positive and negative shapes can shift back and forth as the viewer focuses on one shape and then another. The brightly-colored painted shapes can be seen as positive (foreground) shapes as they contrast with the light tan background (negative) shapes. The blue triangles can be seen as negative in contrast with their red and green (positive) outlines. The light tan shapes are so clear and regular that, if the viewer focuses on them, even they can be seen as positive spaces against the darker green, red, and blue shapes. In some places, orange lines separate painted areas from unpainted tan areas.

The dull, light tan of the rawhide contrasts with the intense colors of the painted decoration. The dominant repetition of triangles unifies the rhythmic pattern. The pattern is bilaterally symmetrical (same on both sides) on both its vertical and horizontal axis.

Short Biography of Art Maker
Each of the hundreds of Native American nations across the country is known for its specific art forms and designs. The central United States is home for the Plains Indians. There are seven councils in South Dakota that make-up this Sioux nation. The Sioux were predominantly a nomadic people who followed the buffalo and elk for food. This lifestyle required mobility as these people used only what they could carry with them. Sioux artwork is reflective of that lifestyle. Women used cases to efficiently organize their possessions. Because different tribes decorated their cases differently and parfleches were an important part of a woman's life, they reinforced their user's cultural identity, that is, the user's membership in the tribe. Generally parfleches reflected the everyday concerns in the lives of Sioux women. Some women used shapes as decoration only, not intending any symbolic meaning. The individual woman who made this case is unknown today and so are her specific intentions.

Artworld Information

The Sioux did not traditionally make art for art sake but rather as useful items. The people who made parfleches did not have words that meant "art" or "artists," because almost everyone in the group made and decorated objects used in daily life. The Sioux created beadwork, leatherwork, featherwork, and quillwork using parts of the buffalo and other available animals, as well as paints and beads received from traders. Parfleches were made exclusively by women. The craft is passed on from generation to generation. Sioux men painted objects such as buffalo robes and shieldcoverings. Men's paintings commonly depicted warriors and horses. Also men exclusively made featherwork.

Each tribe on the Great Plains had its own way of constructing and decorating parfleche cases. The Sioux typically painted shapes first and then outlined the shapes with blue-black lines to clarify the separation between painted and unpainted areas. However, there are exceptions: the Sioux woman who made this parfleche chose not to use blue-black outlines. Other tribes, such as the Crow, typically established a linear structure of colored lines first that predetermined the placement of color areas. One hide made two cases. The two cases were often attached. Each was placed across a horse's back. This is the precursor to the saddlebag.

References

Goble, P. (1996). *The Return of the Buffaloes*. Washington, DC: National Geographic Society.
Sommer, R. (1994). *Native American Art*. New York: Smithmark Publisher.

Collections:

Minneapolis Art Institute; Native American Exhibit (permanent display). Minneapolis, Minnesota.
Sioux Indian Museum, P. O. Box 1504, Rapid City, South Dakota 57709 (605) 348-0557.

The Sioux Parfleche: A Multicultural Experience

Objectives

Students:
1) compare the purpose of Sioux parfleche cases with containers used today.
2) develop a balanced design using geometric shapes.
3) create a case using modern materials and borrowing a cutting and folding process from the Sioux.
4) compare how Sioux women traditionally learned to make parfleche cases with how students learn to make art in school.

Activities

Show the students examples of different types of carriers, i.e., a purse, Tupperware, attache case, backpack, gym bag. Ask students to identify and explain to the class how they are used. Explain to the students that traditionally the Sioux Indians were a nomadic (moving from one area to another) people who followed the buffalo herds from one season to another. In order to move their daily items they made carriers called parfleches. A *parfleche* [par FLECH] served a purpose similar to today's suitcase, backpack etc.

Ask students to tell about how they learned to make some sort of artwork (in art class, from a family member, from a kit, from TV, etc.). Explain that in traditional Sioux culture, women and men made different things. Men exclusively made featherwork and made leather shields. Women made parfleche cases. Explain that different Native Americans of the Great Plains developed different tribal styles. Explain further that older women taught girls how to burn holes for lacings, how to make and apply paint, and how to cut and fold the leather to make a case.

Display a reproduction of a parfleche case. Explain that Sioux decorated most household items with colorful geometric designs. (Review geometric shapes.) Some of the shapes used were symbols for items. For example the triangle could be a teepee or tree. Other designs were taken from the Sioux written picture language or were purely decorative. Define a balanced design as one that has two sides that are mirror images of each other. Point out how the parfleche design is balanced both top to bottom and side to side. Explain that students will make a case using today's materials but constructed and decorated by borrowing traditional Sioux ideas.

1) Have students trace a pattern on tagboard and cut out parfleche case shape.

2) Draw examples on chalkboard of a variety of balanced geometric designs. Assist students in developing their design on separate scrap paper.

3) Transfer design to properly folded tagboard. Outline in black marker and fill-in enclosed shapes with colored markers.

4) Punch holes for closure, secure with ties of yarn or strips of leather. Red felt can be added to folded edges and laced together.

Display completed cases. Ask students to compare how they learned to make their cases with how Sioux girls learned in the 19th century. Ask students to describe and point out examples of balanced geometric designs in their classmates' work.

Assessment

Assessment focuses on:

Use of geometric shapes and a balanced design,

Careful cutting and folding,

Ability to compare today's containers with traditional Sioux parfleche cases, and

Ability to compare their own way of learning about art with 19th century Sioux ways.

Art Supplies and Other Resources

Reproduction of parfleche case

one sheet of tagboard or railroad board per student

various colored markers

red felt scraps

paper punch

rulers

yarn or leather scraps

scissors

parfleche pattern (available online at http://www.nationalgeographic.com/books/9609/buffaloes.html).

Extension Ideas and Other Interdisciplinary Extensions

Interdisciplinary connections could be developed through a social studies unit on Native Americans. A language research project could explore different types of carriers as used by different cultures. An original story reflecting the design on the individual carrier could be developed to use writing skills.

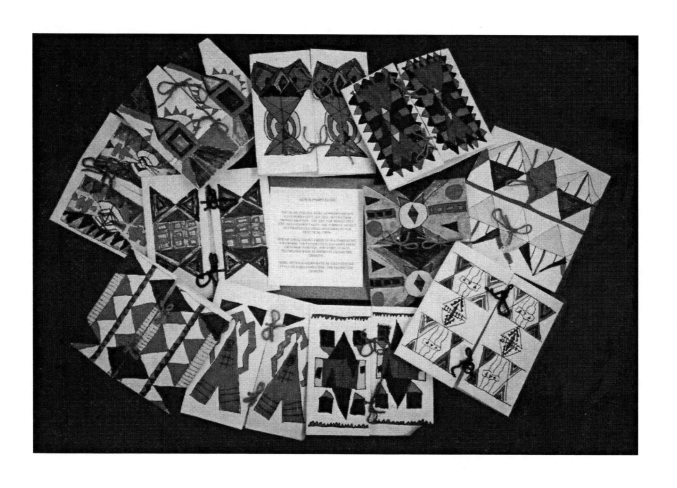

Maus, A Survivor's Tale

Art Maker
Art Spiegelman

Access Information
Spiegelman, A. (1986).
Maus, a survivor's tale. New
York: Pantheon Books

Date of the Artwork
1986.

Location
This artwork is compiled in
the form of an illustrated
book.

Medium
pen and ink drawings

Size
The original art is drawn on
9" x 12" papers. The printed
book is 8" x 11"

Subject Matter

Maus is a family biography of a Holocaust survivor, told by his son. The Jews are all portrayed in the book as mice, the Poles as pigs, and the Nazis as cats. Characters have similar features, yet within the limited form of a mouse Spiegelman coaxes great expressions and variety. Characters also become individuals through the addition of small features, such as glasses, a pipe, or facial wrinkles. Perhaps the most moving depiction of the subject is in the subtle body language of each figure and the powerful settings created for them.

Visual Organization

Important comparisons can be made by placing Spiegelman's pages side by side with a mass produced comic book. Maus uses a free style comic book format. His black-and-white pictures are highly detailed and textured, using expressive hand written words. The dark feeling of the subject can be felt through the black ink that darkens each page. Dramatic shading is an important aspect of each frame. Unlike the glossy sterile look of many comic books, the images in *Maus* are distinctly hand made and personal. When a comic book is opened one has a general impression of the events taking place. In *Maus* each frame needs to be carefully examined and read to gain the full experience. While action unites the look of each ordinary comic book page, in *Maus* a somber mood and a slow pace evolves into a depiction of violence. The fine paper used for the illustrations gives the viewer a sense of looking at a serious visual novel rather than an ordinary comic book.

Short Biography of the Artist/Author

Art Spiegelman was born in Stokholm, Sweden, in 1948 and grew up in Rego Park, New York. He was co-founder of the Avante Garde comic and graphic magazine *Raw.* His work has been published in the *New York Times, The Village Voice,* and the *New Yorker* magazine, and many other publications. Spiegelman's work is an autobiographical statement designed to educate people about the experiences of Holocaust victims. Most of Spiegelman's work is deeply personal as his comics speak openly about his mother's suicide, his troubled relationship with his father and so on. He feels that most art is autobiographical, at least on one level or another, and traces back to the artist's history. He says his work develops because he has a need to do it, and is never certain that it is something he wants to be published. As he says "my art is just a process of trying to understand myself, and trying to understand other things, and my medium for understanding is comics."

Artworld Information

Art Spiegelman's drawings have been exhibited at the Museum of Modern Art in New York, The Jewish Museum, and many major private galleries. For the book *Maus,* he received both the Pulitzer Prize and a Guggenheim Fellowship. He has exhibited his work with many museums across the country, and is currently teaching a course on the History and Aesthetics of Comics, at the University of California, Santa Cruz. Pictures from the book were included in a traveling show, on the history of comic art. Spiegelman has had many offers to do a movie based on the book, but has turned them down saying he does not see this work as a film. Speigelman spends ten hours a day drawing; he feels the consistency of working every day makes him a better artist. As a child Spiegelman felt he was not good on the playground, so he spent a great deal of time in the library and drawing, trying to find something he could do to gain a feeling of mastery and accomplishment.

References

Chicago, J. (1993). *Holocaust Project.* New York: Penguin Books.

Green, G. (1978). *The Artists of Terezin.* New York: Schocken Books.

Greenfeld, H.(1993). *The Hidden children.* New York: Ticknor & Fields.

Kerr, M.E. (1990). *Gentlehands.* New York: Harper/Trophy.

Lowry, L. (1989, 1992). *Number the stars.* New York: Houghton; & Dell.

Orlev, U. (1984). *The Island on Bird Street.* Boston: Hillel Halkin.

Rochman, H. & McCampbell D. (1995). *Bearing witness.* New York: Orchard Books.

Rosenberg, M. (1994). *Hiding to survive.* New York: Clarion Books.

Spiegelman, A. (1986). *Maus, a survivor's tale.* New York: Pantheon Books.

Witer, J. (1989). *Comic Books as history: The narrative art of Jack Jackson, Art Spiegelman and Harry Pekan.* Jackson: University of Mississippi Press.

Music

Shostakovich, *Dem Symphony No. 13 Babi Yar*

Mozart, Wolfgang Amadeus *Requiem*

Grieg, Edvard *Aase's Death*

John William's *Shindler's List.*

Websites

http://cartoon.org/spiegelm.htm

http://cartoon.org/about.htm#top

http://www.ngc.peachnet.edu/Academic /Arts_Let/LangLit/dproyal/spiegel.htm

http://arts.ucsc.edu/derek/Art.html

Institutions

The United States Holocaust Museum

Steven Spielberg's Shoa Foundation, and local synagogues.

The Jewish Museum, New York, NY

Holocaust Studies in the Art Class

Teacher's Statement

I had the good fortune of having a very special guest speaker, my Grandmother Emilie, a survivor of Auschwitz and the death camps of Bergen Belzen. She came to my art class to share her story and her life lessons about the hatred and prejudice of this period in history.

When my dear grandmother, now close to 80, stands before our art class with her kind face and weary eyes, showing her number burned into her arm by the Nazis, there are curious whispers as to why she is here, why the Holocaust is spoken about in an art class.

Ever since her retirement, my grandmother, a survivor of the Holocaust, has lived with us, helping to raise me and, by her courageous life and incredible stories, to inspire our family. A quiet person who never uttered a public word, she decided to battle the ignorance about the past in our state and devote her retirement to teaching the children of Kentucky about the Holocaust, to speak out against any form of hate. In spite of her years, there is a fire in her voice and a sincerity in her very personal appeal, which evokes a unique kind of silence in our art class. She concludes each presentation with a recitation of responsibilities and a charge to future generations. Her un-scripted words come from haunting memories and are spoken from the heart. Her frank images evoke a deep emotional mindscape for our young artists.

Objectives

Students:

1) view the artist as someone with powerful stories or messages to tell.
2) learn that art can be a basic language for expressing human emotions and intellect.
3) recognize the artworld of comics and illustrated books.
4) reflect on how injustices, protest, and historical events played a role in various artworlds.
5) combine images and words to convey stories.

Activities

Dim the lights as students enter the art room. Softly play the musical theme from the film *Schindler's List*. Retire the chairs and school desks to the side of the art room, and occupy center stage armed with the book *Maus* by Art Spiegelman. If possible find a survivor in the community from the Holocaust and invite that person to collaborate in this lesson. The horrors of the Holocaust need to be conveyed by sensitive storytellers. When my Grandmother speaks, there is a sense of a kind, elderly person who is trying to tell a difficult story.

Gather the children around to hear the story of *Maus* from the special guest or the teacher. Present documents, photographs, and illustrations from the book, *Maus,* to show the art and story of the survivor's tale. Discuss how and why Art Speigelman's comics are created and how comics in general are created. Present a brief history of comics and illustrations as an artworld, noting for example: 1. that words and images are often coordinated; 2. that magazines and newspapers and book publishers are influential; 3. that injustice, protest and historical events are often the subject in this artworld. Share information about Spiegelman's artworld. Also show examples of prominent cartoonists and illustrators preferably from several time periods. Ask students to describe cartoons and illustrated books with which they are familar. Read selections from *Maus* as a soft bed time story. Ask students to follow along with their own copies of the pictures and text. You can supply the class with images in a variety of ways. Supply multiple copies of the book; use an overhead projecter; make slides or read to a very small group and share the same book.

Inspired by the solemn state of minds created by the story, ask the students to make a stroyboard illustrating events from *Maus* or from their own lives. After hearing the story and witnessing Holocaust images illustrated in the story, ask students to "recast" and tell their own stories through words and pictures. Ask students to think of key words they feel are expressive of the story or of their own life events. Ask students to then incorporate words into individual drawings and organize them into a storyboard. Display completed storyboards and ask students to present their stories.

Assessment

1) Students can provide examples of illustrations that can create powerful emotions in people.
2) Students can comment on how comics and illustrations are part of a distinctive artworld.
3) Students can explain how Spiegelman used art to tell a story.
4) Assess storyboards as evidence of students' abilities to "recast" or tell their own stories through word and images.

Art Supplies and Other Resources

An old suitcase—this can be used to store materials, for the project. The suitcase is symbolic of the Jews ominous journey and the decisions that had to be made regarding what to save, and what the real valuables were in one's life.

Documents such as passports, photos, and a yellow star.
Copies of illustrations from the book *Maus* (slides, photocopies, overheads, or extra copies of the book)
Drawing paper
Drawing tools such as, pencils, pens and black ink
Heavy stock white drawing paper
Rulers
Brushes
Trays for water
Paper towels
Felt tip pens (Black paint can also be used depending on the age of the students.)

The Peaceable Kingdom of the Branch

Art Maker
Edward Hicks

Access Information
Multiple *Peaceable Kingdoms* and the Richard Westall engraving appear in *Edward Hicks, Painter of the Peaceable Kingdom* by Alice Ford (University of Pennsylvania Press, 1952), *Edward Hicks: His Peaceable Kingdoms and Other Paintings* by Eleanor Price Mather (Newark: University of Delaware Press, 1983), and *The Kingdoms of Edward Hicks* by Carolyn J. Weekley (Harry N. Abrams, Inc., 1999).
Other commercially available reproductions include: *The Peaceable Kingdom* (c.1830), oil on canvas, 17 7/8" x 28 7/8", Metropolitan Museum of Art, in New York from
Art Image Publications; *The Peaceable Kingdom* (1832-1834), oil on canvas from the Abby Aldrich Rockefeller Folk Art Center, Williamsburg, Virginia; and *The Peaceable Kingdom* (1847), oil on canvas from the Denver Art Museum, Denver, Colorado.

Date of Artwork
1822-1825

Location of Artwork
Abby Aldrich Rockefeller Folk Art Center, Williamsburg, Virginia

Medium
oil on canvas

Size
32 1/4" x 37 3/4"

Subject Matter
The painting depicts the Richard Westall composition of a young child with the wild animals listed in Isaiah 11:6-8, a lion, ox, leopard, kid, lamb, and wolf. There is also a much smaller group of people that are readily identifiable as William Penn signing a peace treaty with the Leni-Lenape Indians. Both vignettes are within a natural landscape with a large stone bridge on the left and a large overhanging branch on the right.

Visual Organization
The painting is horizontal in format. It is compositionally divided in half. The foreground on the right depicts the Richard Westall grouping with the child's face as the focal point. This group is balanced by the stone bridge on the left that shields the William Penn group. Both the three-dimensionality of the bridge and a stream meandering into the distance create a sense of depth. The large branch coming onto the scene from the right leads one's eye along the bridge and back to the child and animals. The colors are the muted greens, browns, and grays associated with a natural scene.

Short Biography of Art Maker
Edward Hicks, born in 1780, was not a birthright Quaker. His Anglican parents were quite affluent and owned extensive property in Bucks County (outside Philadelphia). In the year of Edward's birth, his grandfather, an official representing the British colonial government, was accused of being a Tory sympathizer and the Hicks lands were confiscated and sold. Edward's mother died when he was 18 months old and as the father could not afford to keep the family together, Edward went to live with Elizabeth and David Twining. At age 13, he was apprenticed to a local coachmaker named Tomlinson where he learned coach and ornamental painting. At one point, the coach shop burned and did not reopen for two years. During that time, the Tomlinsons and their apprentices worked in a tavern; Edward served as a lackey, shoeblack, hostler, and bartender where he was "too often exposed to the worst of company" (Weekley, 1999, p. 20). He was also so inspired by the sights and sounds of the militia that he actually enrolled. This interest was short-lived, however, and he resigned in 1801. At age 20, his apprenticeship ended and he began his own painting business. During the early years, he frequently went to Philadelphia to drink, dance, and "frolic." After a period of introspection and regret, he vowed to change. He began attending Friends Meeting and by 1813 was acknowledged as a Quaker minister.

Hicks received criticism of his painting, because its decorative nature was incompatible with conservative Quaker faith. As a result, Hicks gave up painting in 1815 and attempted farming, but within a year had gone deeply into debt. (He did not earn any income from his ministerial work.) Bankruptcy meant a loss of church membership, so he was helped financially by friends and returned to painting in 1816. His conscience was eased by a liberal interpretation of Quaker codes (performing a "useful" trade and earning a living by "honest" work). He also began easel painting, choosing a theme that was compatible with the Quaker belief in pacifism. Working from the Old Testament scripture of Isaiah 11:6-8, he began a series (more than 60) of Peaceable Kingdoms, depicting a prophetic peaceful coexistence of people and animals. He continued painting this theme until his death in 1849, although the pictures took on increasing symbolic significance of opposing and eventually separating Quaker factions. He continued his preaching/traveling ministry as well, at one point discussing the interpretation of the animals and how they related to Quaker theology in a sermon at Goose Creek, Virginia. This sermon remains the most important source for understanding Hicks's work.

Artworld Information

Edward Hicks is unique as an artist in that he attempted to straddle two (and at times, opposing) worlds. As a Quaker (and a minister), he received criticism for working in a field that was considered at best decorative (and not part of a simplistic, pious life) and at worst sinful (painting a tavern sign). He had to find peace with his own conscience as well as answer others. There was also an economic dimension to his dilemma in that he was financially successful in painting and was unable to support his family through farming and preaching.

At the time Hicks began his *Peaceable Kingdom* series, he had quite a bit of experience in ornamental painting but little of easel painting. He salved his conscience and silenced his critics by choosing a theme that was acceptable to the faith. Over a period of 33 years, he used the medium not only to depict a major tenet of Quaker theology, but also to reflect his concerns about the church.

As a 13-year-old apprentice, Edward had learned the skills to create a variety of types of decorative painting and finishes. His shop work included ornamenting and gilding horse-drawn vehicles, furniture, and sign painting. Once he had his own business, other workers in the shop included Morris Croasdale, Luis Jones, Thomas Hicks (Edward's cousin), and possibly Martin Johnson Heade. Thomas Hicks and Heade became noted academic painters later in the century. (Weekley, 1999, p. 71)

Although Edward Hicks has been identified as the "first" Quaker to paint decorative pictures in America, there were other Friends who produced images as well. Charles Wilson Peale is remembered for his portraits, William Bartram (famous Philadelphia botanist) for his drawings of native plants, and surveyor Benjamin Ferris for his sketches of buildings. Art patronage among Quakers was limited with only the more wealthy urban Quakers commissioning artwork while those living in rural areas advocated a "simple" lifestyle.

Edward borrowed compositions from other artists. His Delaware River signboard is taken from an engraving by George S. Lang after Thomas Sully, *Washington at the Passage of the Delaware,* 1819. Benjamin West's famous painting of *Penn's Treaty with the Indians* (1771-1772), made popular through an engraving by John Hall, was the likely source for a similar grouping in his *Peaceable Kingdoms.* The child and lion composition (spoken of in Isaiah 11) was taken directly from *The Peaceable Kingdom of the Branch* by Richard Westall, 1815, an engraving printed in the Bible.

Hicks's popularity as a folk artist remains secure today. The appeal perhaps lies not only in the aesthetics of his painting style but in his subject matter and our desire for a simple, peaceful existence in our world so often marred by violence. There is also a challenge in interpreting his work, unique in having available 62 images on the same theme painted over a period of 33 years. These offer us insights into the man, the preacher, and the artist.

References
Ford, A. (1952). *Edward Hicks: Painter of the Peaceable Kingdom.* Philadelphia: University of Pennsylvania Press.
Mather. E.P. (1983). *Edward Hicks: Peaceable Kingdoms and other paintings.* Newark: University of Delaware Press.
Weekley, C.J. (1999). *The kingdoms of Edward Hicks.* New York: Harry N. Abrams, Inc.

Blessed are the Peacemakers

Objectives

Students learn:
1) the meaning of the terms "folk artist" and "fine artist."
2) that Edward Hicks had a dilemma as a Quaker minister/artist.
3) that an artist's artworld (people and circumstances) affects his/ her art production.
4) how to interpret a *Peaceable Kingdom.*
5) how to create their own version of a *Peaceable Kingdom.*

6) how to articulate their thought process in depicting a peace theme.
7) to value the contributions made by folk artists to the artworld.
8) to appreciate their own folk art heritage.

Activities

Initiate a class discussion on the definition of "art." This can be done orally or by asking for written definitions and then discussing the responses. Continue the discussion by narrowing the focus to the differences between fine art and folk art. Explain that both forms are valued as art. Offer working definitions to help students gain in their understanding. Fine art can be defined as art that requires highly developed techniques and skills. It is produced primarily for beauty rather than utility. Folk art originates from the common people of a nation or region and usually reflects their traditional culture. Often folk artists are anonymous and have no formal academic training in the arts. Ask students for examples of folk art within their own families/community. Why and how were they created? Where are they now? How are they valuable? How would they be valued by another community? Is their value measurable?

Consult the Short Biography of the Art Maker and Artworld Information about the *Peaceable Kingdom* to identify specific information to share with your students. Introduce events in Edward Hick's early life including his apprenticeship through which he learned coach and ornamental painting and his early painting business. Explain that when he became a Quaker his paintings were criticized for being decorative and that eventually he chose to use the Peaceable Kingdom theme from the Old Testament. Explain also that even though he was not formally trained as an artist, he did borrow ideas from the work of other artists of his time.

Show Edward Hicks's *Peaceable Kingdom of the Branch*, 1822-1825, as an example of folk art and briefly tell the story of Hicks' life and the events and circumstances leading him to paint 62 images on the same theme. Assist the students in interpreting the painting with these questions:

1) How does Hicks convey a message of peaceful coexistence? (Child and wild animals together, William Penn signing a peace treaty with the Leni-Lenape Indians, natural scenery, scripture border)

2) What is the focal point of the picture? (Child/Lion.) It is the animal grouping, particularly the lion that is so fascinating to watch develop throughout the *Peaceable Kingdom* series. By associating the lion, long a symbol of the British Empire, with the American Revolution, Hicks was reminding viewers of the dangers inherent in secular kingdoms.)

3) Edward Hicks's early *Peaceable Kingdoms* include a paraphrase of the Isaiah scripture as a border. Why do you think he did so? (Reflects his work as a sign painter or perhaps he wanted to clearly identify his intent, much like children who label their drawings.)

4) What ideas did he borrow from Richard Westall's 1815 engraving? (Child and animal composition and grape clusters held by the child.)

5) In what way did he change Richard Westall's work? (included the William Penn scene and a natural stone bridge, from Virginia, that shields the William Penn group.)

You may want to use additional slides and/or reproductions in order to compare Hicks' early, middle, and late *Peaceable Kingdoms*; or *Peaceable Kingdoms* by other artists such as contemporary folk artist Malcah Zeldis (1931-present) or graphic artists from *Images for Survival* from the Shoshin Society, Inc. in Washington, D.C. You might ask students to compare and contrast two *Peaceable Kingdoms*.

Once students have gained an understanding of Edward Hicks' work, ask them to begin to brainstorm possible "peaceable kingdoms" of their own. They can depict animals that in the natural world would be in a predator/prey relationship. They can develop ideas from their knowledge of history and/or current events. (You may want to plan a trip to the library or get the Social Studies teacher involved.) They can offer a visual solution to a contemporary social problem such as racism.

After developing and choosing their ideas, the students draw them on canvas board and complete their paintings in acrylic paints. Each student also completes a brief written analysis of his or her work on an index card that is displayed with the painting. Lead a discussion about whether their *Peaceable Kingdoms* are or are not examples of folk art and about the contributions of folk art.

Assessment

Assess students' paintings and written statements noting whether they are able to express the theme of *Peaceable Kingdom* both visually and in words.

Assess discussions of folk art throughout the lesson noting whether students can identify features that commonly distinguish folk art from so-called fine art and can identify contributions made by folk artists.

Art Supplies and Resources

slides/ reproductions
acrylic paints/mediums
12" x 16" manila paper
brushes
12" x 16" canvas board

Extension Ideas

1) If the work of Malcah Zeldis is included in the preliminary discussions, students could send photos of their paintings to her with written explanations of their *Peaceable Kingdoms*.

2) Connections could be made to other subject areas such as Social Studies (colonial history, Pennsylvania State history, and current events) or used in the teaching of conflict resolution.

My painting symbolizes the road of life heading toward heaven. At the top is where the peacable kingdom is.

—Cailin Arena

In my peacable Kingdom, I tried to portray the lion laying down with the lamb. This was mentioned in Isaih 11:6 where it talksabout all the animals living in peace.

I also included a snake, hawk, and mouse who are all known enemies in the real world. Maybe one day we all will live in peace together, Blacks and Whites, Christians and Buddist. If not on earth, definately in heaven with Christ.

Political Self-Portrait #3 (Class)

Art Maker
Adrian Piper

Access Information
An image of this work can be found in *ContemporaryAmerican Women Artists* page 64, published in 1991 by Cedco Writing Group, San Rafael, CA. The book may be ordered through Amazon.com at:http://www. amazon.com/exec/obidos/ ASIN/ 1559122528/ qid=924185774/sr=1-8/ 002-8205475-5371660.

Date of Artwork
1980

Location of Artwork
John Weber Gallery, New York City

Medium
Photostat

Size
unknown

Subject Matter

In *Political Self-Portrait # 3 (Class)*, Adrian Piper typeset the story of her young realization of color and class and imposed the text over the entire surface of her photographed self-portrait. The story describes her visits to school friends' homes on 5th Avenue in New York City. After one particular visit, Piper rushed to her own Harlem home to tell her mother that she had found a wonderful place where her family should move. It was not until this point in her life that Piper realized that who and what she was dictated where and how she lived, as well as her future.

Visual Organization

Black text covers the entire surface of the picture plane and is superimposed over a monochromatic green toned photograph of a young female teenager. (color/ organization). The viewer may be drawn to first look at the young woman's face (focal point). However, her gaze does not include the viewer. She looks away to the viewer's right as her hands dig into the pockets of her four-buttoned coat (direction). The hood and drawstrings of her coat direct the viewer's gaze to a large tag, similar to a price tag attached to the sleeve of the coat that reads "Bonwit Teller" (balance/repetition). The stark contrast of values in the photograph makes the reading of the text a difficult task (value). The blurred and irregular typeface looks to have come from an old typewriter and appears to reveal a secret story (association). And, indeed it does. For as the reader deciphers the text, she or he discovers a very personal and revealing story of the artist's youth. Through this arduous deciphering task, the viewer/reader may be engaged in a similar form of self-reflection to that of the artist as she becomes aware of cultural, racial, class, and gender bias (interpretation).

Short Biography of Art Maker

Adrian Piper is an African-American female artist who was born in New York City in 1948. She received her A.A. at the School of Visual Arts in New York in 1969, her B.A. from City College of New York in 1974, her M.A. from Harvard University in 1977 and her Ph.D. from Harvard in 1981. Piper has pointed out that she often feels her light skinned features require that she announces her racial identity to people. She works in a variety of media: installation, photographs, charts, photo-text collage, video, drawing, mixed-media, and descriptive language. She focuses her artwork on issues of racism, xenophobia and racial stereotyping. Piper's often "in your face" tactics cause critics such as Berger (1990) to write that she has "shifted the involvement of the spectator; neither artist nor viewer is permitted the usual defensive rationalizations that exempt us from the political responsibility of examining our own racism" (p. 5). A biography of Adrian Piper can be found at: http://www.personal.psu.edu/users/d/d/ddt105/danielle's_cat/ bio_7.html.

Artworld Information

The purpose in Piper's work is political in its both angry and hopeful terms. She looks to the agendas of color-blind idealism and racial militancy as she challenges the viewers of her work to understand that their reactions to racism are political choices that they themselves make. Piper says, "For a white audience, it often has a didactic function: It communicates information and experiences that are new, or that challenge preconceptions about oneself and one's relation to blacks. For a Black audience, it often has an affirmative or cathartic function: It expresses shared emotions-of pride, rage, impatience, defiance, hope-that remind us of the values and experiences we share in common" (Cedco, 1991, p. 62).

Piper has had a number of solo and group exhibitions including the Whitney Museum of American Art (NY) in 1990, the John Weber Gallery (NY) in 1989, the Alternative Museum (NY) in 1987, the And/Or gallery (Seattle) in 1981, the Wadsworth Athenueum Gallery (Hartford) in 1980, the Wexner Center for the Visual Arts (Ohio State University) and Contemporary Arts Center (Buffalo) in 1990, Cincinnati Art Museum in 1989, Maryland Institute of Art (Baltimore) in 1988, The Studio Museum (NY) in 1985 and the New Museum (NY) in 1983.

References
Berger, M. (1990). The critique of pure racism: An interview with Adrian Piper. *Afterimage, 18* (3), 5-9.
Cedco Writing Group (1991). *Contemporary American women artists,* San Rafael, CA.: Cedco Publishing Co.
Piper, A. (1996*). Out of order, out of sight. Volume 1: Selected writings in meta-art 1968-1992.* Cambridge, MA: The MIT Press.
Wolcott, A. (1996). Is what you see what you get? A postmodern approach to understanding works of art. *Studies in Art Education, 37* (2), 69-79.

Websites
Self-portrait exaggerating my negroid features. is posted at http://www.christina-thomas.de/bvk/piper.htm.
Decide who you are #27: Test Tube Babies, 1992. Courtesy Paula Cooper Gallery, New York. *The Myth is Being: Getting Back #3.* Courtesy John Weber Gallery are posted at:
http://www.louisiana.dk/nowhere/incand/adriand.html .
Gallery of Pipers work is posted at:
http://parallel.park.uga.edu/~lisaboyd/240G/w98/piper.html.
More art works are posted at:
http://www.personal.psu.edu/users/d/d/ddt105/danielle's_cat/artwork_7.1.html
How to handle black people is posted at http://www.ejafa.com/adrian_piper.html
Passing for white, passing for black is posted at:
http://www.pbs.org/wgbh/pages/frontline/shows/secret/readings/piper.html

Differences are Not Worlds Apart: Challenging the Notion of Fitting in Through the Art of Adrian Piper

Objectives
Students:
> 1) through critical and comparative analysis of Piper's work, will write about, discuss, and reflect upon the ways that identity (whether defined through race, gender, class, or personal history) is not always visually apparent.
> 2) write and discuss the ways that their experiences reveal the need to take time to know and understand people before stereotyping, judging or labeling.
> 3) borrow Piper's technique by typesetting their own stories of difference and overlaying drawings of scenes or symbols of their stories over the text.
> 4) use balance, focal point, direction, contrast, and color choice as organizational strategies.
> 5) identify the different audiences of artworlds and identify characteristics of Piper's artworld.

Activities
Display Piper's work, *Political Self-Portrait #3 (Class),* read the title, and ask students: What do you see? What is going on in this work? Who is this person and what is she trying to tell us? What do you think the artist means by class? Class is usually determined by economics, isn't it? What else does class mean to you? What groups or classes of people are in this school? Typically, students begin talking about groups at this time. As the students begin naming groups, write them on the board (for example, some of the groups may include: geeks, Blacks,

wannabes, do-gooders, preps, rednecks, artsy crowd, jocks, cheerleaders, and dead heads). Ask the students to describe these groups. You may write some of the descriptions on the board as well or allow this time for students to discuss openly the issues and concerns of each of these groups in the school. Be careful as the students begin describing the groups and allow for defense from some of the group members that may be in the class. Let this be a time for the students to both defend and air their differences.

Have the students assist you as you try and read the story that is typeset on Piper's work (It is important that the students work with you to decipher the words and that they realize this is not easy.)

Next have the class discuss how Adrian Piper feels that her light-skinned features require that she announce her racial identity to people. You may share some of Piper's other works that deal even more about her racial identity such as*: Self-Portrait Exaggerating my Negroid Features and The Myth is Being: Getting Back #3.* Ask students if they feel differently about this work of art or this artist after hearing the story. As the discussion continues, work to guide the students to see that we can not know, understand, or label people simply by what they look like, wear, or even the way they act. Discuss how stereotyping, judging, and labeling people through mere observation or hearsay may not always be a correct or fair analysis. Discuss how the formation of cliques that exclude from conversation and activities those students who do not "fit in" is not only hurtful but sometimes an inaccurate assumption. Talk about how harassment of people in vehement and hurtful ways may serve to further the kinds of stereotypes that certain groups say are incorrect. Discuss how reading and understanding the words in Piper's work was not an easy task. "We had to work together as we tried to decipher some of the words. How is this a metaphor for our lives? How can we try harder to understand each other? Do we need to take time to know and understand people who we consider different from ourselves? What can you do to help people understand your story or your feelings of difference?"

Ask the students: "Do you feel that you 'fit in' with any one group? Why or why not? Think about your own lives and the stories that you feel may change the way you are perceived by other people." Have the students work on writing their stories in their journals. For homework, they should complete the story that they will typeset using a computer or word processor in the next class. Ask them to also think of what image, symbol, scene, or object they could use as a metaphor for their story.

The next class will involve the students in typing and printing their stories. This can be done in the art room if you have a computer, library, or computer lab. Most likely this will involve the students in taking turns. While they are waiting or after they have completed this task they can look for references for their drawings and begin making sketches that will determine where on the page they will place their drawings over their text. Discuss such organizational strategies as symmetrical and asymmetrical balance, focal point, direction or flow of the viewer's gaze, contrast, and color choices. "Will you follow Piper in a monochromatic color scheme? Do you want to create contrast through complementary colors or create more unity with analogous color choices?" Discuss techniques such as: (1) Overlaying colors in the colored pencil medium produces intensity as well as a mixing of colors. This is preferable to too much pencil pressure as the hazing or surface shininess from pressing too hard may interfere with the reading of the text as well as result in a surface quality that is not desired. (2) White colored pencils may be used as a blending agent for light colors and will take away some of the graininess of light pencil pressure. (3) The white of the paper however, should be used for highlights as the white colored pencil will not completely cover another color. (4) Graphite pencils should not be used in conjunction with colored pencils as they will mix and produce a dirty appearance. (5) Make sure that the ink of the type is dry and set before drawing to reduce the possibility of blurring the text. (6) Print several copies of the text to practice placement and composition.

Introduce students to the idea that the audience as well as artists are important people in the artworld. Explain what Piper thinks about the audience for her artwork. For instance in Piper's art titled *Art for the Art-World Surface Pattern,* Piper attempted to create a work that would confront the notion of "depoliticizing" or neutralizing the effect that the aesthetic stance in contemporary art has on the issues raised by minority and other politically concerned artists. Her intention was to bombard the viewer with political information concerning various catastrophes and situations around the world, and simultaneously to block recourse to the "aestheticizing" response by incorporating it satirically onto the work itself. Piper wants the viewer to register the political information immediately without using the ideals of aesthetics to dismiss the reality of the real and artworld (Piper, 1996, p.164-165). In Piper's artwork, she casts the artist as an agent of social change and the viewer as a political agent. Ask students to consider how different audiences might view their artwork.

Assessment

Self-critique in student journals may include the following questions: "Describe your work in words. How does your work reflect your understanding of difference? How do you think it will affect the viewer's understanding of you? Review the student objectives that are written on the board and explain how you: 1.) wrote, discussed, and reflected upon the ways that identity (whether defined through race, gender, class, or personal history) is not always visually apparent; 2.) wrote and took part in the discussion of the ways that their experiences reveal the need to take time to know and understand people before stereotyping, judging or labeling; 3.) borrowed Piper's technique by creating a work of art of your own story of difference; and 4.) considered the audience for your artwork. Group critique may be an extension or sharing of the journal entries.

Grading of the projects will include looking at the degree to which the students: 1.) wrote their stories and whether their stories indicated an understanding of the objectives of the unit; 2.) wrote in consistent style, grammar, and syntax; 3.) meaningfully participated in discussion; 4.) chose sophisticated metaphor associations for their pictorial images or settled for trite or predictable symbols; 5.) were thoughtful in their journal entries or made a perfunctory attempt at answering the questions; 6.) used balance, focal point, direction, contrast, and color choice as organizational strategies; and 7.) were proficient with their artmaking techniques properly overlaying colored pencils.

Art Supplies and Other Resources

Computer or word processor
Printer
Colored pencils
Journals
Pencils
Access to aesthetic philosophies (reference books, the Internet, and/or a teacher/student constructed aesthetic philosophy handout with quotes from artists, critics, and philosophers)

Extension Ideas or Interdisciplinary Connections

Writing of both the story and the critical observations and self evaluation are obviously connected to English composition class. Granted, many word-processing computer programs have tools such as spelling and grammar check. However, the need for in-depth discussion and editing is important throughout the students' writing activities. I have found that including an oral presentation of the stories (either to the class or in private with the teacher) is an excellent way for the students to understand the need for careful consideration of their writing structure. Another excellent connection is to enlist the help of the English teacher in the writing of the stories. Because the high school art class is typically made up of students in a variety of grade levels, the students do not all have the same English class or teacher. Therefore, student-initiated connections are more applicable. For example, the students could approach their own English teacher for assistance and guidance as well as share with the art class literature that may connect to the artist's works, such as *Black Like Me* often read in 9th grade. Connections can also be made with the Social Studies class study of the Equal Rights Amendment and Martin Luther King. Students could be challenged to critically look and connect the issues that Adrian Piper addresses in her work with the information that is presented or not presented in their history books.

Kopper Kart

Art Maker
George Barris

Access Information
Barris, G., & Fetherston, D.
(1994). *Barris kustoms
of the 1950's.* Oscela,
WI: Motorbooks
International Publishers
& Wholesales, p. 66.
(1-800-826-6600 or
www.motorbooks.com).
Consumer Guide. (1978).
*Grease machines: A
complete guide to hot
rods & customized cars
of the fifties.* NY:
Beekman House, p. 32.

Date of Artwork
Circa 1957

Location of Artwork
Unknown, may no longer
exist; according to Barris,
last seen in the early 1960s,
abandoned in a field near
Morris Town, Ohio

Medium
A six-cylinder 1956
Chevrolet truck, heavily
modified

Size
When customized, became
shorter than the stock
pickup truck

Subject Matter
The car does not depict anything, that is, it has no subject matter.

Visual Organization
Modifications include a shortened body (5.5"), lowered roof (4"), removal of door handles (replaced with electric pushbuttons) and original ornaments, addition of copper plating, and redesign of the hood, fenders, and rear of the truck. A new front end was created that includes recessed quad headlights and a hand formed grille. "Barris Kustom autos" is written on the door's copper panels, and "Kopper Kart," centered in large letters above the license plate, is flanked by pinstripe designs. Because the chassis is lowered, the exhaust pipes extending below the doors of the car nearly touch the pavement. Broad stripes on the roof and truck bed cover contrast with the fenders' long, narrow stripes, which allude to speed as they taper to points. Copper hues (on panels, stripes, and pinstripes) and whites (car body, tires, license plate, and lettering on door panels) create a simplified color scheme. The copper look is repeated on hubcap covers, lights, and exhaust pipe trim. This radical customizing resulted in a streamlined, organic, unified form, an award-winning machine that Tom Wolfe (1965) would label "sculpture," meant more for a pedestal than for the road.

Short Biography of the Art Maker
Often referred to as "King of the Kustomizers," Barris could also be called the Picasso of the Custom Car Artworld. Born in Chicago in 1926 and growing up near Sacramento, California, Barris and his older brother Sam were young car enthusiasts who customized their first car while in their early teens. In high school they both took mechanical drawing, wood, and metal shop classes; were apprentices at local auto body shops, and customized beat-up cars that came into their possession. After high school, George took design classes for a year at a local art center. By 1945 the brothers owned a body shop in the Los Angeles area where, as inventive designers and exceptional craftsmen, their business quickly flourished. For car owners interested in showing and cruising, they pioneered many customizing techniques and they also helped perfect the use of the new candy apple lacquer paints becoming popular at the time. Sam's metal crafting skills combined with George's skills in design, painting, management, and promotion made them the premier custom shop in California. Throughout the late 1940s and 50s they developed a national reputation as their work won awards at auto shows across the country and was featured in automotive magazines. George became even more involved in the national custom car scene by photographing professionally at auto shows and writing for hot rod and custom magazines.

After Sam left the business in the late 1950s, and although custom work peaked by 1959, car owners avidly sought George's designs and the skills of his shop specialists. Barris' reputation escalated as toy manufacturers translated his custom and hot rod designs into popular plastic car model kits. His innovative styling ideas influenced Detroit automakers who hired him as a design consultant. From the late 1950s into the 1990s, Barris and his shop designed and constructed automobiles for hundreds of movies and television programs, e.g., the hot rod driven by James Dean in *Rebel Without a Cause*, cars for James Bond movies, the original Batmobile for the 1960s *Batman* TV series, the driverless Ford Explorer in *Jurassic Park*, and the Flintmobile in *The Flintstones* movie. Barris also customized vehicles for numerous celebrities, including Elvis Presley, John Lennon, Cher, Clint Eastwood, and John Travolta.

In semi-retirement, Barris continues to run Barris Kustom Industries in North Hollywood, and recently, he was inducted into *Hot Rod Magazine's* 50th Anniversary Hall of Fame, and his Star Car Museum opened in Gatlinburg, Tennessee.

Artworld Information

A custom car artworld didn't exist until after World War II when interest in customizing skyrocketed among teenagers and young men, particularly in California. People headed west for jobs; more money was available; cars were scarce; and the new ones weren't attractive to young people who preferred more aerodynamic designs. Many first-time car owners also wanted to express their individuality by taking used vehicles of the 1930's and early 40s and modifying them in a variety of ways. Two groups formed within this artworld culture—those who modified to achieve a low, streamlined appearance, and those who modified hot rods for speed. Cruising to show off cars and drag racing became favorite teen pasttimes. The California weather stimulated outdoor activities, and open land and roadways provided space for drag racing. Subgroups formed under the two umbrellas—for cruising and looks, the lead sleds, lowriders, and street rods; for speed, the hot rods and the later street machines and muscle cars.

Cruising to the first drive-in restaurants, joining car clubs, hanging out at body shops, visiting auto shows, reading the new auto magazines—all these activities contributed to the burgeoning custom car artworld. Skills for customizing were developed in high school industrial arts and art classes, in body shops where the youthful customizers practiced under the guidance of shop owners, and in backyards where they restyled their own cars.

At first, custom cars were meant to be seen and appreciated by friends who shared a passion for cars. Cruising became a ritual, a way to impress and seek approval in a communal setting. New designs and skilled workmanship attracted attention and respect as well as business from club members and others. Likewise, the quarter-mile drag race was a communal event for teenagers, and success in the race would glorify the driver and his car. Reputations and incomes grew as innovators in the field won awards at growing numbers of auto shows across the country and their cars were seen on covers of major auto magazines (*Motor Trend, Hot Rod, Road and Track*). These publications served not only to showcase the masters in the field, but also to explain technical processes to the novices. Customizing often meant collaboration—the car owner with an initial idea, the body shop owner who may have served as a design consultant, and employees who became increasingly specialized—someone with metal fabrication expertise, another who excelled in painting, and still others who worked with engineering aspects of the electrical systems and engine.

As Detroit auto designers became influenced by streamlined custom styling, interest in radical modifications was replaced by greater attention to paint jobs, the graphics and the appearance of the paint surface. Radical body changes were also more costly; a flashy paint job was less expensive, yet it individualized the car, one of the goals of customizing. In recent years, as older cars became scarce, molds from popular models were created and cast into fiberglass bodies, resulting in the "look" of an old car made entirely from new parts.

Judges at auto shows are usually experienced customizers affiliated with The International Car Show Association. Cars are judged in categories (e.g., low rider, hot rod, street rod, and roadster) using various criteria, e.g., detailing, workmanship, overall paint job, graphics, engine, interior, a car's "attitude" and "stance." Points are awarded or taken away, and tallied. Competitors are ranked by their point totals at the end of the year, and big winners receive prizes. Today, an extensive show circuit continues to attract many competitors and viewers with the Oakland Roadster Show in California continuing to be the premier event. The Good Guys Rod & Custom Association, a prominent organization, sponsors a national competition and numerous regional shows. Local car groups continue to organize weekly cruises to drive-in restaurants and shopping malls.

Trends in customizing have existed over the years:radical versus minor modifications, flashy versus subtle paint jobs, old versus new cars, slow versus fast-interest. Participation remains high among all subgroups within this artworld. Barris recently said, "The best part of it, I'm going into my sixth decade of customizing cars, and I don't see an end." (interview, www.nashville.com)

References

Barris, G. (1997*). Barris kustom techniques of the 50's, Vol. 4: Flames, scallops, and striping.* Sebastopol, CA: Thaxton Press.

Barris, G. & Fetherston, D. (1994). *Barris kustoms of the 1950's*. Oscela, WI: Motorbooks International Publishers & Wholesales.

Burnham, C. (1980). *Customizing cars*. New York: Arco Publishing, Inc.

Consumer Guide. (1978*). Grease machines: A complete guide to hot rods & customized cars of the fifties*. NY: Beekman House.

Harris, M.F. (1988). *Art on the road*. Minneapolis: Pogo Press, Inc.

Padilla, C. (1999). *Low 'n slow: Lowriding in New Mexico*. Santa Fe, NM: Museum of New Mexico Press.

Wolfe, T. (1965). *The kandy-kolored tangerine*flake streamline baby*. NY: Farrar, Straus, & Giroux.

Websites:

www.barris.com (Barris web page), www.goodguysgoodtimes.com (Good Guys Rod & Custom Association web page), www.kustomkars.com, www.motorbooks.com, and www.nashville.net (go to George Barris links for 1996 interview).

Note: The major source for car publications, including a 2000 George Barris custom car calendar is Classic Motorbooks, P.O. Box 1, Osceola, WI 54020-0001. 1-800-826-6600. An extensive reference list can be obtained from the author, School of Art, Bowling Green State University, Bowling Green, OH 43403.

Cruising with Kustom Cars

Objectives

Students
1) identify important features that define an artworld as a distinct culture.
2) identify several subgroup cultures within the custom car artworld.
3) explain influences on the development of and changes in the custom car artworld.
4) describe visual qualities of a selection of customized vehicles.
5) formulate interpretive statements, supported with reasons, about expressive qualities as well as meanings perceived in the graphics on custom cars.
6) working from tracings of vehicles, create original custom designs that result in a restyled vehicle with unity in form.
7) create custom designs that include one or more body modifications used by customizers.
8) create "paint job" designs based on themes or ideas which reflect their interests and life experiences.
9) produce designs that exhibit craftsmanship.
10) taking roles of automotive journalists, write about an exhibit of their custom cars stating criteria for awards they give to car designs.
11) provide reasoned responses as they consider several aesthetic issues related to the custom car artworld.

Activities

Introduce students to the concept of artworlds by asking what kinds of objects they think of as "art" and where they see them. Seek a range of art examples, e.g., paintings and sculptures (art museums), quilts (at home or county fair), CD covers (music stores), children's picture books (public library), comic books (magazine store), and others. After several different forms of art are mentioned, refer to an artworld as a culture with specific places, people, activities, and ideas that relate to a particular kind of art. Questions to ask could include: Where do we see famous paintings from the history of art? Who designs CD covers? Athletic shoes? How are designs for CD covers and athletic shoes judged differently by the people in corporations who pick the designs to be manufactured? Are some kinds of art displayed in "art museums" and other kinds shown in other places? Talk about how people (the creators, the viewers or users, the judges) participate in different artworlds, depending on what they create, value, and enjoy as art.

Tell students that some artists take something that already exists and change it in some way. Ask what it means to customize something. Do they or their family own anything they have customized? Why do people customize something? Give an example of personal customizing, such as adding decals or pins to a baseball hat or adding designs with puffy paint to a sweatshirt.

Ask students to consider the world of customized cars as one of many artworlds. Tell students that over the years, many teenagers and adults who loved cars, became interested in customizing their cars to have them reflect individual interests or personalities. Find out what they already know about customized cars. Where have they seen them? Do they know someone who owns one? What was done to the car? Has anyone been to a custom car show or seen them displayed at a shopping mall? Make a list on the chalkboard or on large paper to record responses. Explain that today the costs of customizing can range from minimal changes that are inexpensive, to many thousands of dollars.

Introduce *Kopper Kart,* one of the earlier designs of George Barris, a 1956 Chevrolet pickup truck with extensive customizing. Ask students to describe what is unusual about this truck. What was removed? What was added? Why is it called *Kopper Kart?* How do the stripes affect the looks of the truck? Why do all the parts of this redesigned truck seem to fit together so well, i.e., have unity? Explain that Tom Wolfe, a well known thinker and writer about art, referred to customized cars as "sculpture." Do students agree with Wolfe? Why or why not? Tell students about the Barris brothers, their innovations, the various roles they took from inception to completion of a custom car, their participation in auto shows, and their cars being featured in auto magazines. Explain that the *Kopper Kart* was one of their early show cars, that they traveled in it throughout the country to custom car shows, and used it to promote their business. (You may want to extend your discussion to include additional examples of customized cars reproduced in some of the electronic and print references provided with the Access Information.)

Explain to students that almost anything can be done to customize a car, but that it always reflects the owner's personality and taste, a way to express the self. Tell students that they will design customized vehicles, starting with the body of an old or a newer vehicle, and decide on a theme or main idea for their "paint job" (take time to brainstorm with class). Show students a selection of several large tracings of automobiles from which they can choose, for example 1950s Mercury, 1950s Corvette, recent VW Bug, sports utility vehicle, minivan, station wagon, and sedan.

Steps in the process include:

1) Decide on the vehicle body to be customized.

2) Students may obtain a car body from several approaches: teacher traces a car tracing which students transfer to large, white paper; students complete a tracing from an auto company brochure (enlarge if needed); students complete a free hand drawing of a vehicle.

3) During the idea generation process, encourage students to write lists, draw design ideas, browse through books, look at photographs on bulletin board, and view cars on Internet websites.

4) Make more complete sketches as decisions are made about intended themes and changes in the auto body. Symmetry is an important design element for those who choose a frontal view of car. Aim for unity in the final design.

5) Decide on medium-markers or colored pencil; or a combination.

6) Lightly draw on body modifications and graphics ideas.

7) Exhibit craftsmanship in use of markers/colored pencils.

8) Display completed designs in parade format on classroom walls or elsewhere.

9) As students finish their designs, they write a paragraph that provides a title for the car, an explanation of theme, and how the car body was modified.

10) When all designs are completed, direct students to form groups of three to take roles of automotive journalists and collaborate to write a newspaper article about an exhibit of their custom cars, citing three awards they would give, and including criteria to support their assessments. The teacher can provide a scoring sheet with listed criteria or the teacher and students can collaborate to decide on judging criteria and/or award categories.

Assessment

Student art learning will be assessed based on achievement levels for the following criteria: Ability to:

1) Identify features characteristic of various artworlds, especially the custom car artworld.

2) Identify similarities and differences among various customs cars, through discussion of modification made on car bodies, designs/graphics on car surface, and use of color.

3) Create a unique, unified design for their customized vehicles.

4) Develop a theme or idea that reflects their interests and life experiences.

5) Create a restyled body design that includes two or more body modifications used by customizers.

6) Exhibit craftsmanship in the designing process with use of markers and/or colored pencils.

7) Give reasoned responses, orally or in writing, to aesthetic questions.

Art Supplies and Other Resources

80# (or heavier) white drawing paper (12"x18" minimum, larger preferred)

Assorted color markers with various point tips (very fine to broad)

Pencils

Colored pencils (optional)

Tracing paper

Light table (if available)

Bulletin board display of customized cars and photos of early vehicles

Brochures and pamphlets from car dealers

Slides or other reproductions of Barris' *Kopper Kart*,

Additional reproductions of customized cars (optional).

Extension Ideas and Interdisciplinary Connections

Aesthetics extension

Working in small groups, students focus on questions such as the following and present their views to the class-mates, who may also comment as the dialogue progresses.

1) Are customized vehicles works of art? Why or why not?

2) In the custom car artworld collaboration often takes place among two or more people during the customizing process. Are there artists today in the "fine art" world who collaborate? Is collaboration acceptable in some artworlds and not others? What are the benefits of collaboration? The drawbacks?

3) Customizers take pre-existing vehicles, change them, and exhibit them as a redesigned object. In the "fine art" world this is called "appropriation." How does appropriation differ from a painter, such as Roy Lichtenstein, who paints a Matisse composition in his own style, from the appropriation done by the customizers? Is appropriation acceptable in some artworlds and not others?

4) Many award-winning custom cars no long exist. Barris's *Kopper Kart* may now be a pile of rusted metal in a junkyard. Yet, in the "fine art" world there is concern about permanence, that important artworks should be preserved and protected in special places. How important is preservation in the custom car artworld? Is preservation more important in some artworlds than in others? Should preservation become more valued in the custom car artworld?

5) How do criteria for judging custom cars differ from those used for judging paintings or sculptures seen in museums and galleries? Can certain criteria be used for all kinds of art, in all artworlds?

Custom Car Artworld Extensions

Students investigate and report on issues such as the following:

1) What did people think, believe, or do that affected the development of the customized car artworld? What was happening in America that was affecting the custom car culture?

2) What art ideas, beliefs, and activities were important to the early car customizers? Has the customized car artworld changed over time? If so, in what ways?

3) Explain some of the trends in customizing over the years? What influenced changes that took place?

4) How were Detroit automakers influenced by the customizers?

Additional Car and Vehicle Extension Ideas

Focus on:

1) Chicano lowriders.

2) Custom cars in movies and television.

3) Cross-cultural study of decorated vehicles—rickshaws (Bangladesh), Tap-taps (Haiti), buses (Panama), chivas (Colombia), ox carts (Costa Rica). See reference list.

4) The "art car" movement in the United States

5) "Cars in Art," a broad theme, that includes contemporary artists who use actual cars in their art, e.g., Cadillac Ranch near Amarillo, Texas; Gilbert Lujan's painted car; and John Chamberlin's abstract sculptures made from junked cars.

Interdisciplinary Extensions

1) Social Studies: The impact of the automobile in American society or the car culture in America.
2) Music: The automobile in music.
3) Language Arts: The automobile in literature, e.g., early novels about hotrodding and others.
4) Science: Technology that affected automotive design and performance throughout the 20th century.

Artwork completed by eighth grade students.

Artwork completed by eighth grade students.

The Wedding

Art Maker
Jonathan Green

Access Information
Jonathan Green Studios
316 Morgan Road
Naples, Florida 34114-2562
(941) 775-9999
FAX (941) 775-9129
Publications Distributor:
P.O. Box 66 Yemassee, SC
29945 Office: (843) 846-8319;
Fax: (843) 845-8467
Items available for purchase;
Wall calendar, book of post-
cards (30 images), posters,
book entitled, *Gullah Images:
The Art of Jonathan Green* by
Pat Conroy. (1996). Columbia,
SC: University of South
Carolina Press. (image located
on page 69)

Date of the Artwork
1988

Location of Artwork
Private collection

Medium
Oil on masonite

Size
48" x 48"

Subject Matter

This artwork shows Green's representations of a special event he may have observed as a child growing up in rural South Carolina. Celebrations have played a vital role in the life of African-American communities for generations. This work shows people who are gathered for an outdoor wedding ceremony. The people in the foreground are preparing for the reception. Persons in the middle ground are participants in witnessing the ceremony, while people in the background are walking towards the joyous event.

The wedding takes place on the front porch of a golden colored building (perhaps a house). A crowd of people are in attendance. The foreground shows two ladies in the front left hand corner preparing the reception food and drink, they are facing us. A wedding cake sits on the table.

The middleground shows people entrenched in the ceremony as well as people who are walking toward the joyous event all carrying items (gifts?). Behind them, three other women are either wearing hats or carrying items on their heads. A small building is behind them. The people depicted are all sizes, heights, and ages.

Visual Organization

The painting is filled with brilliant color except for the faces of the people, which are solid black and a few other lighter skin tones. No details such as eyes, mouths, and noses are included. People in the foreground are larger and the people further away walking up to the event are painted smaller. Depth is shown by the way in which the crowd of people are overlapping one another. Green leads us around the painting up to the front porch where the actual ceremony is taking place (center of interest). The house takes up a great deal of space. The painting is balanced by the people over to the left side who are walking up towards the special event.

Short Biography of the Art Maker

Jonathan Green was born in 1955 and raised in Gardens Corner, South Carolina. He was the second of seven children. Jonathan was raised by his grandmother, from whom he learned to speak the Gullah dialect and discovered the oral traditions which had been passed from generation to generation in the African American community. Jonathan Green was considered a special person at birth because he was born with a fetal membrane (veil) covering his head. In Gullah culture, the veil is a sign that a person possesses unnatural powers and magic to benefit and nurture the community (Goforth, 1996-97). Jonathan Green is a visual storyteller. Green (1998) stated that "through listening to stories, young people gain a sense of their culture and also learn how to relate to other people and how to live in the world" (p. 1). Green didn't always appreciate his cultural heritage. Greene (1990) stated that "Like many others, he had to leave his home and journey to a far place to comprehend the value of his Gullah roots" (p. 44).

His brilliant colored images are drawn from his childhood and express a sacredness of tradition, heritage, and community. His paintings celebrate and rejuvenate his grandmother's legacy, expressing the Gullah culture that is unique to the coastal islands of South Carolina and Georgia. The Gullah way of life developed during slavery as a synthesis of predominately Gold Coast African cultures and European culture. African influence remained strong on isolated coastal island plantations because new slave arrivals continued on the islands until the late 1850s. After the Emancipation, many of the Gullah remained on the islands to become landowners, farmers, teachers, nurses, blacksmiths, doctors, and fishermen. Because many of the island communities remained isolated, the Gullah people were able to preserve a strong community identity, their language and many ancestral customs, despite dislocation and the adversity of slavery.

Although Jonathan hasn't lived in Gardens Corner since he was a teenager, through his art he is able to preserve images of his childhood as if he were still there (Branch, 1995). Jonathan Green lives and paints in Naples, Florida.

Artworld Information

Jonathan Green's art was heavily influenced by his emotional, spiritual, and cultural upbringing. His paintings celebrate the legacy of his grandmother, Ms. Eloise Johnson, and the Gullah culture that is unique to the coastal islands of South Carolina and Georgia.

While studying at the Art Institute in Chicago, Jonathan immersed himself in literature pertaining to Africa, Caribbean, Mexico, and South America. Class discussion was geared towards assisting students in exploring their own lives within a wider cultural framework. In art school, the focus was on mainstream modernism therefore, opportunities to study African American art were limited. Students were to be expressive with subject matter and to reject narrative art. Jonathan felt that this creative mandate was challenging. He believed that being personally creative and innovative outside one's own cultural experience required cultural denial. After Green graduated from the Art Institute, he traveled widely throughout the United States including Canada and Mexico, the West Indies, Switzerland, Germany, England, and France.

His work is highly received and recognized by the people who live in the state of South Carolina. In October of 1996, a festival was held at the University of South Carolina's McKissick Museum. This festival celebrated Green's work as a painter of the Gullah culture as well as the release of a book entitled *Gullah Images: The Art of Jonathan Green* (Goforth, 1996-97, p. 25). He was also awarded an honorary doctorate in the arts. According to Carroll Greene, a consultant on African American culture and a Savannah collector of African American art "for people who live in the low country Jonathan's work is special because he has explored aesthetically an African American lifestyle and he has done it with love." Jonathan has been the keynote speaker for the South Carolina Art Education Association at the annual state conference. Many local art educators incorporate discussions of his work into their curriculum.

Since 1982, Jonathan has had four traveling exhibitions through the United States and numerous solo exhibitions and group exhibitions. His work has been included and reviewed in major art publications and cultural journals. Green (1998) postulated that, "I am drawn to rural environments that afford a sense of space and silence and an opportunity to unobtrusively observe daily functions of others as we all pursue life's mission of work, love, and belonging. Agrarian life allows me to experience how we work in harmony with the mysterious and changing fabric of nature. It is the small, but critical tasks of daily life that I find most stimulating and reflective of the quality of essential, personal, community, and social values." (p. 1)

References

Branch, M. (1995). *The water brought us.* New York: Cobblehill Books.
Conroy, P. (1996). *Gullah Images: The Art of Jonathan Green.* Columbia, SC: University of South Carolina Press.
Goforth, T. (1996-1997). *Jonathan Green: Painter of Gullah Culture.* Sandlapper. *The Magazine of South Carolina.* 7, 25-28.
Greene, C. (1990, February). "Coming home again artist Jonathan Green returns to his gullah roots," *American Visions,* 5, 44-52.
Green, J. (1998). Biographical statement from unpublished monograph. Jonathan Green Studios.
McKissick Museum. (1995). *Traveling exhibit presents lyrical images of an exotic* nearby culture. Columbia: University of South Carolina, 13.

A Celebration in Three-Dimensions

Objectives

Students:

1) examine how one's cultural heritage (values, family, community and traditions) instilled in an artist at an early age can influence his or her art.

2) identify their own unique family traditions and celebrations.

3) create a three-dimensional painting of themselves with two other people participating in a special celebration.

4) identify Modernist art ideas that Green accepted and those he rejected.

Activities

Display an art reproduction entitled *The Wedding,* by Jonathan Green. Have students name things they see in the work. Specifically have students discuss Green's use of bright color, size, and placement of figures in the work and the celebration depicted. For example, have students examine the size of figures and notice that figures in the background space are smaller than the ones in the front of the painting. Introduce overlapping as a vocabulary word. Point to examples of overlapping in the work.

Ask students to raise their hands if they have ever attended a wedding? What do people wear? Have students describe weddings they have attended or participated in. What other celebrations have they participated in? Have them describe what they wore or would wear to this event. Was any special music played? What events took place as part of the ritual of their particular celebration?

Day One

Give students a piece of construction paper (white) and a crayon to draw three people participating in a celebration. Encourage them to draw large and add details in faces and clothing. Have them think about actual clothing worn for their celebration, i.e., graduation cap and gown, birthday hat. Remind students that each individual figure will be cut out. Next, hand out white construction paper and discuss how the background will look. Did the celebration take place indoors or outdoors? What objects did you see? What can you include to provide clues of the special celebraton? Again, have them use a crayon to draw the background. Encourage students to draw large shapes due to the fact that their works will be painted.

Day Two

Review background information on Jonathan Green. Briefly discuss his use of bright color, patterned clothing, and lack of facial features. Encourage students to mix skin tone colors for the faces of persons drawn. Provide students with general directions for painting. Allow them the opportunity to use a variety of large and small paintbrushes. Remind students to dry paint brushes on paper towels before they use a new color (to keep colors from running). Tell students that they may want to paint the skin colors on all of the body parts then move on to painting the clothes. Last, have students paint small details such as the eyes, mouth, nose, etc.

Pass out the background drawings. Have students paint the background, reminding them to paint the large sections first. Let dry. You may want students to use a black felt marker to outline some parts, and add facial details that may have disappeared while painting. Next, pass out the scissors. Have the students cut out the figures. Review the lesson on the foreground, middle-ground, and background and the way in which Green used space in his paintings. Explain that Green accepted and used some ideas from the Modernist artworld, (such as use of foreground, middle-ground, background, and overlapping) but rejected other ideas (such as avoidance of narrative subject matter). Have students think about where they want to place their figures. Review the concept of overlapping. Have students point to examples of overlapping seen in Green's work.

Next, pass out tabs of varying sizes and have students use glue to attach the figures to the background painting. The teacher should demonstrate first. Remind students to make sure the tab does not show when attached to the cut out figures. Next, have students add glue to the tab and attach entire piece to the background paper. Let dry. When dry, ask for volunteers to show their works to their classmates. Ask students to describe their special celebration.

Assessment

Criteria:

Identified objects in the reproduction.

Verbalized factors that influenced Green's art and subject matter.

Described own family traditions and important ceremonies unique to their family.

Able to describe Green's use of space. (foreground, middleground, and background, overlapping).

Incorporated a foreground, middle ground, and background into their own paintings.

Able to paint at least three people involved in a celebration.

Able to identify Modernist ideas tha Green used (foreground, middleground, background) and rejected (avoidance of narrative subject matter).

Art Supplies and Other Resources

Two sheets of white construction paper (12" by 18")

Crayons (one per child)

Tempera paints (assorted colors) include skin tone colors

Paintbrushes (variety of sizes)

Water containers

Paper towels

Newspaper to cover tables /desks

Scissors

Tabs (prepared by the teacher)

Elmer's glue

Art reproduction: *The Wedding* by Jonathan Green

Examples of other celebrations painted by Jonathan Green

Kalachakra: The Wheel of Time Mandala

Art Maker
Tibetan Buddhist monks in the United States

Access Information
Kalachakra Sand Mandala: The Wheel of Time is available at http://www.buddhanet.net/kalimage.htm and at http://buddhanet.net/kalackak.htm.

Date of Artwork
Mandalas have been made in Asia for many centuries. *The Wheel of Time Mandala* was first presented in the United States in New York in 1988.

Location of Artwork
A permanent mandala is on exhibit on the floor of Asian art in the Denver Art Museum. However, most mandalas are dismantled in a prayer ceremony after they are made. Mandalas are made by the Tibetan monks at sites around the United States.

Medium
The sand mandala is made of colored sand on the floor. Originally, crushed colored rock was used.

Size
The sand mandala often has a diameter of 5' to 7'.

Subject Matter
Buddhists sometimes use *yantras* to help them to pray and meditate. Yantras are ways to help people concentrate. One of the Yantras is the mandala. The *mandala,* or circle, is an important symbol of Buddhism. It sometimes represents a palace or the whole universe. The mandala can also be a representation for the human body.

The four arms of the *Wheel of Time Mandala* represent the four directions: north, south, east, and west. The main arms of the mandala suggest the connection to the center of the universe from which the four directons come. The shape of the mandala also reflects the structure of the universe with the four arms reflecting the four "gates" guarded by various deities. Deities are sometimes represented by Sanskrit syllables.

Looking at a mandala from above is like looking at a palace from the air. The squares inside the other squares represent the levels of the palace. The different levels have different meanings: e.g., Mandala of Enlightened Wisdom, or Mandala of Enlightened Mind. The various concentric squares and circles contain intricate designs which are symbols with precise meanings. The center of the mandala can signify the core of the universe. Sometimes, the center is the home of the deity.

There are many mandala forms. The *Kalachakra* mandala represents the five-story palace of the Wheel of Time deity called Kalachakra and his enlightened universe of compassion and wisdom. The circle can represent many things, such as the lotus flower, the buddha, etc. Also, mandalas show pictures of buddhas, humans, bodhisattvas, words, clouds, animals. Colors, shapes, and objects signify many levels of traditional meanings used to help in meditation on the "Path of Enlightenment."

The outer circle symbolizes the lotus and represents the outer edge of the universe. "In his meditation, the person imagines a lotus unfolding in his heart which then magically expands to become the universe" (Blofield, 1992, pp.102-14).

Visual Organization
The mandala is a round, symmetrical composition with many symbols in the form of geometric shapes, circles, squares, and lines.

Short Biography Art Makers
In many countries of the world, especially Asia, many people practice a religion known as Buddhism. Buddhism started in India with the teachings of a prince. His name was Prince Gautama, later known as Sakyamuni. He was a great teacher who lived in India a very long time ago in the 6th century BCE. Because of his achievements, he was given the name Buddha, meaning the Enlightened One. The term, Buddha, can also apply to other beings and to the spiritual principles of Buddhism.

People were very impressed by Sakyamuni's ideas. Many people followed him, listening to his ideas. The religion of Buddhism tells people that they should work to control their minds and try to reach a state of much wisdom. Therefore, many people who are Buddhists spend much time praying and meditating. When meditating, they concentrate on ideas about life and their world. They meditate for very long periods of time. Some people spend their whole lives in prayer and meditation. These people are called *monks* (men) and *nuns* (women).

In Tibet, a nation in the mountains of Asia, the culture of the people is based on Buddhism. Many people in Tibet had to flee their country when the Chinese government came into their land. The Tibetan monks also escaped to India. They established a monastery there. Many Tibetan Buddhists also came to the United States and created places to live and practice their religion.

In Denver, Colorado, several monks from a Buddhist monastery in India came to make a very large mandala to help them pray for the healing of injuries caused by gang violence in Denver. The monks worked together many days to make the mandala in the Denver Art Museum. They worked long hours every day. Many people came to watch as they prayed and worked on their mandala. The television stations and the newspaper reporters came to tell people at home about the mandala.

Artworld Information
The monks who make mandalas go through many years of training in a place called a monastery. Monks memorize exact details of making mandalas and then practice with a master. Making a mandala is a time of meditation. To begin the mandala, the monks, following the ancient texts, prayerfully draw the mandala outline on a surface on the floor. They draw the mandala very carefully. The mandala has the same shape on each side.

After drawing the mandala in white chalk, the monks slowly apply sand starting at the center of the design. The sand, which is dyed with colors, is applied through a *chakpu* and a *shinga*. The *chakpu* a tool with a special metal funnel which is used to apply the colored sand. The *shinga* is a wooden scraper used to straighten the lines of sand. The sand makes little mounds upon the surface. The monks help each other as they make the mandala. Monks pray during the days that they are making a mandala.

In Denver after the mandala was completed, the monks said many prayers. The deities were requested to return to their homes. Then the monks gathered up all the sand and offered the sand to the river of the city as a gesture of purification for the environment.

References
Blofield, J. (1992). *The tantric mysticism of Tibet: A practical guide.* New York: Penguin Books, Arkana.
Bryant, B. (1994). *The wheel of time sand mandala calendar.* New York: Samaya Press. (802-439-5031),
    www.samaya.org, or samaya@samaya.org
No Author. (1995). *Mandala.* New York: Thames and Hudson.
Trungpa, Chogyam & Rinpoche. (1975). *Visual Dharma: The Buddhist art of Tibet.*
    Berkeley, California: Shambhala Publications, Inc.

Websites
Hansen, J. *Mandala.* available at: http://www.jyh.dk/indengl.htm.
Mandala Internet resource site available at: http://www.northnet.org/mwcsart/mandala.htm
Mandalas on the Web available at: http://www.abgoodwin.com/mandala/ccweb.shtml or email at:
    alan@abgoodwin.com
Mandala: Buddhist tantric diagrams available at: http://ccat.sas.upenn.edu/george/mandala.html

Videos and Posters
There are many resources available from Snowlion Publications, PO Box 6483, Ithica, NY 14851-6483 and
    http://snowlionpub.com/index.html

The Mandala

Objectives
Students will:
    1) identify examples of Buddhist mandalas. (The student will be able to tell why mandalas, usually made in Asia, are now also made in the United States by Tibetan monks.)

2) identify the symmetrical organization and repeat lines, shapes, and colors within a mandala.
3) identify Buddhist symbols in the geometric shapes of a Buddhist mandala.
4) create a mandala with their own personal symbols.
5) use symmetry, repeat lines, shapes, and colors to create their own unified mandala.

Activities

Discussion

Gather the students in front of a reproduction of a Tibetan Kalachakra mandala. You may want to show other mandalas as well. Consult the Short Biography of Art Makers and Artworld Information about Tibetan mandalas. Explain the process of making mandalas, why they are made, where they are made, who makes them, and why some mandalas are now being made by Tibetan exiles in the United States. Display a map of Asia and indicate the locations of Tibet and India.

While the students are looking at the reproduction, ask the following questions: (For younger students) What do you think about when looking at this picture? Describe the shapes that you see in the mandala. (For older students) How do the monks get the sand on the mandala exactly in place? Where should we start exploring this picture? Why is the mandala round?

Give each student a packet of information on the mandala that includes the outline of a basic mandala. Define *symmetry* as unity created by repetition on both (or all) sides of an artwork. Explain that the lines, shapes, and colors of a mandala are symmetrically repeated on all four sides. Ask the students such questions as: What areas of the mandala look the same? What do the monks do before and while they are making the mandala? What are the tools the monks use? What was the purpose for making this mandala? Ask the students to search for lines, shapes, or colors in the mandala that may not be obvious to others. Encourage the students to ask questions and give opinions.

Art Making

Ask students to create a mandala using the traditional Tibetan form. They should use the shapes of the universal circle symbol, emphasizing the four directions. They should use their own symbols. Ask students to think of objects or shapes, which represent them or objects and events in their lives. For example, some students think that a circle or diamond shape may represent them. Students may think of themselves as best represented by a certain color. Clouds or stars may represent the spiritual side of their lives.

Provide students with white drawing paper, colored pencils, crayons, or fine-line markers. Ask students to develop a four-sided symmetrical mandala. Ask them also to use repeat lines, shapes, and colors to help unify their mandala. If time is limited, or the class is mainly a lecture class, students may use the preprinted mandala outline.

Analysis

Display students' mandalas. Ask students to explain shapes and colors in the mandalas to other students to show their understanding of the mandala's history and symbolism. Ask students to write or tell how they used symmetry and repeated lines, shapes, and colors to unify their mandalas.

Assessment

Assess students' participation in the discussion of the Kalachakra mandala for understanding of the role of mandalas in Tibetan Buddhist culture (in Tibet and also in exile in India and in the United States) and how monks and nuns learn the symbols and methods of making mandalas.

Assess students' mandalas for four-sided symmetry and repeated lines, shapes, and colors.

Assess the students' participation in the analysis of the mandala for their ability to identify symbols, recognize symmetry, and explain how they unified their mandala.

Art Supplies and Other Resources

    Printouts or a reproduction of the Kalachakra mandala

    Map of Asia

    Handout of an outline of basic mandala form, compasses (optional)

    White drawing paper

    Colored pencils

    Crayons

    Fine-line markers.

Extension Ideas or Other Interdisciplinary Extensions

Comparisons might be made with Navajo sand paintings or medieval European rose windows. The lesson might be incorporated into a unit on Asian studies.

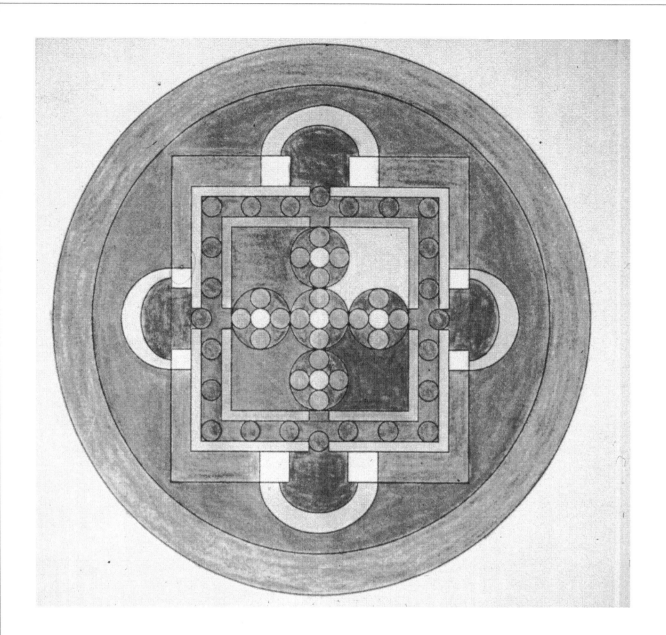

Zydeco

Art Maker
Jean-Michel Basquiat

Access Information
Guenther, S., H. (1992).
Jean-Michel Basquiat, The blue ribbon paintings.
Thames: Mount Holyoke College

Date of the Artwork
1984

Location of Artwork
Private Collection

Medium
Wax Crayon, Acrylic, and Oil on canvas

Size
86" x 204"

Subject Matter

A man with accordion is depicted in the middle of the triptych. The word Zydeco is represented three times in the middle panel. Outlines of objects, such as four male heads, two crowns, and an icebox are depicted in the first panel. A still camera, a man with a movie camera, and seven heads are recorded in the third panel.

Visual Organization

A Zydeco musician holding an accordion between his arms is the focal point of the canvas triptych. The musician is juxtaposed against a green and white background. A white male head is repeated on the first and third panels. Thin contour lines are used to draw simple shapes such as circles, squares, triangles, and rectangles. These shapes are used to construct objects including the accordion, icebox, still camera, and movie camera.

Short Biography of Art Maker

Jean-Michel Basquiat, contemporary African American artist, was born and raised in a middle-class Brooklyn neighborhood in New York City. Jean-Michel's father is Haitian and his mother is Puerto Rican. Jean-Michel left home at a young age to live his life as an artist. Basquiat developed fascinating methods of organizing a variety of historical images and facts in graphic visual presentations. The images are commanding, comical, maddening, and depressing. His artwork contains many graphic elements that symbolize political issues in our culture. Jean-Michel's artwork addressed political issues of racism. He represented the pride, the passion, and the pain of being Black in America through the organization of symbols. His goal was to challenge people to understand the role racism has played during the 1980s. The purpose of his artwork was to address cultural democracy and define who he was. A large male head wearing a three-pointed crown represents a symbol of the nobility of the African American male. He used the copyright symbol, official-looking seals, and stamps to signal the end of the artwork. The brain, ear, intestines, pelvises, and other anatomy suggest the way by which we know the world through the function of our five senses. In 1988, Jean-Michel died of a drug overdose at age 27.

Artworld Information

Jean-Michael Basquiat began his career by drawing and lettering graffiti on building walls on the streets of SoHo. With a friend, he tagged art on buildings with "SAMOc." By the mid-1980s Basquiat had progressed through one-man and group exhibitions with top New York galleries. His mentor and friend was Andy Warhol. Many of this friends, fellow artists, and patrons were celebrities. Patrons of his artwork include musicians and movie stars such as Madonna. Connections may be seen between his work and other artists of this century such as Jean Debuffet, Jasper Johns, Wilhem de Kooning, and graffiti artists during the 1980s. For example, there is likeness between Wilhem de Kooning's painting method of swift vigorous gestures and Basquiat's quick application of brush strokes. In addition, Jean Debuffet's, *Jazz Band*, 1944, a simplistic, child-like representation of band members, is similar to Basquiat's approach for depicting figures.

References

Angelou, M. (1993). *Life doesn't frighten me.* New York: Stewart, Tabori & Chang.
Chalfant H. & Prigoff, J. (1987). *Spray can art.* New York: Thames and Hudson.
Cheim, R. (1990). *Basquiat drawings.* Boston: Little, Brown and Company.
Guenther, S.H. (1992). *Jean-Michel Basquiat, The blue ribbon paintings.*
    Thames: Mount Holyoke College.
The 20th Century Art Book. London: Phaidon Press Limited.
Yenawine, P. (1995) *Key art terms for beginners.* New York: Harry N. Abrams, Inc.

Contemporary Ethnic and Activist Research

Objectives

Students:

    1) express ideas and feelings about their world when they make artwork.

    2) use observations of people, places, objects, and events as sources of ideas for art making.

    3) use both spontaneous and deliberate approaches in their art making.

    4) identify and discuss meanings in Basquiat's works.

    5) communicate their ideas about their own and others' artwork.

    6) relate Basquiat's work to the study of the graffiti movement in New York during the 1980s.

Activities

Display a reproduction of *Zydeco*. Pose questions to students to identify and discuss meanings of the painting. Zydeco, is a popular music from southern Louisiana that combines tunes of French origin with elements of Caribbean music and the blues. It is a form of Cajun music. Specific questions may include: What is going on in this painting? What do you think Basquiat was trying to express about the African American culture in this piece? What kind of shapes did Basquiat use? What kind of lines did he use? What colors do you notice? While talking about *Zydeco*, play Zydeco music in the background. After listening to the music, talk about how the music sounds. Discuss how the music and the artwork are similar or different. For example, compare the pattern, rhythm, repetition, and movement of the artwork with sounds of the music. Next relate Basquiat's work to the graffiti movement during the 1980s. Discuss Basquiat's drawing and lettering on the sides of New York buildings with spray paint. Show the students images of graffiti art in the book *Spray Can Art* by Henry Chalfant and James Prigoff. Look at the images in the book and define the nature of a graffiti writer: someone who represents words and images with spray paint on walls of buildings. In addition, discuss the controversies such as the Anti-Graffiti Network task force to end graffiti writing during the 1980s.

After a discussion of *Zydeco*, ask students to draw upon their observations of people, places, objects, and events in their neighborhood as a source of ideas to make a painting that expresses either something about an intolerable situation in their neighborhood or something beautiful about their neighborhood. Some difficult problems may include starvation, homelessness, abuse, noise and air pollution, littering, and exclusion. Students may also choose to express something beautiful about their neighborhood instead. Ask students to brainstorm existing situations in their neighborhood. Ask students to work for a few minutes in small groups to express their ideas and feelings about their existing problems before drawing. Ask students to express how they will represent their neighborhood and listen to comments and questions about their ideas. You may help students express their ideas visually by using motivational dialogue. For example, the teacher may pose questions to the students about what they see in their environment. Other questions include: Who do you see walking by your house? How does your neighborhood smell? What noises do you hear? These questions help children visualize the subject matter. Then transition the students to their drawing by asking more questions, such as: What will you draw first? Where will you draw it? Will you draw it near or far away?

After small group and teacher led discussions, ask students to draw events in their neighborhood with a pencil onto white drawing paper. Next, ask students to discuss their drawings with the teacher before painting. In this teacher and student discussion, you should be looking for details student may add to his/her drawing. The teacher may nudge the student to add more details that can give the drawing more information about the events in the neighborhood. After students have discussed their ideas and feelings about their neighborhood and the events they chose to represent, ask them to deliberately plan areas of their drawing to apply acrylic paint and/or wax crayons to add color to their drawings. Encourage students to experiment with spontaneous approaches to using the acrylic paint and wax crayons together. Remind students that Basquiat also used acrylic paint and wax crayons to make paintings. See the assessment section for a culminating activity in the form of a performance assessment.

Assessment

The assessment procedure is a group discussion, a performance assessment strategy. When students have completed their paintings about an existing situation in their neighborhood, ask them to communicate their ideas about their own and others' artworks. Ask questions to help students reflect upon their work, such as: What issue do you think Johnny's drawing tells us about what is happening in his neighborhood? What do you see that helps you know? Ask each student to discuss what is happening in his/her artwork and the process s/he went through to represent the idea. In addition, ask other students to direct comments and questions to the student discussing the artwork. Assess art understanding by asking students questions about the similarities and differences between their drawings and Basquiat's piece. Questions teachers may use to help students explain connections between their work and Basquiat's painting include: How does your subject matter seem similar to or different to from Basquiat's painting? What kinds of lines did you draw to make shapes? Did you put together several shapes to make the objects in your drawing? Did you work in a slow speed or a fast speed while drawing and painting? During this discussion, ask students to will re-look at Basquiat's painting to make artworld connections. Does his work show influences from his early experience as a Graffiti tagger? How has his work been received by artists and orgaizations of the mainstream artworld? Write anecdotal notes on note cards that will be put into each student's portfolio. The anecdotal notes will include how the students discussed the artwork and how the students listened to and responded to others' work. The anecdotal notes may include the students identifying objects in the artwork, communicating the process to compose the art elements, supporting ideas and interpretation of the artwork with relevant reasons and finding artworld connections. This discussion provides insight about what the class learned through this lesson. After the discussion, ask students to respond to what happened in the discussion. Ask them to reflect and write about what more they learned through the discussion about their work, other students' work, and Basquiat's work.

Art Supplies and Other Resources

Reproduction of *Zydeco*
White drawing paper
Acrylic paints
Wax crayons
Pencils
Brushes
Water containers
Paper towels
Zydeco music

Kwakwaka'wakw Transformation Mask: Raven and the Raven of the Sea

Art Maker
The mask was probably carved by a man of the Kwakwaka'wakw (formerly Kwakiutl) culture.

Access Information
Jonaitus, A. & Myers, S. S. (1991) *The land of the totem poles: The Northwest Coast Indians art collections of the American Museum of Natural History.* Seattle, WA: American Museum of Natural History in association with the University of Washington Press, 177, plate 78.

Date of Artwork
The artwork was made in or before 1901, since Hunt collected it in 1901 during the Jessup Expedition.

Location
American Museum of Natural History, New York City

Medium
The mask was carved from wood and decorated with mineral paints; graphite and magnetite for black, celadonite for blue, and hematite for red. The minerals were then mixed with salmon eggs that had been chewed. Paint brushes made of porcupine guard hairs may have been used.

Size
83 cm long and 38.2 cm high

Subject Matter
This mask represents the head of the Raven when closed and the Raven of the Sea (with sharp-toothed creatures facing inward inside its beak) when opened. The Raven of the Sea appears to have human characteristics because of the eyebrows and the mouth that appear below the mask. This human appearance suggests the oneness of all creatures. The Raven was the most important of all the creatures to the people of the Northwest Pacific. The Raven took many forms. He was a Creator, a Transformer, and a Trickster. The Raven could dive beneath the sea, maneuvering tides so that the people could harvest the bounty of the sea and the beach. The Raven placed the lakes and rivers and filled them with fish.

Visual Organization
The Raven mask has a large beak that opens and closes during dances to symbolize the transformation of the Raven. Black is the primary design color. The black lines are bold and describe the outlines of the Raven and of the creatures inside Raven's beak. The creatures' bodies are made up of "U" shapes that are turned different ways. The Raven's eyes are long and pointed at either end of the eye socket. Red is the second color used in designs. The areas that are painted red are areas that are considered of secondary importance. The Kwakwaka'wakw also add a tertiary color such as blue, but may also add a fourth color such as green in this Transformation mask.

Short Biography of Art Maker
The maker of the Transformation mask lived in the Northwest Pacific region, which covers an area from northern Washington State up the west coast of Canada, to the southern part of Alaska. The land located between the mainland and the sea is a very rich environment, but also one that changes rapidly. There are the movement of the tides, the mixing of fresh water and salt water, cycles of drying by the wind and the sun, and the Pacific Ocean storms. The people had little power over various aspects of their lives such as illness, death, bad weather, fish runs, and other natural disasters. To control these, the people looked to their *shamans*, men who had acquired special abilities, to interact with the supernatural world.

In the past, the people of the Northwest Pacific build immense houses in which 50 or more related individuals reside. Wealthy families could increase their power and status by engaging in elaborate ceremonies.

Women and men traditionally worked with different materials. Because men carved wood, this mask was probably made by a man.

Artworld Information
"The Northwest Coast is the only area in North America where heraldic and ceremonial carving and painting was in the hands of professional artists who could be supported by the upper class from economic surplus" (Feest, 1980, pp. 27-8). The mask carvers learned through apprenticeships and were held to high standards of craftsmanship and the desire to constantly improve their skills. The decorations on the objects were statements of social identity and also reminders of rights and prerogatives bestowed on their ancestors by supernatural beings, or of lessons taught to them by myths, encounters with birds, fish, or other beings.

Mask makers follow stylistic traditions passed down in their culture, such as the use of a limited color scheme (with black as the primary color and red as next most important), symmetry, formlines (gently expanding and contracting lines), ovoids (rounded rectangles), and "U" shapes. Representing eyes with long, pointed sockets is a design feature that differentiates Kwalwaka'wakw artwork from that made by other Northwest Pacific peoples.

Powerful families headed by chiefs own the rights to use certain visual images. These images, or family crests such as Raven, represent beings from the distant past before the world came to be as we know it. Families, or sometimes entire villages, consider these beings to be their ancestors. "Nobody used motifs that did not belong to him or her; that would be stealing at a profound level" (Kirk, 1986, p. 49).

The Transformation mask would have been worn at elaborate Winter Dance ceremonies. "Face masks are robust, with features emphasized by painting, and supernatural bird masks [such as Raven] are often wildly inventive and elaborate; some have enormous beaks that open and close during dances—to symbolize transformation—an outer mask that opens to reveal an inner mask" (Stewart, 1979, pp. 97-8). Art making has evolved since the arrival of European American explorers. Art makers made items tailored to the needs of the explorers and European Americans commissioned work from them. The Kwakwaka'wakw were quick to start using commercial paints when they became available and experimented with other colors; they return, however, to the traditional colors. Today many Northwest Pacific art makers sell their work to European and American art collectors and tourists.

References

Carnegie Museum of Natural History. (1998). *North-south-east-west American Indians and nature: north: the Tlingit of the northwest.* Pittsburgh: Rinehart.

Cole, J. (Ed). (1982). The raven brings light. *In Best-loved folktakes of the world.* Garden City, NY: Doubleday, pp. 719-21.

Feest, C.F. (1980). *Native arts of North America.* New York and Toronto: Oxford University Press.

Kirk, R. (1986). *Tradition & change on the northwest coast.* Seattle: University of Washington Press in association with the Royal British Columbia Museum.

Normandin, C. (Ed.) 1997. Raven and sea gull. In *Echoes of the elders: The stories and paintings of Chief Lelooska.* New York: DK Publishing, 22-27.

Stewart, H. (1979). *Looking at Indian art of the northwest coast.* Vancouver and Toronto: University of Washington Press.

Websites

American Museum of Natural History. Jessup Exhibition. http://www.amnh.org/Exhibitions/Jesup/.

Burke Museum (1998). Anthropology Division. http://www.washington.edu/burke museum/anthro.html.

Northwest Pacific Masks and Papier Mach Mask

Objectives

Students:
1) point out the location of the Northwest Pacific region within North America.
2) recognize that stories and rituals are associated with the masks from the Pacific Northwest region.
3) identify visual qualitites of masks passed down through apprenticeships of Northwest Pacific mask makers (such as the use of a limited color schemes, symmetry, formlines, ovoids, "U" shapes, and exaggeration).
4) distinguish additive and subtractive sculpture.
5) use a sketch as a part of the process of making art and to consider why they make changes in their artwork.

Activities

Display examples of Pacific Northwest Native American masks focusing on the Kwakwaka'wakw Transformation Mask. Questions to ask are: What are these? What do the masks look like they are made of? How would the artist create these shapes out of wood? (Explain that when masks are carved, material is taken away, and that process is called subtractive sculpture.) What elements of art do you see? (Focus on the limited color scheme.) What principles of composition do you see? (Focus on asymmetry and symmetry.) Do you see people or animals? What might these people or animals represent? What shapes are exaggerated? How do the exaggerated shapes on specific masks make you feel?

Consult the Short Biography of the Art Maker and Artworld Information. Share with students information about the Northwest Pacific region, apprenticeships, traditional attention to craftsmanship among mask makers, and the role of the mask in ceremonies. Ask students what sort of rituals or celebrations they participate in that are similar or different from the rituals or celebrations of Northwest Pacific Native Americans.

Tell students that they will be making their own masks. Explain that they may not directly copy these masks as they are used for Native American rituals and stories. Ask students what stories they could tell about their lives through a mask design. Could a mask represent a wonderful family celebration? Could a mask have a religious significance to you? Is there an animal that is important to your life? What animal would you choose to represent you? What features would you exaggerate? Would you create a headdress for the mask?

Explain that Northwest Pacific Native American mask makers learned how to make masks by first serving as apprentices. Only a few young men were selected as apprentices to learn the secrets of mask making. Explain also that they were held to standards of craftsmanship and constantly worked to improve their skills. Explain that mask makers followed traditions passed down to them, such as the use of limited color schemes, formlines, ovoids, "U" shapes, and exaggeration. (See Visual Organization and Artworld Information.)

After discussing ideas for masks with the students, give them each a 9"x12" piece of newsprint and asked them to design two mask ideas. Explain that artists sometime do several sketches of an idea before they create a work of art, so the students are going to do two sketches. Be sure that students keep their sketches throughout the process so that they can refer back to their original idea. Model an idea in front of the class on a sheet of paper on which you design a mask that tells something about yourself. Remind students that this is your idea and they are not to use it.

After the students have had time to work on the sketches, go around and discuss the designs with each student and approve each design or makes suggestions for improving them. Focus on using exaggeration to make the design show up (and be easier to paint) and the use of a limited color scheme. Masks will not be carved but will be sculpted out of paper. Explain that the technique the students will use is called additive sculpture.

Pass out the 9"x12" tag board. Demonstrate to the students how to transfer the mask shape onto the tag board. Some areas of the mask, for example a headdress, could be attached on with pipe cleaners or yarn or may need to be constructed with additional tag board pieces.

Next the students draw a line in each corner of the tag board. With elementary children suggest that the line be as long as their thumb. Then the teacher demonstrates cutting the line in each corner. Then the corners are folded together and stapled.

Ask students to think about which parts of their mask they would like to have stick out and which areas they will paint. Explain that at least one area of the mask must stick up from the surface. Demonstrate how to fold, bunch, and crumple paper to make shapes to raise the surface of the mask.

After students have had a chance to work on the surface of the mask, demonstrate how to cut shapes that could be add-ons to the mask for ears or a headdress. Provide extra tag board for the students working on these ideas.

If the students have not used papier maché before, you may want to talk about the maché paste so that the students are not surprised by its texture. Demonstrate how to tear the newspaper into strips. Then demonstrate how to put on the first layer. First, the newspaper strip is dipped into the papier maché paste. Then the excess paste is wiped off. This layer will be placed on the mask vertically going from top of the mask to the bottom. As each strip is laid on demonstrate how to smooth and sculpt the papier maché strip around the mask form and how to wrap the end of the strip around the edge of the mask.

After the students have completed the first layer of papier maché, demonstrate how to add the second layer of papier maché. Then demonstrate how to lay the second layer on horizontally, from side to side, smoothing and sculpting as each piece is laid down. Emphasize to the students that they need to smooth down all the newspaper. When the masks are placed on shelves to dry you may want to have the students ball up a piece of newspaper to place under the mask to support it, especially if a student has used too much papier maché paste. This will help the masks maintain their original form.

When the masks are dry, the students will be able to paint them. Talk about the Northwest Pacific masks again and ask what colors are used. Talk about the colors that appear in the masks, such as red and black and several values of blue to green. Tell the students that they, like Northwest Pacific mask makers, will be using a limited color scheme.

Instruct the students to look at their sketches and to decide on an overall color or a background color for their mask and to paint their mask all one color first. If they need to put on a second layer of paint, they may do so after the first layer dries. Next, ask students to paint their designs on top of the background going from large areas to small areas.

Be sure to point out that the opaque nature of tempera paint allows them to paint over if they make mistakes. Ask students to paint the designs directly on the mask. Remind the students that they are following the sketch that they created. Because the designs change once they are put on a three-dimensional surface, encourage students to verbalize the changes they sometimes need to make in their mask design.

When the painting is done, provide students with the opportunity to add items to their masks to enhance them or create textural effects that would be difficult with papier maché. Ask students to punch holes in the side of the masks, string yarn through the holes, and hang up the masks.

Assessment

Display the students' masks and allow them to see the choices everyone made. Encourage the students to talk about their masks.
1) Did the students add on or raise one area of the mask?
2) Did the students use some Northwest Pacific art traditions (the limited color scheme or exaggeration)?
3) Did the students use their sketch to guide the process of making the mask?
4) Can the students locate the Northwest Pacific region on a map of North America?
5) Can students tell how Northwest Pacific mask makers learn how to make masks?

Art Supplies and Other Resources
Newsprint
Pencils
Tag board
Staplers
Masking tape
Newspaper
Scissors
Paper towels
Papier maché paste
Paint brushes of various sizes
Tempera paints colors (Be sure to include red, turquoise, black, and white)
Bowls to hold the papier maché mixture
Extra newspapers for the tables
Hole punch
Various materials to add onto the masks (e.g., yarn, beads, glitter, feathers).

Nine Mojo Secrets

Art Maker
Betye Saar

Access Information
Walker, H. (1999). African American art: A Los Angeles Legacy [on line]. Available: http://www.getty.edu/artsednet/resources/African/Saar/index.html

Date of the Artwork
1971

Location of Artwork
California Afro-American Museum, Los Angeles

Medium
wooden frame, paint, photo, paper, feathers, plastic figures, fiber, seeds, and beads.

Size
49 3/4" x 23 1/2" x 1 3/4"

Subject Matter

A rectangular wooden frame with a round top, resembling the shape of a stained glass window, is divided into sections. In the center is a photograph of the Luba people of Central Africa with a large brown hand containing a mystic eye above them. The spaces around the central section contain symbols of the sun, moon and stars. Below the central section, the corner squares each contain small feathers and a plastic skeleton, and between them is a space with a small radiating sun, a white mask, and a lion. A skirt of fiber, beads and seeds hangs from the bottom of the frame.

Visual Organization

The artwork repeats the symbols of sun, moon, and stars. The symmetrical balance of these symbols is offset by a red space with a dark moon covering the sun, and a dark space with a crescent moon in the shadow of the Earth. Feathers and skeletons are repeated in the two symmetrically balanced bottom spaces. The artwork also repeats the idea of mask. In the center of *Nine Mojo Secrets*, the Luba people are performing a ceremony. Wooden masks are a part of costumes that cover the entire body in many traditional African ceremonies that honor beloved ancestors. The fiber skirt beneath the wooden frame of the artwork repeats the idea of mask by referring to the raffia beneath the wooden headpiece of an African masquerader's costume. In the bottom square of *Nine Mojo Secrets* there is another mask, but in this case it is a small white mask that is meant to conceal part of the face.

A Short Biography of the Artist

Born in Pasadena, California in 1926, Betye Saar was influenced by artistry in the world around her. Because her mother worked as a seamstress, she grew up in an environment containing colorful scraps of material and sewn objects. She was also exposed to the many traditional forms of Asian and Mexican art that are visible in Los Angeles. During the summers, Saar visited her grandmother who lived in Watts, just blocks from the towers that Italian immigrant Simon Rodia was building when she was a child. The metal spires decorated with castoff materials fascinated her. Saar, too, had a passion for collecting stray objects, sometimes picking up stones and pieces of glass, shells, and even bits of dirt (Munro, 1979). Later Saar studied design at the University of California Los Angeles and worked as a designer and graphic artist. After marrying and having three children, she went back to California State University for graduate work. Some of her early work consisted of prints combined with drawings framed in windows, which Saar considered symbolic structures that allow viewers to access the spiritual world. In 1966, for the first time, she used an actual object, a discarded window frame, for a print composed of compartmentalized images. Upon viewing an exhibition of surrealist artist Joseph Cornell's boxes, Saar was further encouraged to explore the possibilities of contained space and recycled objects. During the late 1960s, she did a series of assemblages on African American stereotypes, which she intended to heal those psyches that had been harmed by negative social images. Since then her work has evolved to include altars, installations, and public art using discarded objects to draw viewers into ritual healing and the celebration of life.

Artworld Information

The Dada and Surrealist movements and their use of dream-like narrative influenced Betye Saar. However, Saar's emphasis on the ritual of the artistic process and on the power of discarded objects places her within the artworld of a number of post-modern artists of color and feminist artists who draw from ancient spiritual traditions in art. These artists, from diverse cultural backgrounds, are involved in synthesizing (combining the energy of) the multiple art traditions that influence the culture of the United States.

Saar has also been considered part of the artworld of the Black Arts and Women's Art movements. When she created *Nine Mojo Secrets* in the early 1970s, the United States was immersed in radical upheaval. The idealism of the Civil Rights Movement, which sought inclusion for African Americans in society, had changed to despair. After the murder of Dr. Martin Luther King, Jr. in 1968, some African Americans turned to ideas of Black nationalism, which inspired the art, music, and literature known as the Black Arts Movement. In the 1970s women also began to protest for their rights. Saar's series *Liberation of Aunt Jemina* [http://www.getty.edu/artsednet/images/X/jemima.html]with its stereotyped images of an African American woman and raised Black fist, became a symbol for the women's movement, although she felt that it was more about "the rights of African Americans, the rage that came up was my concern at the time" (Lovelace, 1977, p. 144).

In 1971, African Americans and others were disillusioned by promises not fulfilled and needed to begin to heal. Just as Navajo sandpaintings are pictures used in a ceremony to promote healing, *Nine Mojo Secrets* might be considered an artwork to meet survival needs of a community. As a *mojo*, this artwork can be thought of as a charm that calls on the beloved ancestors for protection, an object to heal the pain of being Black in a racist society, or an amulet to promote harmony, equality, and acceptance. Instead of the raised Black fist as a symbol of rage, it has spiritual symbols from all over the world that promote healing.

References
Lovelace, C. (1977, May). Weighing in on feminism. *Art News*. 140-144.
Munro, E. (1979). *Originals: American women artists*. New York: Simon and Schuster.

Collecting, Creativity, and Collaboration

Objectives

Students:
1) give examples of symbols and how they are used in society.
2) describe how the intended viewers of an artwork might understand and appreciate a particular artwork.
3) identify and draw upon a range of experiences to express personal meaning in their artmaking.
4) communicate interpretations of artworks supported with reasons.

Activities

Bring in pictures of contemporary and historic symbols and spend some time talking with students about what these symbols mean and what is meant by a symbol. Begin making a bulletin board of pictures of symbols you have collected and ask students to locate pictures from photographs, books, and magazines to contribute to the bulletin board. Ask them to categorize the symbols by thinking about their geographic places of origin, or group them according to whether they are from ancient cultures, from traditional or contemporary popular culture, or from their own regional culture or family.

Ask students to think about how symbols can be used; for example, often they have spiritual or religious meanings, they can be a way to identify with a group, or they can be very personal. Explain that from ancient to contemporary time, a hand print has been considered a symbol of human presence, and often it is the signature of the artist. Ask them to describe the power of a symbol of human presence and to think about why an artist would be symbolized by a hand. Ask students to trace their own hands, paint, sign, and decorate them, cut them out, and add them to the symbols on the bulletin board.

Give students copies of *Nine Mojo Secrets* and ask them to identify the symbols they notice. List the symbols on the board so they can think about where these symbols come from and what they might mean. Explain to students that the picture in the center is of a ceremony in Central Africa (since it will be difficult for them to recognize.) Ask students to think about the name *mojo*. Explain that it is a word often used in the lyrics to blues music, and that it means a special charm or protection. Tell them that the artist, Betye Saar, is a woman who has African, Native American and Irish ancestors, and that she was born under the sign of Leo. Then ask them to explain how some of the symbols in this artwork could have personal meaning to the artist. Discuss the Civil Rights and Black Arts movement with students, and ask them to think about the possible meaning this artwork could have for African Americans, and for people who live in the United States. Ask them to speculate on the reason she named the artwork *Nine Mojo Secrets*.

Explain to students that this artwork is considered an assemblage because it is made with both two-dimensional and three-dimensional objects that Saar collected and arranged inside a wooden frame. Tell them that you would like them to collect some discarded objects for an assemblage that has personal meaning to them. They will need a three-dimensional object for the frame. They should also collect objects with a variety of textures and colors that appeal to them, for example: small rocks, feathers, sticks, leaves, shells, popsicle sticks, junk jewelry, small pieces of metal, postcards, photographs, fabrics, lace, strings and ribbons, textured papers, small mirrors, small plastic figurines, or pieces of discarded toys.

When students bring the objects that will provide the frames for their assemblages and their collections to class, ask them to keep in mind that what they will make should have a personal meaning for them. Allow them to keep their collections visible in their work space. In this way they can see what they have to work with and try out objects until they feel that they have made something that fits well together. Encourage them to play with the design and experiment with how they feel about various arrangements. Invite imagination and risk taking. Tell students they may use paint if they wish, cover their frames with fabric, paper, ribbons, etc.; glue several small boxes together; decorate a cover for their assemblage; or try out other imaginative ideas.

When students have glued things in place, allow them time to think of a symbolic name for their assemblage. Display their work and ask students to comment on the designs, the symbolism of the objects they have used, and how this design is personally meaningful.

Assessment

Students can provide examples of symbols and categorize them by their use in society.

Students can describe in a sketch for a political cartoon how some intended viewers of *Nine Mojo Secrets* such as mainstream museum collectors, members of the Black Arts movement, or diverse groups of people from the many cultures that make up the United States might understand and appreciate it.

Students can comment on the personal meaning and symbolism in the assemblage.

Students can communicate an interpretation of their assemblage by naming it and explaining their meaning either through poetic verse, or with lyrics to a song.

Art Supplies and Other Resources

Copies of *Nine Mojo Secrets*.
For hand prints: paper, crayons, markers, and paint
For assemblages: paint, markers, crayons for color and a variety of means for attaching objects such as glue, tape, wire, string, and staples
Additionally each student will need:
An object that will provide the frame, such as small sturdy cardboard boxes, a tray, or a small wooden drawer or cigar box.
A collection of small discarded objects of various shapes, colors, and textures.

Extension Ideas or Interdisciplinary Connections

Extend this lesson by comparing the symbolism in *Nine Mojo Secrets* with
the symbolism in the Chumash Rock Painting. [Available: http://www.getty.edu/artsednet/images/P/chumash.html]
How do both of these artworks refer to the place of human beings in the universe? (Both artworks have cosmic

symbols. The Chumash may have used the rock painting site as a place to celebrate the winter solstice, when the sun's journey appears to turn and days begin to lengthen.) How might contemporary viewers use *Nine Mojo Secrets* as a celebration?

Science: Use models of the earth, sun, and moon to explain the shadows that cause the crescent shapes of the moon and solar and lunar eclipses. Have students do a drawing of the moon's journey around the earth after this demonstration. Ask students to check the *Farmer's Almanac* to find information on when to expect eclipses to occur and when to expect changes in the moon's appearance. Assign them to watch the moon for one month and construct a visual chart of what they observe. Ask them to compare and discuss how what they see from the viewpoint on earth can help them understand how the moon travels through space. Ask them to compare their observations to ideas about the passage of time and the invention of a calendar.

Literature: Research the mythology of various cultures to find out about beliefs about the moon. Compare what is similar and what is different in these stories.

Part Three: Resources

In this final section the reader will find key resources that support the curriculum unit, Protest and Persuasion, which Faith Clover outlines in Chapter Three and the effectiveness of which Mary Erickson reports on Chapter Four.

The artworks and information in this section come from two complex and overlapping artworlds: one based in Mexico and Chicana/o communities; the other in African American culture. Often artists interested in getting their messages of protest or persuasion to many people without a large expense for each artwork choose printmaking as their medium. The artworks we have selected are all prints. Printmaking allows artists to devote a good deal of time and effort to making a block, plate, silkscreen, or other intermediate form, which they can then use to produce multiple original artworks.

Mexico's great political printmaking tradition is rooted in the work of the prolific popular printmaker José Guadalupe Posada. In the era of the Mexican Revolution of 1910 Mexican Posada's political satire advocated against the 35-year dictatorship of Porfirio Díaz and celebrated revolutionary heroes such as Emiliano Zapata. After the revolution the ruling *Partido Revolucionario Institucional* (PRI) officially encouraged art making that continued to pass on the glories of the Revolution. Printmakers established the *Taller de Gráfica Popular* (Workshop of the People's Graphics) to support progressive ideas and democracy. At the same time the Mexican muralists Alfaro Siqueiros, Diego Rivera, and José Clemente Orozco were known around the world for their revolutionary art.

As Bernard Young notes at the end of the first chapter, "Multicultural Challenges in Art Education," in the middle decades of the 20th century, a shared interest in protest and persuasion brought together artists from the African American and Mexican artworlds. Issues such as segregation and social injustice motivated some prominent African Americans to visit and seek collaboration with well-established Mexican muralists and printmakers working in Mexico City. In later decades many Mexican American artists who sought political solidarity and improved social conditions modeled their efforts on the successes of Mexican printmakers and muralists. Cooperative printmaking workshops thrive in many urban centers around the United States. Community murals also appear in African American and Mexican American neighborhoods in most United States cities.

The eight prints reproduced in this section exemplify the complexity of the enduring, evolving, and overlapping artworlds of African American, Mexican American, and Mexican cultures.

This section concludes with Artworld Analysis worksheets, which present instructions teachers and students can use to extend their understanding of artworlds beyond those provided here. We invite teachers to use these worksheets to prepare lessons and to guide students' appreciation of the artworlds that are most important to their students and communities.

Calavera Revolucionaria[1]

Art Maker
José Guadalupe Posada

Date of Artwork
Circa 1910

Location of Artwork
Calavera Revolutionaria was mass produced as a broadside and found its way into numerous art and culture collections.

Medium
This print is the central image from a larger broadside. José Guadalupe Posada drew the image onto a zinc plate with a greasy medium that protected the marked areas from acid. He then submerged the plate in a light acid bath. The acid eroded into the plate leaving the drawn lines standing in relief. After the acid was rinsed off, a roller was used to ink the plate. The ink adheres to the raised surfaces that had been protected from the acid. The plate was put in a press and the image was printed, usually on newsprint. The image, like most prints, is reversed. That is, the print image is a mirror image of the plate.

Size
The entire broadside, including smaller surrounding images and text, is 14 1/2" x 10 1/2".

Subject Matter
The print shows a female *calavera* (skull/skeleton) riding a horse and swinging a lasso over her head with her right hand. She wears a black scalloped sombrero-type hat and is dressed in a tucked-in sailor blouse with a dark collar. She wears a belt and her skirt flies up exposing her button-up boots or leggings. The *calavera* is riding astride, not side saddle. She also wears a bullet belt with gun slung around her waist.

Her horse is dark with a long white blaze down the middle of its face. The horse's nostrils are flared and its eyes are wide open. The horse is in full gallop with its tail swooping up while it lunges forward. Three of the horse's feet are in the air and only one foot is on the ground. The horse has a medallion around its neck.

At the bottom of the print, under the horse's feet are the small figures of four *campesinos* (farm workers). On the far left is a "living" agricultural worker running with two other "living dead" male *calaveras*. All three wear sombreros. The female *calavera* on the right wears a ribbon on her head. These tiny *calaveras* are overwhelmed by the galloping horse and all are running with their hands in the air. The landscape is mountainous with some vegetation. There are four birds flying in the upper right corner. A decorative, linear, scroll-like design with notches frames the entire image.

Visual Organization
The image is created by printing black ink on light colored paper. The illusion of gray is created by the close proximity of lines. Line variations include thin, thick, scalloped, and curvilinear. Because there are only some very small areas that do not have any marks, the image has an energetic quality.

The composition centers around the triangular shape of the *calavera* and her horse, the images with the highest contrasts in value (light and dark). The repeated lines in the background create a roughly gray effect. Because of this overall grayish tone of the background, viewers may miss details (like birds and mountains) if they do not focus on background areas.

The illusion of shadows, made by the hatched lines, creates a rhythmic quality. The main focal points are the heads of the *calavera revolucionaria* and her horse. Movement is created by the repetition of lines in her skirt and in the horse's tail. The large scale of the *calavera* and her horse emphasizes the importance of these central figures. With only one foot on the ground, the rider and horse illustrate a sense of instability, urgency, power, and speed. The smaller *calaveras* are dominated, trampled under foot, and are left behind in a swirling turbulence of lines.

Short Biography of the Art Maker
José Guadalupe Posada Aguilar was born in Aguascalientes, Mexico, in 1852. He was one of nine male children. As a child, he worked for his uncle, Manuel Posada, in his pottery shop and later assisted his brother who was a rural teacher. At the age of 18, Posada attended art school.

José Posada became an apprentice to José Trinidad Pedroza, a publisher, printer, and graphic artist. Pedroza taught Posada the printmaking techniques for lithography and engraving on wood and metal. It was at this print shop that Posada began political satire. The local government was not hospitable to

Pedroza's and Posada's commentaries. The hostility finally forced them to move to the city León de las Aldamas, in the state of Guanajuato. Here they established a lithography and printing shop. Pedroza moved away and left Posada as the head of the shop, which Posada later bought. In 1888, a terrible flood struck León and Posada was forced to return to Aguascalientes. A few months after, he moved to Mexico City.

There in Mexico City in 1892, José Posada began work and soon became the chief artist with the Publishing House of Don Antonio Vanegas Arroyo, the publisher of newspapers and periodicals. These broadsides and chapbooks were cheap and accessible to the general public, and were disseminated sometimes by the thousands. For the rest of his life, Posada would work closely with Vanegas Arroyo.

José Posada's imagery included natural disasters such as floods, storms, and earthquakes, satirical commentary concerning politics and the common people, ballads, heroes, assassins, tragedy, miracles, death, and revolution. Posada was Mexico's most prolific printmaker. The number of works produced is estimated at 20,000. José Posada died in 1913 at the age of 61 years.

Artworld Information

José Guadalupe Posada was not considered a "fine artist" by the established artworld of his lifetime. He did not paint, nor did his art reflect the romanticism of the Industrial Age. His subject matter pertained to the everyday life and tragedy of the common people. His art communicated the important (and trivial) facts that engaged his audience in history and in popular culture. His art reflects the events of his time.

Although José Posada was not considered a member of the established fine artworld in Mexico City, he was an important artist in the popular artworld of his time. He received his art training through apprenticeships rather than through education at an art academy. Posada was an apprentice to José Trinidad Pedroza, a publisher, printer, and graphic artist. Pedroza taught Posada the printmaking techniques for lithography and engraving on wood and metal. Posada later bought one of Pedroza's commercial shops. Eventually Posada moved to Mexico City and worked as the chief artist of broadsides for Antonio Vanegas Arroyo, the publisher of newspapers and periodicals. These broadsides and chapbooks cost only a few cents and were accessible to the common people.

Calavera Revolutionaria, along with many other of José Guadalupe Posada's works, is taken from a popular broadside. These were inexpensive prints distributed throughout Mexico and were read by many people. The illustrated publications of Vanegas Arroyo allowed those that were illiterate to understand the events of their times. Posada's images could be easily understood by all. They functioned as records, commentary, and satire of events of his time. He did not try to further the glory of Mexico, nor did he have wealthy patrons. His audience was composed of the working class, whose concerns he addressed.

References

Erickson, M. & Keller Cárdenas, G. (1997-9). *Chicana and Chicano Space.*
[On Line]. Available: http://mati.eas.asu.edu:8421/ChicanArte.
The Mexican Fine Arts Center Museum, (1989). *José Guadalupe Posada Aguilar*. Chicago: The Mexican Fine Arts
    Center Museum.

[1]Information about this print is an edited version of text published on *Chicana and Chicano Space* (Erickson & Keller Cárdenas, 1997-9) and used with permission.

Calavera Revolucionaria by José Guadalupe Posada

Untitled Woodcut[1]

Art Maker
Alfredo Zalce

Date of Artwork
1941

Location of Artwork
Collection of Gilberto
Cárdenas

Size
15" x 18"

Medium

Alfredo Zalce's untitled print is a woodcut. Zalce cut into the surface of a block of wood using a gouge. The gouge cut more smoothly and easily with, than against, the linear grain of the wood. The predominance of horizontal lines in Zalce's print suggest that the grain in his block ran horizontally. Straight lines are easier than curved lines to cut into a hard wooden surface. Zalce also executed even, curved forms.

After the artist completed the image, the block was printed onto a sheet of paper. The artist applied ink to the surface of the block with a brayer (roller). The brayer rolled across the uncut surfaces of the block distributing ink, but did not reach down to ink the gouged areas. The artist placed a sheet of paper over the inked block and applied pressure. When the paper was removed it presented a reverse image of the block.

Zalce's paper was larger than the block. The block was only as large as the outermost areas of black on the print. The white areas of Zalce's print are untouched paper. The black areas were printed with the ink from the uncut top surfaces of the block. When Zalce planned his print he had to work backwards, making marks where there would be untouched paper in his print and placing guns on the left, if he wanted them to appear on the right in his final print.

Subject Matter

The woodcut depicts a scene containing well-known features of the Mexican Revolution of 1910-1919. In the foreground lies a humble, wounded Mexican revolutionary of Indian stock. He wears the traditional dress and sandals (called *huaraches*) of the Mexican peasant. His barefoot female companion is tending to his head wound. She is identified as one of the *rieleras* (camp followers, riding the comandeered trains with their male revolutionary counterparts) through reference to the locomotive that fills the upper left background. In the right foreground, rifles are arrayed in a self-supporting tripod, in the middle of a large cache of ammunition, including cartridge belts. In the right background appear Mexican peasants against a backdrop of mountains or large hills. One is a male revolutionary with a rifle and three are women carrying loads.

Visual Organization

Alfredo Zalce's print includes a variety of textured areas, for example, thin, parallel, straight lines in the train engine; long, slightly curved, tapered gouges in the sky; shorter gouges in many directions in the mountains; and quite short, almost triangular gouges on the ground.

There is a strong formal contrast between, on the one hand, vertical and horizontal lines, and, on the other, diagonals. The vertical and horizontal lines are prominent in the recumbent, ailing revolutionary, the horizontal railroad tracks, and the locomotive. Set against these and somewhat in opposition to them are the diagonals that characterize the rifles and the woman. The diagonals that frame the woman especially contrast with the horizontals that set off the man. In this formal use of line, in the subject matter (a woman nursing a wounded man with a bandage), and in the dynamic posture of the woman, caught in mid-movement, partially kneeling and steadied by her covered right leg and tense left foot, which is supporting her weight, there is an echo of the Pietás and similar images of women comforting Christ or a saint that were common to the Old Masters.

Short Biography of the Art Maker

Alfredo Zalce was born January 12, 1908 in Patzcuaro, Michoacán, Mexico. His father and mother were both professional photographers. Zalce attended elementary and high school in Mexico City; during these years he also helped his parents develop film. He studied art (supporting himself as a photographer) at the *Escuela Central de Artes Plásticas*. When he was 20 his works were exhibited in the Mexican pavilion of the *Exposición de Artes e Industrias,* Seville, Spain (1928), where he won second place in the category of painting.

In 1930 the Mexican government gave him the assignment to found a painting school in Taxco, Guerrero. In 1931 he began attending the lithography workshop of Emilio Amero and he has produced numerous lithographs dating from that year. In 1932 he became an art teacher working for the Mexican Secretariat of Public Education and he completed two al fresco murals at two separate public schools.

His first one-man show (both prints arts and paintings) was in 1932 at the *Sala de Arte de la Secretaría de Educación Pública*. The following year he exhibited in Chicago.

Zalce was a very active member of politically progressive groups including the *Liga de Escritores y Artistas Revolucionarios* (League of Revolutionary Writers and Artists, 1933-dissolved in 1937), and in 1937 he was one of the cofounders of the *Taller de Gráfica Popular* (Workshop of the People's Graphics). He completed important commissions and his work as exhibited widely.

In 1950 he became the director of the *Escuela Popular de Bellas Artes de Morelia* (sponsored by the University of Michoacán) and the *Escuela de Pintura y Artesanías de Morelia* (sponsored by the *Instituto Nacional de Bellas Artes*).

In 1960, 17 of his prints formed part of the collective exhibition of, the TGP, "450 años de lucha. Homenaje al pueblo mexicano." In 1981, the *Museo de Arte Moderno de Chapultepec* (Mexico City) had a major retrospective celebrating 50 years of his work in which were exhibited 200 works of painting, sculpture, textiles, drawings, and graphics.

Artworld Information

In the 1940s the artists of the *Taller de Gráfica Popular*, depicted the Mexican Revolution or other images of workers, peasants and ordinary Mexicans without self-consciousness or a sense that they were being coopted for public relations purposes by the Mexican government. The *Taller de Gráfica Popular* emerged out of the earlier *Liga de Escritores y Artistas Revolucionarios* (League of Revolutionary Writers and Artists, 1933-1937), as a leftwing, progressive group of artists in response to and encouraged by the administration of Mexican president Lázaro Cárdenas.

This was a period where there was a close correlation between the creation of art and political activities. The "Declaration of Principles" of the *Taller de Gráfica Popular* makes that clear, stating: "The TGP undergoes a constant effort, in order to benefit by its works the progressive and democratic people, especially in the fight against fascist reaction. Considering that the social aim of plastic art is inseparable from good artistic quality, the TGP strives to develop the individual technical capacity of its members. The TGP lends its professional cooperation to similar workshops and cultural institutions, to popular or labor organizations and to all progressive movements and institutions" (Taller de Gráfica Popular, 1949).

Writing in 1947, Alfredo Zalce expressed his general views about the goals of the TGP. That statement well summarized Zalce's intention about the untitled woodcut: "The goals of those of us who founded the TGP were to do graphics for the people: our clients were workers, organizations. Prints had an established function and a real consumer, not a hypothetical client. The TGP did not enter contests nor did we win prizes or honorifics. We did not follow fashions because our work was vital. With all frankness, if a print was not liked by those who had asked for it or by other members of the TGP, it was redone and that was that. If critics liked it or didn't like our art was of no importance because our efforts reflected our participation in an anti-Nazi celebration, the founding of a school, or a First of May celebration. A specific social climate caused our art to flower" (Zalce, 1987, p. 179).

The viewers for whom the work was created were the common or humble Mexican workers and peasants, both men and women. The work has a certain didactic purpose, to illustrate a liberating aspect of the Mexican revolution in which men and women worked together for a common purpose. The artwork was part of a government-supported and sanctioned corpus of popular, widely circulated revolutionary images. While the images were stirring, militant, and often violent, they were not controversial. The Mexican citizenry of the 1930s and 1940s reflected back on its Revolution with great pride and for the most part strongly supported the Mexican government and the *Partido Revolucionario Institucional* (PRI), which had inherited that Revolution.

References

Erickson, M. & Keller Cárdenas, G. (1997-9). *Chicana and Chicano Space.* [On Line]. Available: http://mati.eas.asu.edu:8421/ChicanArte.

El Taller de Gráfica Popular. (1949). *El Taller de Gráfica Popular.: doce años de obra artística colectiva/The Workshop for Popular Graphic Art: A Record of Twelve Years of Collective Work.* Mexico City: La Estampa Mexicana.

Zalce, A. (1987). Alfredo Zalce letter to Antonio Rodríguez, 1949. In Raquel Tibol, *Gráficas y neográficas en México,* Trans. by Gary D. Keller Cárdenas.Mexico City: Secretaría de Educación Pública/Universidad Nacional de México, 1987.

[1]Information about this print is an edited version of text published on *Chicana and Chicano Space* (Erickson & Keller Cárdenas, 1997-9) and used with permission.

Untitled Woodcut by Alfredo Zalce

Untitled Linocut[1]

Art Maker
Carlos Cortez Koyokuikatl

Date of Artwork
1978

Location of Artwork
Collection of Gary D. Keller Cárdenas

Medium
Carlos Cortez's print is a linoleum block print or linocut. Linoleum printing is a relatively recent relief-printing technique. Cortez could cut freely in any direction in making an image on a linoleum block because linoleum, unlike wood, has no grain. As with the much older woodcut technique, the artist carved away the sections to remain untouched by ink (in this case the white areas), leaving the areas to be printed (in this case the black areas) untouched. After he rolled over the untouched surfaces and placed a sheet of paper over the inked linoleum block, he applied pressure to produce the print. The printed image is a mirror image of the linoleum block. So in order to make readable letters on the manifesto, Cortez had to not only leave the letters standing while he carved out the white, negative spaces around them, he also had to do this while carving in reverse.

Size
29 1/2" x 19 1/2"

Subject Matter

Carlos Cortez's woodcut depicts the Mexican Revolutionary, Ricardo Flores Magón (1873-1922) from his cell in the Leavenworth Federal Penitentiary. Magón is wearing a prison suit and stands before prison bars. He stands at a 3/4 angle to the viewer. He has thick hair, eyeglasses, a mustache, and strong features. In his right hand Magón holds a fountain pen and in his left a sheet of paper with printed words and his signature. The paper displays a manifesto that he has just completed and signed that criticizes "art for art's sake." The translation of the letter is as follows:

> This stuff of "art for its own sake" is an absurdity and its defenders have always gotten on my nerves. I feel such a reverent admiration and love for art that it causes me great distress to see it prostituted by individuals who, incapable of having others feel what they feel nor think what they think, hide their impotence behind the slogan of "art for art's sake."

The name and address of a Chicano art organization appear at the bottom of the print.

Visual Organization

Carlos Cortez's print uses only black and white. Cortez used high value contrast to great advantage. This is vividly apparent in Flores Magón's striped prison suit; the interlacing of the white bars and the black spaces between them; the white face set against the foreground of the black mustache, eyeglasses, and hair; the black pen held in the white hand; and the manifesto that appears in black against a white sheet of paper. The contrasts of black and white reinforce the manifesto itself which is neither subtle nor nuanced, but rather, expresses direct antagonism toward the notion of "art for art's sake."

The viewer is situated in the same space, the prison cell, as Flores Magón. Thus, the perspective is from the inside with the viewer able to see nothing outside of the cell bars except black spaces. The figure of Flores Magón, particularly his head and hands, is drawn primarily with softer, rounder contours that contrast sharply with the horizontal stripes of the prisoner's outfit, which he is forced to wear. The prison bars, which also are imposed upon him, feature austere vertical and horizontal lines filled with black spaces.

Short Biography of the Art Maker

Researcher Archie Green tells us that Industrial Workers of the World artists "have been modest in telling their life-stories," and "within this laconic tradition, Carlos Cortez reports key facts" (Green, 1997, p. 5). These facts include the following: Carlos Cortez was born on August 13, 1923 in Milwaukee, Wisconsin. He was the son of Alfredo Cortez, a Mexican partisan of the Industrial Workers of the World (acronym, IWW, popularly known as "Wobblies"), and a German socialist-pacifist Augusta Cortez. He grew up in Milwaukee and later moved to Chicago. He spent two years in federal prison (Sandstone, Minnesota) during World War II as a conscientious objector "because he did not want to kill living things" (Nelson, 1997, p. 6).

Upon his release from federal detention in 1947 he joined the IWW and has remained active for five decades as a graphic artist, poet, and advisor within that organization. In 1985 at the Gato Negro Press (Black Cat Press) he printed a catalog for a touring exhibition of cartoons, *Wobbly: 80 Years of Rebel Art.*

Cortez has been a muralist, woodblock and linoleum-block artist, and cartoonist. He added the name Koyokuikatl (using the Náhuatl word for coyote) as an adult, but usually does not include it in identifying his poetry. He typically signs his art with the letters CAC, the imprint of a coyote baying upward, and a date.

His formal art training consisted of two years of art basics in high school and later night classes at Layton Art School (uncredited).

He says of his current life: "After some 40 years of being a construction laborer, record salesman, bookseller, factory stiff and janitor, I am no longer punching a clock for some employer and am now engaged in the most productive phase of my life" (Cortez, 1997).

Carlos Cortez has had numerous exhibits in Illinois, California, New York, Colorado, Mexico, Canada, and Germany. Cortez has given a multitude of workshops, demonstrations, and lectures at numerous elementary and high schools and colleges in the greater Chicago area and at the Field Museum and the Chicago Art Institute Children's Museum, the University of California, Santa Cruz and the University of Wisconsin, Green Bay.

Carlos Cortez is also a well-known poet whose poems have been published as books and in magazines. Some of his poems have been reprinted in school textbooks as examples of argumentation.

Artworld Information

Carlos Cortez has been a "Wobbly" for over 50 years. The organization was founded in 1905 in Chicago when syndicalists, trade-unionists and socialists gathered together to create the Industrial Workers of the World (IWW) in order to work toward "a commonwealth of toil—a revolutionary order to be achieved within a decade" (Green, 1997, p. 5).

The Wobblies have been very active not only in labor economics but art and literature. They rejected Marxism, the Communist Party/Popular Front politics of the 1930s-40s, and the notion of a "party line" in art and culture, that is an officially sanctioned form of art. In contrast to Communist Party cultural activities, the IWW artists are notable for their exuberance and diversity. While most of their art is realist in nature, some Wobblies worked in expressionism and some even experimented with the modernism of James Joyce and Pablo Picasso. The Wobblies internationalized issues of gender and ethnicity and the support of environmentalism long before craft unionists generally, and faced challenges even before many radicals.

The IWW was similar to the Mexican *Taller de Gráfica Popular* of the 1940s in that there was a close correlation between the creation of art and political activities. There was one major difference however, in that the Wobblies were self-supported from the funds of its worker membership while the *Taller de Gráfica Popular* was an officially supported institution of the Mexican government of the period, which identified itself as "revolutionary" in nature.

At the lower left of the linocut the words *Movimiento Artístico Chicano* (Chicano Art Movement) appear and at the lower right are the box number and address where copies of the linocut can be obtained. The reference to the *Movimiento Artístico Chicano* is an important link between the early 20th century Mexican hero who is being depicted and the Chicanos of the 1970s who have been inspired by him.

References

Cortez, C. (1997). Unpublished resume submitted by the artist.

Green, A. (1997). Carlos Cortez and Wobbly artistry, In C. Cortez, *Where are the voices and other Wobbly poems?* Chicago: Charles H. Kerr.

Nelson, E. (1997). Introduction. In C. Cortez, *Where are the voices and other Wobbly poems?* Chicago: Charles H. Kerr.

[1]Information about this print is an editied version of a text published on *Chicana and Chicano Space* (Erickson & Keller Cárdenas. 1997-9) and used with permission.

Untitled Linocut by Carlos Cortez Koyokuikatl

Divides and Conquers[1]

Art Maker
Lisza Jaurigue

Date of the Artwork
1998

Location of the Artwork
Collection of Mary Erickson

Size
9" x 12"

Medium

Divides and Conquers is a linoleum block print or linocut. The image was printed on a thick, heavy, absorbent acid-free paper. Using a variety of "u" and "v" shaped cutting tools, the image was carved out of a piece of linoleum. The negative/white areas were cut away. The raised linoleum was then inked using a rubber roller. The acrylic ink and a drying retarder were mixed to a consistency similar to a self-leveling honey. Before inking the linoleum, the artist first rolled out a square to assure that the roller was evenly inked. A thin layer of ink was then applied onto the linoleum using the roller.

After inking the plate, Lisza Jaurigue prepared the paper. After soaking the paper in water for a couple of minutes, she placed it between two sheets of dry paper. She next used a rolling pin and rolled over the papers to soak up any excess water. She removed the damp sheet of paper and placed it in the middle of another dry sheet of paper. Before printing, she aligned the block in the middle of the paper leaving equal space at the top and at the sides and about double the space at the bottom. She then placed the inked block onto the damp paper.

Jaurigue next carefully flipped the block and paper so the block is at the bottom. Using the back of her knife, which has a rounded bottom, she proceeded to rub every area of the plate. Spoons can also be used to rub the block. She knew she was finished when the image and its outline could be seen on the paper. She carefully peeled the paper from the plate.

Divides and Conquers is the first in an edition. It is not however the first print made from the block. The very first print was the artist's proof. Jaurigue used this proof to gauge how much pressure and ink were required to achieve the printed results she wants. There are 15 prints made in the edition. More prints may be made in the future, depending on demand, but no more than a total of 80 prints will be made.

Subject Matter

In *Divides and Conquers,* there are two rows of clenched fists. Four rows of barbed wire divide the fists from each other. Some of the hands belong to women, indicated by their long fingernails.

Lisza Juarigue writes "In *Divides and Conquers*, I wanted the fists to show signs of strength, unity, and stability. But I also wanted the print to give a feeling of division and confusion. In so doing I eliminated deep space in the work and wanted everything to be pushed forward, in order to give a sense of immediate action" (Jaurigue, 1998).

The concept of *Divides and Conquers* portrays a specific type of protest. That which is being protested—barbed wire, literally and conceptually divides the imagery of Divides and Conquers. The wire conceptually symbolizes the issues involved concerning the *frontera* (southern border of the United States) and the division of the people its fences were intended to keep out.

Visual Organization

The visual elements that are particularly important in this artwork are line, shape, mass, space, and value (light and dark). Lines create the mass of the images, while light and dark create the imagery. The positive and negative shapes determine the space of the entire image.

The composition of *Divides and Conquers* moves from the triangular shape of the three middle fists, outward toward the other fists behind the wires. Horizontal rhythm is created by the barbed wires that interlace between the fists, while also holding the fists back. The fists form a repeated pattern of lights and darks. These darks and lights are in a stark contrast with each other.

Short Biography of the Art Maker

Lisza Jaurigue was born, raised, and went to school in Phoenix, Arizona. She is of Xicana (Juarigue's preferred spelling of Chicana), Yaqui Indian, and Spanish (Basque) descent. She received her B.A. from Vassar College in philosophy, with minors in studio art and Spanish literature. She received a master's degree from Arizona State University. Jaurigue has also lived in New York, Berlin, and Ecuador. She has taught philosophy, world and Native religions, art history, and Mexican art history at the Guadalupe Learning Center, in the town of Guadalupe, Arizona known for its large Yaqui community, as well as other community colleges. She has taught at Arizona State University and served as teacher or speaker in many other settings, including the Phoenix Art Museum, art galleries across Arizona, and in programs sponsored by Chicanos por La Causa, Free Arts for Abused Children, and the Boys' and Girls' Clubs of the greater Phoenix area. Jaurigue created the graphics used Chicana and Chicano Space, a Website of Arizona State University's Hispanic Research Center (Erickson & Keller Cárdenas, 1997-9). She lives with her artist husband, Marcus Zilliox, in Tempe, Arizona.

Artworld Information

From early childhood Lisza Jaurigue's Nana (Grandmother), Lupe, taught her a variety of sculptural media including textiles and ceramics. Her mother and aunts taught her how to draw. She studied art at Vassar. She cites Käthe Kollwitz, Malaquias Montoya, Carmen de Novais and Zarco Guerrero among the artists whose work has influenced her own.

Jaurigue is currently involved in many ways with the artworlds of the metropolitan Phoenix area. The Chicana/o artworld is a major contributor among various artworlds in the greater Phoenix area. The Chicana/o movement in Phoenix was pioneered by a handful of local artists during the 1970s. Many of the founding artists are very involved in raising artistic experience and awareness that continue today. These artists established organizations, such as MARS Artspace (*Movimiento Artistico del Rio Salado*), and Xicanindio Arts that still provide space for art and artists.

Often community organizations, such as El Museo Chicano and the Cultural Coalition, sponsor activities and opportunities for artists and community involvement. There are strong ties within the Chicana/o arts community. Zarco Guerrero early on helped in the establishment of Chicana/o organizations and in mobilizing the Mexican communities in the greater Phoenix area. Among the variety of experiences provided by these organizations, are Mexican celebrations including *Día de Los Muertos* (Day of the Dead). These festivities bring the Mexican/ Chicana/o communities together along with other communities that share an interest. These festivities provide opportunities for local artists to develop, organize, and participate in a variety of different mediums, from music to dance, and installations/*ofrendas* (altars). For *Dia de Los Muertos* fiestas, Native American and African communities also participate in the presentation of music and dance. Juarigue builds *ofrendas*/installations for many *Día de Los Muertos* celebrations in the area.

Juarigue has curated shows, received numerous commissions, and participated in many solo and group shows. She is best known for her paintings that use glitter exclusively for color. Her work has been exhibited in Arizona, California, Texas, Colorado, New York, Mexico, India, and Germany.

References

Jaurigue, L. (1998). Questions and answers about Lisza Jaurigue's *Divides and Conquers*. (unpublished manuscript).
Erickson, M.& Keller Cárdenas, G. (1997-9). *Chicana and Chicano Space*. [OnLine]. http://mati.eas.asu.edu.: ChicanArte.

[1]Information about this print is an edited version of text originally written by the artist under contract with the Getty Education Institute (Jaurigue, 1998).

Divides And Conquers By Lisza Jaurigue

Solid as a Rock

Art Maker
Charles White

Date of Artwork
1963

Location of Artwork
Reproduced in book,
*Images of Dignity: The
Drawings of Charles White*
(Belafonte, 1967).

Size
Unknown

Medium

A linocut is a print made from a design cut into a mounted piece of linoleum. It is a member of the relief family of prints. Relief prints result from a raised printing surface. The portion of the block or plate meant to take the ink is raised, while the non-printing areas are cut away below the surface. The most common form of relief printing is the woodcut. In this method an image is drawn on a wood block, and then the non-image areas are cut away with sharp tools. Variations of the relief process include linoleum block printing (linocut) and wood engraving.

Linocuts are relief prints. The design is drawn on the surface of mounted linoleum. The areas that are to be blank are cut away, leaving raised the design that is to be printed. Ink is then rolled or daubed over the raised area. A sheet of paper is placed on top of the block and pressed against it, either in a press or by hand. This pressure transfers the ink to the paper. Since the print is the mirror image of the design on the block, the image must be conceived in the reverse. A rubber stamp is a common example of relief printing process.

Subject Matter

Solid As a Rock is a solid female figure that looks as if it were carved from a solid rock. A tall image of an African-American figure appears to be a hero, standing still, wearing a long robe. The rows around her neck that could be carved beads emphasize the large strong structure of her neck. The figure is built like a Black goddess that is prepared to take on any unknown forces that may arrive to attack. The figure has large muscular arms, hands, feet, and a serious face that appears to be chiseled from a rock. The figure appears to represent a victorious leader.

The title of the work indicates that the artist believes leaders for African Americans were important, needed, and had to be solid as a rock. The leaders White portrayed had to be solid morally and solid physically to lead an oppressed people in the United States. The image takes up the entire surface of the plate with the exception of a few spaces surrounding the figure, which are white and highlight the shape and form of the figure. The left hand and feet of the figure also show the strength of the figure.

Charles White was inspired by the dignity of African Americans and a love for spirituals. Negro spirituals are religious or sacred songs that originated among slaves in the southern part of the United States. Some of these songs were developed years after slavery and were taken directly out of stories in the Christian Bible. Many of these songs dealt with spiritual issues rather than material matters. Some Negro spirituals reflect an identification with suffering and the belief of being delivered from sorrows of this world. *Go Down Moses, I'm Marching to Zion, Steal Away,* and *Together On Our Knees* are just a few songs that basically created imagery and words of how the Spirit of God would eventually deliver African Americans from their earthly trials and tribulations. The spirituals affirmed a complete trust in God to make right in the next world what was wrong in this world.

These songs, as well as the titles of many of White's drawings and paintings, are of hope and despair. Often scriptures describe a graphic historical story of early

African Americans much like the art of storytelling used by Africans during the same time period. It is very likely the figure in "Solid as a Rock" may very well represent a character from one of the spirituals Charles White respected and often created in his work.

Visual Organization

The organization of the image is contained in the figure of the linocut. The use of linocut is detailed with hundreds of lines that create a massive figure looking into the future. All the important characteristics of this print are contained in this figure. The texture and intricate cuts are in a dominating figure that emits power from within. The background is cut with less detail to give the foreground the emphasis of force and texture. The black and white print makes great use of the dark, gray, and white areas that define the space of the figure.

Short Biography of the Art Maker

Charles White's grandfather was a slave in Mississippi, and his mother lived most of her life in the South. White was born on April 2, 1918, to Ethel Gary and Charles White, Sr., in Chicago, where the family had migrated. His father was a railroad and construction worker and his mother was a domestic worker. His father died when White was very young. White, an only child, and his mother took care of each other.

White began his formal training in art when he was about 15 years old taking art classes at the South Side Settlement House. He later won a scholarship to the Chicago Art Institute that allowed him to qualify for employment with the Works Progress Administration (WPA) art program for three years. This was his first opportunity to work full time with other artists. In 1939 he was invited to show his work at Howard University with artists such as Archibald John Motley, Charles David, Eldzier Cortor and others. During this period he started speaking in community centers about Negro heroes of American history and painting pictures of them. One mural was called *Five Great American Negroes*. By the age of 22 in 1940, Charles White's career was off to a great start as he continued to receive coveted commissions, publicity, and respect from his peers.

The titles of many of his works are named after spirituals: *Move On Up A Little Higher* depicts a woman with her palms stretched towards heaven; *Take My Mother Home* (1957) is a drawing that focuses on the plight of elderly African Americans, who are often denied nursing home care. Possessing the richness, power, and moving simplicity of spirituals, the graphic art and paintings of Charles White have illustrated that democracy and equality are for all Americans. His meticulously rendered drawings and paintings of African Americans have won him the distinction of being labeled one of the finest draftsman in contemporary America.

In looking at the work of Charles White it must not be overlooked that he had a profound influence on his students and younger African American artists, such as John Biggers, David Hammons, Richard Wyatt, and John Wilson, to name a few. John Biggers said that for a number of years he turned out "little Charles Whites." Biggers further relates that many of his colleagues as well as himself have taught Charles White as a major subject to art students through the years. (Young, 2001, p. 80). He was the second African American artist (after Henry Ossawa Tanner in 1927) to be elected a full member of the National Academy of Design in 1973. His work is found in 49 museums in the United States, Mexico and Europe.

Artworld Information

There are many people in the African American Artworld. Not all of them are involved in protest art or printmaking. A few of the printmakers from the African-American Artworld include: Charles White, Elizabeth Catlett, John Scott, William Smith, Jacob Lawrence, Romare Bearden, Allan Edmunds, Willie Robert Middlebrook, James Lesesne Wells, Lois Mailou Jones, John Biggers, Rip Woods, Alvin Loving, Sam Gilliam, Leon Hicks, David Hammons, and a host of others.

There are other people in this artworld who are not necessarily artists, like Samella Lewis and Sharon F. Patton, David C. Driskell, Leslie King-Hammond and Lowery S. Sims. These are a few of the people who are African American art historians and curators at major museums of art in America. Some of these people are both art historians and artists.

African American art can be seen in most major museums in this country. Each museum may not have many pieces of work by African Americans, but if you inquire you will locate the artwork. A concentrated effort of this art can be found in museums that specialize in the work of African American artists and multicultural artists such as Robert Blackburn's Printmaking Workshop in New York (opened in 1948), the Schomburg Center for Research on Black Culture in New York, Brandywine Workshop in Philadelphia, the Studio Museum in Harlem, California Afro-American Museum, DuSable Museum in Chicago, Hampton University in Virginia, George Washington Carver Museum in Austin, Texas, Museum of African-American Life and Culture in Dallas, Texas. These are only a few of the places where you can study about African American art and culture.

References
Belafonte, H., Porter, J. & Horwitz, B. (1967). Images of dignity: The drawings of Charles White. Los Angeles, CA: W. Ritchie Press.
Young, B. (2001, July) *African American Arts and Cultures*. Unpublished manuscript.

Solid As A Rock By Charles White

St. George

Art Maker
John T. Scott

Date of Artwork
1992

Location of Artwork
Brandywine Workshop,
Philadelphia, Pennsylvania

Medium
Linocut

Size
Approxiately 9" x 11.5"

Subject Matter

The linoleum print of *St. George*, is a highly detailed print of an African American soldier in a civil war union army uniform, that is ready for war. His designation as a saint seems to indicate that he is a warrior that protects the church and what it represents. The object he is holding is a symbol of a cross, the right side of his chest holds a cross, his hands and clothing are decorated with small crosses, and the silhouette behind his head is the symbol of a cross. While this soldier may not have the look of a traditional saint, he does have the stature of a noble soldier. It is common for Scott to use puns as he does in this print. According to John Scott, St. George is ready to fight and conquer the dragon with his spear. The dragon that is not present in the picture is racial injustice in the United States.

Visual Organization

This bold print uses every bit of the printing area to create a bold black-and-white texture. Some of the linoleum cuts appear to be bold unrelated lines that fall into place once you look at the entire print to create the larger image of a fighter. The image of St. George is dynamic with enlarged African American facial features that have been common trademarks in pictures over the years. What is not common is the image of an African American leader that is dressed in gear ready to go to war for spiritual or territorial reasons. As a true king or general of legends of soldiers, this sage character is ready for action. St. George complete with symbolism in the forms of the cross represents that there is good and evil. Certainly this print represents that good will win out over evil.

Short Biography of the Art Maker

John T. Scott, was born in New Orleans in 1940, Louisiana. He received a B.A. in 1960 from Xavier University of Louisiana; in 1965 he earned a Master of Fine Arts degree from Michigan State University. He is also the recipient of three honorary Doctoral degrees.

From 1965 to the present he has been a professor of fine arts at Xavier University. He is a versatile artist with exceptional skills in numerous areas. He has taught sculpture, modeling, carving (wood, stone), casting (bronze, aluminum), printmaking (relief, silk screening, etching, stone lithography, collagraph, design, (two- and three-dimensional), drawing, papermaking, and calligraphy. He also served as the department chairman from 1974-80.

In 1992 he won the prestigious John D. MacArthur Fellowship. In describing his work he has said, "What I've been trying to do for the last thirty-something years is make a piece that would be similar to what African American musicians have done with gospel and blues and jazz. So that when you hear it, it wraps your soul."

Since the 1970s, Scott's work has shifted from a figurative style to a more abstract style, and back and forth with combinations of both styles. Most recently he has made sculptures that are kinetic works that are inspired by African instruments or forms.

upbringing as a Catholic. He attended Holy Cross Church in New Orleans and the public schools until he attended a Catholic university. While at Xavier University, Scott was influenced by the determination and spiritual strength of his teachers. He states that he has been striving to become a spiritual thinker or a jazz thinker for years. Jazz music, the musicians, his spiritual upbringing, and his heritage from the continent of Africa influence his work.

Artworld Information

Just as in the Chicana/o culture African Americans are involved in a tradition of activities involving protest and persuasion, organizational meetings in churches, and in the streets, speeches, petitions, marches, sit-ins, strikes, boycotts and battles in the Supreme Court and lower courts.

Alain Locke the philosopher thought the goals for "New Negro" artists in the 1920s should use African art as the formal foundation for their works, and this is a position still held by many artists today.

Political and social agitation inspired the images of African American art during the 1960s. Some people believe that all of these artists had to use protest and persuasion in order to be considered "Black" artists.

The art activist and historian Edmund B. Gaither believed that only those who based their art on African culture and African American culture and history qualified as "Black" artists. This certainly raised numerous debates about defining Black art.

Literary critic Addison Gayle published a book (1971) which outlined an agenda for a new Black art movement. He believed there was a "Black Art Aesthetic" that uniquely belonged to African Americans. He also believed this was part of a political revolution that would help Blacks to stop having a "double-consciousness," a sense of always looking at one's self through the eyes of others, which must be overcome in order to arrive at true self-worth. John Scott's work represents the combined thinking of the old and the new in African American art. His older work uses representational images to depict protest and persuasion and his new abstract work symbolizes African-American thought and the traditions of Gospel, Blues, and Jazz. The kinetic aspects of his work create conceptual environments that engage the viewer into thinking about the art piece as an experience. His sculptures that emphasize kinetic art have mechanical parts that can be set in motion. For example, his sculpture *T-2 Harriet* (1988), painted steel of life-size dowels, appears to play musical sounds as wind and light hit the steel. *Akhanten Rowboat* is painted wood and brass that creates the environment of a rowboat while it lacks the mass and physical elements of a rowboat. His nonrepresentational works are conceptual visual constructions and art experiences.

References
Gayle, A. (1971) *The Black Aesthetic*. New York: Doubleday.
Interview with John Scott, by B. Young at ASU, April 24, 1998.

St. George By John T. Scott

Defense Worker

Art Maker
Dox Thrash

Date of Artwork
1941

Location of Artwork
Federal Works Agency,
Works Progress Administration
on deposit at the Philadelphia
Museum of Art

Medium
Carbograph

Size
9 1/2" x 8 1/4"

The Defense Worker is a Carbograph, or Carborundum print. From 1935 to 1942 Thrash worked in the Graphic Arts Division of the WPA, where he invented and refined the Carborundum print technique. Dox Thrash and a group of artists under his direction created the carborundum print technique. The carborundum tint process is a copperplate intaglio print-making method. Using carborundum as a grinding agent to prepare engraving plates, the artists were able to achieve new levels of shade and tone in their prints. The printing of a carborundum tint is almost identical to that of an etching except that the process is on the whole simpler. Experiments with the process proved that it was quite possible to combine line, either bitten or dry-point, with the carborundum tone, by etching the plate before the abrasive is used.

One day, in the studio, Thrash decided to use carborundum to make changes and variations to lines in an etching and the result became his discovery, the Carborundum Print Process. Later as he further experimented he developed the Carborundum Print, the Carborundum Etching, and the Color Carborundum Print.

Subject Matter

Thrash's image of the *Defense Worker* (1941) is an example of the Carborundum Print. The subject matter and the process that was used by Thrash go hand in hand in describing the subject. The *Defense Worker* demonstrates not only this new printing method and the nation's involvement with World War II, but also one of the first involvements of African Americans in the defense industry. Before 1941 this industry was segregated and African Americans were not permitted to work on armaments. This print serves as a symbol of an American war effort with race unity. The *Defense Worker* is an image of a worker drilling into the ground during World War II and symbolizes what it's like to be an African American during the second world war that is intentionally making a political and social statement about working in an open and free society, a society that still has problems with the questions about race and equity.

Visual Organization

The *Defense Worker* is a large image of a proud man that is darkly etched in lines highlighted and contrasted before a bright background of light, which, in turn is surrounded in black. The curved, dark, form of the central figure is dramatically set off by strongly contrasting white negative spaces. A flame-like cloud of billowing white defines the figure on right and left. The most powerful light-dark contrast defines the figure's hand on the drill and his trousered legs. Rounded shapes and lines unify both the positive and negative areas of the print. A circle (button?) appears on the figure's jacket or shirt. His cap and its bill are curved as are his cheeks, trouser cuffs, shoe soles, glove tops, rings on his drill, and the air hose and its shadow as they cross the contour of his leg. The arched form of the figure emphasizes the strong central vertical of the drill. The image may represent the same insufferable treatment Thrash received during this same period of time he applied for employment in civil defense work.

Short Biography of the Art Maker

Dox Thrash was born to Gus and Ophelia Thrash March 22, the year is believed to be 1893, in Griffin, a small rural town in Georgia. He was one of four children, nothing is known about his father and it is believed that his mother raised him and his siblings as a single parent. The Thrash family lived on the outskirts of town in a former slave cabin built on a small tract of land that lead to the city of Atlanta. Many of Thrash's prints made during the 1930s and 1940s are based on his memories of growing up in rural Georgia. He started to dream of his future career as an artist at a young age. He nurtured his talent for drawing by studying art through correspondence courses and this activity continued after he left home in 1908 at the age of fifteen. In April, 1917 his studies were interrupted, he joined the army as the United States entered World War I. He severed as a private in the 365th Infantry Regiment, 183rd Brigade of the all–black 92nd Division. After Thrash completed his service in the Army he took evening classes before enrolling in the Art Institute of Chicago as a full-time student in the fall of 1920. For the next three years Thrash studied continuously and enrolled in painting, drawing, graphic design, mural making and a combination of commercial art courses. In the 1930s he started to receive some recognition for his art abilities and mural painting.

The period of the 1930s was filled with the excitement of artistic growth and revitalization. Federal funding during the Depression provided by the Works Progress Administration / Federal Art Project (WPA/FAP) supported regional workshops where artists were encouraged to experiment with a wide variety of artmaking processes. Philadelphia had the only Graphic Arts Division of the WPA that was devoted entirely to the development and production of fine art prints. Dox Thrash became the head of the Graphic Division. His formal education at the School of the Art Institute of Chicago and the Philadelphia Graphic Art Sketch Club (now the Fleisher Art Memorial) laid a firm foundation for his career. From 1935-1942 he produced 47 prints with the Federal Arts Project. His prints covered a wide range of subjects including landscapes, portraits, and some interesting dark views of Philadelphia Slum neighborhoods. Thrash's work that includes over one hundred prints, drawings, and watercolors is well represented in the collections of The Philadelphia Museum of Art, The Free Library of Philadelphia and the National Museum of American History at the Smithsonian Institution.

Artworld Information

In 1935 Franklin Delano Roosevelt formed the Works Progress Administration (later renamed the Works Project Administration—WPA) to create jobs that would allow individuals to maintain their sense of self-esteem. The national government supported programs for artists that placed emphasis on community participation in the arts. The WPA/Fine Arts Program (WPA/FAP) originated out of a fear that artists' skills would deteriorate if not used. In September 1935, the United States government appointed Holger Cahill—writer, museum curator, and art expert— as director of the WPA/FAP. He hired many sculptors, painters, printmakers, and designers to produce art throughout the United States. Many well-known artists who benefited from the program were Thomas Hart Benton, Grant Wood, Ben Shahn, David Siqueros, and Diego Rivera. A number of African American artists such as: Samuel Brown, Jacob Lawerence, Dox Thrash, Charles Alston, Vertis Hayes, Gwendolyn Bennett, Eldzier Cortor, William E. Smith, and others benefited from this program, as well. Their artwork included cultural reflections of the Depression era, scenes of contemporary America, and Mexican murals. Many of the individuals that participated in the WPA are represented in the archives of the Library of Congress. Dox Thrash is one of these artists. Many of these materials created during the WPA were acquired for the Library largely through the efforts of Archibald MacLeish while he was Librarian of Congress from 1939 to 1944.

References

Ittmann, J. (2001). *Dox Thrash an African American Master Printmaker Rediscovered*. Philadelphia Museum of
    Art. Department of Publishing.
Porter, J. A. (1992). *Modern Negro Art*. Washington, D.C.: Howard University Press,. (First published in 1943, The
Dryden Press, N.Y.) .
Wood, J. (1940, December). A new print process. *The Crisis, 40* (11), 379,389.
Young, B. (2002, May) African American Arts and Cultures. Unpublished manuscript.

Website References

African American mosaic, WPA. (19916). Library of Congress [on line] available: http://www.loc.gov/
exhibits/african/wpa.html
Philadelphia Museum of Art: Dox Thrash: An African American master printmaker rediscovered. (2001) [on
    line] available: http://www.philamuseum.org/exhibitions/exhibits/thrash.shtml

Author Note

The print used in this book by Dox Thrash is not the print that was used in the original study referred to in Faith Clover's chapter and used by teachers in the study reported in Mary Erickson's research chapter. The print used was *Bill Johnson as Emperor Jones* by William E. Smith. Because we could not obtain permission to use and reproduce this print, we choose the Dox Thrash print which is readily available for teacher use in museums throughout the country. The Smith print can be found in the journal *The International Review of African American Art*, vol. 6, (4) 1985, p. 15. Both artists can be viewed on the website listed.

Dox Thrash, *Defense Worker*, c.1941, carborundum mezzotint over etched guidelines. Federal Works Agency, Works Projects Administratoin, on deposit at the Philadelphia Museum of Art, 2-1943-275 (18).

Harriet

Art Maker
Elizabeth Catlett

Date of Artwork
1975

Location of Artwork
High Museum of Art,
Atlanta, Georgia

Medium
Linocut

Size
32 cm x 25.5 cm

Subject Matter

This print is of Harriet Tubman, the monumental leader and former slave who escaped from slavery in Maryland, and returned 19 times to lead over 300 slaves to freedom in Canada. Elizabeth Catlett has portrayed Harriet Tubman in print three times between 1946 and 1975 to impress us with this powerful woman's strength and leadership. The linocut shows "Harriet," the leader often referred to as General Moses, pointing the way to freedom. It shows Tubman an abolitionist leader, born into slavery, conducting a group of slaves out of slavery. The print depicts a disciplined leader pointing the way for a group of adults and one child who is being carried by a women who we can believe is the child's mother. Tubman was known by different names, such as "The Conductor," and as "Moses," which compared her to the biblical figure who led the Jews out of Egypt. In 1849, she escaped to the North to freedom. This print shows Tubman on one of her returns to the South to lead other slaves, including her aged parents, her sister, and her two children, to freedom along the route known as the Underground Railroad. Perhaps this print shows the actual underground railroad with a stormy sky and a journey of courage. Without question this black and white print shows Harriet Tubman as a remarkable conductor and leader of the Underground Railroad. It also shows the commitment Catlett has in depicting the struggle of African American people, and especially the deep respect she has for women of color.

Visual Organization

The central figure in this powerful print is Harriet Tubman. The numerous lines carved into the linocut display the energy of Tubman leading her people to freedom. Her arm stretches forward and points to freedom; while the intensity of the people concentrates on moving forward, only one person in this print looks back, and he is in the background directing additional people to move forward. The foreground and sky area of this print are radical with lines cut to show this journey was one that was not easy. The road is rough and the sky is not friendly. Most of the print is taken up with the people being depicted, with little space left for the environmental aspects of the print.

Short Biography of the Art Maker

Elizabeth Catlett was born in 1919 in Washington, DC. Catlett is without doubt the most prominent living African American woman artist. She has long been recognized as one of America's leading sculptors and printmakers. The themes of her work have developed around the respect for mothers and children, historical figures, women, human conditions, social justice, and dignity. After studying under James Porter and James Wells at Howard University and teaching high school briefly in North Carolina, she returned to school, at the University of Iowa, to study under the famous regional artist, Grant Wood. In Iowa she earned a Master of Fine Arts degree. Grant Wood had a profound effect on Catlett's artistic philosophy. He encouraged her to pursue subjects she knew most intimately. He prompted Catlett to look to her people for inspiration. In the early 1940s she met the artist (former husband) Charles White and they were married and received teaching assignments at Hampton Institute in Virginia. While there the leading art educator and psychologist Viktor Lowenfeld encouraged her to use art to discuss social injustice and human dignity. In 1946 Catlett and her husband went to Mexico on an extension of her Rosenwald Fellowship to complete a series of prints, paintings, and sculptures on the theme of African

American women. While there, her strained relationship with her husband Charles White ended in divorce. Catlett's trip to Mexico opened new vistas for her. She studied ceramic sculpture with Franciso Zúñiga. She had time to concentrate on her prints while working with artists at the Taller de Gráfica Popular (Workshop of the People's Graphics). At the workshop she discovered a new philosophy in her work and political views, and she met the Mexican artist Francisco Mora, who later became her husband.

Catlett's sculptures and prints are realistic and are created to demonstrate liberation and the self-determination of African Americans. She believes the purpose of art should serve mankind beyond the visual pleasures of aesthetics and design elements. Abstract art is often not understood by the masses. Catlett believes her realistic, powerful images can better reach the masses of people from all social classes.

In 1958, Catlett became the first woman hired as a professor of sculpture at the National University of Mexico's School of Fine Arts. Catlett became a Mexican citizen in 1962. She remained at the university until her retirement in 1976. Her powerful sculptures often focus on African American women and frequently convey themes of mother-hood, suffering, and triumph. Catlett capitalizes on the expressive power of line and form to convey emotion to her viewer. Over the years her primary concern in creating art has been to bring to the forefront the dignity of African American heritage. Her sculptures and prints combine modernism, culture, and liberation.

Artworld Information

Elizabeth Catlett used her sculptures and prints to resist injustice and to promote self-determination. Jacob Lawrence, John Biggers, and many others resisted injustice and promoted equality with paint and prints. In 1946, as a mature artist Catlett left the United States and went to live in Mexico. Her art as well as her life is a cultural mixture of experiences in both countries. After four decades of working in Mexico, Catlett still maintains some to the themes of her earlier work. Some of her work has been collected in major institutions such as The Metropolitan Museum of Art, The Wadsworth Atheneum, and The Studio Museum in Harlem. She puts her work to use and makes it accessible to the people, in churches, universities, and community centers. She has received international recognition while remaining steadfast using themes that were filled with political and historical figures.

In 1946 Catlett moved to Mexico City and began working in Taller de Gráfica Popular, which was a workshop against Imperialism. Catlett has said. "It was a workshop for the liberation of all peoples" (Gedeon, 1998, p. 34). It was at this workshop that Catlett made radical and sometimes revolutionary two- and three-dimensional work with the popular appeal that represented the hearts and lives of African American and other non-Western peoples and traditions. The spirit of the workshop in this artworld was one of collaboration rather than competition among the artists.

References
Gedeon, L.H. (1998). *Elizabeth Catlett sculpture, A fifty-year retrospective*. Neuberger.

Harriet By Elizabeth Catlett

Artworld Analysis

Name _____

There are, and always have been, many artworlds in North America and around the world. Identify an artworld that you d like to learn more about.

Name of Artworld _____

Activities

1. There are many ways to get involved with an artworld. Identify the kind of artwork made in the artworld you ve chosen and describe the activity involved in making it.

2. Besides making artworks, people in an artworld also create a community and provide support that makes it possible for art makers to do their work. Describe some art activity in the artworld you have chosen that does not directly involve making art.

People

3. Many different kinds of people are involved in an artworld. Name a person who is well known in the artworld you have chosen and explain why you think the person is important in that world.

4. Name another person you know about who is involved in the artworld you ve chosen and explain why you think the person is important in that world.

Places

5. People meet in a variety of specific places to get involved in an artworld. Name a place in the artworld you ve chosen and explain why people of that artworld meet there.

6. Name another place where members of the artworld you have chosen meet and explain why they go there.

Ideas

7. People have some very different ideas about why art is important. Explain why you think art is important. (If you do not think it is important, explain why not.)

8. Think of someone who is a member of the artworld you ve chosen whom you think has another idea about why art is important. Explain why you think that s/he believes that art is important.